MANILA ESPIONAGE

Manila Espionage

By

Claire "High Pockets" Phillips

and

Myron B. Goldsmith

Bowsprit Books
2018

CHAPTER 1

A Fool Rushes In

As WE DOCKED AT PIER NUMBER SEVEN, I spotted my close friend Louise De Martini, waving excitedly, and calling my name.

September 20th, 1941 and journey's end at Manila. Twenty six days voyaging across the frequently not-so-pacific Pacific on a slow Swedish freighter is not a picnic. Add to this the care of a small child, mal-de-mar [sea sickness], boredom and the inescapable smorgasbord [buffet]. These are a few of the many reasons why I was happy to reach my destination.

In a manner, it was coming home. I might as well recite that closed bitter-sweet chapter of my past life briefly, and then slam the book shut with a decided bang.

Some years before I had played Manila with a touring American musical stock company, and only expected to remain there about six months. I met Mr. Wrong, [instead of Mr. Right] married him, and deemed myself settled as a carefree, station-wagon driving housewife. We acquired a comfortable suburban home, a baby girl, servants, friends, and for a time all was well.

Next to death, marriage is probably one of the greatest of life's adventures. Mine culminated in a misadventure and as the aftermath, I took my infant daughter, Dian, and returned home.

Call it restlessness, fate, wanderlust or the whirligig of chance. Bill Shakespeare said that "all the world's a stage" and maybe I was not fond of sitting in the wings, so for some unexplainable reason the States soon lost their lure for me. Despite the dire warnings and vehement protests of my well-meaning family, I packed my bags, took Dian in my arms, and walked up the gangplank of the *S. S. Annie Johnson* at Wilmington.

Now I was back. As the motley assortment of gold miners [headed for the gold ore rich veins in the mountains of Luzon or Baguio, or perhaps a small strike elsewhere] and Filipino students, my erstwhile fellow passengers, courteously made way, Dian and I went ashore.

"Honey, I'm glad to see you," Louise greeted, as we hugged and kissed. "But I think that you're a crazy fool."

"That's a fine way to welcome [back] a pal," I returned, somewhat surprised. "Why am I so foolish?"

"Mr. Whiskers has been frantically urging all of the American women and children in the Islands to return home for the past six months, and here you come barging in."

"Well, what of it?"

Louise clapped her hand to her brow in mock horror.

"What of it, she says. Didn't it occur to you that the navy escorted your tub into the Bay because it is mined? Take a look at the army and navy activity on the waterfront."

"So what?"

"So there may be a war, and Manila will be a very unhealthy spot."

"You mean the Japs?" I returned, undaunted. "That's newspaper talk. They threaten and bluff, but I don't think that they will ever fight us. They are not that crazy."

"This world is chock full of crazy people," said Louise with a gesture of finality as she led the way to her car.

We stowed ourselves and luggage in it, and drove off. The form of half-forgotten things now began to shape itself in my mind. As we sped through the streets of the ancient city, I became acutely aware of the depressing heat and the pungent ammonia-like odor resulting from the universal human and animal promiscuity. We narrowly averted numerous collisions with carromatas... those quaint little native vehicles drawn by diminutive flea-bitten nags.

"We're having practice blackouts," Louise remarked casually.

"That's interesting. I hope they will have one soon."

"Well, I don't! I may be a pessimist, but don't let me get you down. I am glad that you've returned."

"Then I am not a fool?"

"Of course, you are," Louise shot back. "But we're birds of a feather. Plenty of people keep telling me that I should go home, but here I am."

Louise had two rooms in readiness for us in her attractive bachelor-girl apartment. I liked them and told her so.

"Why not settle down here permanently," she invited. "And be my family?"

"Oh yes," I laughed. "We will stay here 'permanently' until I can get some singing jobs and a place of my own."

I soon discovered that whenever three people assembled at Louise's apartment, a party was under way. Sometimes it was only a quiet tea party. Then again, cocktails or champagne would appear as if by magic; more people would drop out of the blue, and ideas as well as corks would start popping. After some of these shindigs, Louise and I would chin far into the night, discussing mutual friends, both old and new.

One couple, both intrigued and worried us. "Mona" so dubbed because of her "Mona Lisa" smile, and her adoring "Wop," Charley De Maio, Chief Petty Officer, U.S. Navy, he had good-naturedly "wopped" her right back, for both were of Italian ancestry. I liked him at once because of his infectious grin, his expressive Latin eyes and his impulsive, warm-hearted mannerisms. Charley was good-looking, stocky, and not too tall but tall enough for his petite, red-headed girlfriend.

Mona was about twenty when I met her, very pretty and cute, with smooth olive skin, plus dimples that she could turn on and off like her charm. When she was crossed, her temper flared like her hair. Mona could not "possibly live" on the generous allowance that her father gave her, so she was constantly asking her friends to help her out of her financial difficulties "just until the end of the month." Wop laughingly commented several times, "I'm engaged to Mona all right, but I'm damned if I know if she's engaged to me!" Louise said that it certainly did not look like it when Wop's ship was out. I remember that De Maio told me "Just let me catch Mona two-timing me. I'll put her right across my knee." I hastened to let him know that the idea was a good one, adding, "It would be a better one to forget her. She will never be serious about anyone but herself."

I enjoyed the gossip, the assorted pleasure-loving crowd and the good times we shared, but like all things mortal, this, too, came to an end when I lined up the kind of singing jobs that I wanted. This was not difficult as with few passable American singers around, competition was not too keen. My professional experience, plus my collection of new songs and gowns, fresh from the States, was also a helpful factor. Billed under my stage name of "Claire De La Taste," I was soon singing for special parties; first at the Manila Hotel ballroom, and then at the ultra-modernistic Alcazar Club.

Ignoring Louise's well-intentioned protests, I moved to the Dakota Apartments, an airy modern building in Ermeta, one of the most attractive residential sections of the city. My little ménage was soon running smoothly with the aid of Lolita, a young Filipino nurse, plus Maria, an elderly native cook-housekeeper. Lolita was more than just a mere servant from the moment she entered my employ. I left Dian in her keeping on the nights I was working, knowing that the baby would be well cared for. Lolita could "live in" as her husband had recently joined the Philippine Constabulary and was constantly on maneuvers.

The romantic setting of the Alcazar Club, where I sang nostalgic torch songs under a soft cascade of shifting pastel lights, may have been responsible for what happened next. However, it was destined to be, and the result would have been the same if the locale had been a frozen tundra in the Arctic Circle.

No one could miss that soldier!

I saw him almost as soon as he arrived with a group of his friends... over six feet of erect, well-proportioned he-man... brown hair with a wave in it... deep, heavily-lashed eyes under straight brows. The quiet type, I thought, watching his slow, graceful manner of dancing. I had never seen a more handsome man.

When I stepped up on the dais in front of the orchestra for an encore, I sang... and I might as well confess it... to him. The soldier listened attentively as though he loved and understood music. My selection was a sentimental one that was sweeping the States when I left them:

"I don't want to set the world on fire,
I just want to start a flame in your heart..."

Our eyes met, held, and lingered. The soldier looked at me in the manner that a woman longs to be gazed at earnestly... by the right man.

"In my heart I have but one desire
And that is you, no other but you..."

A faint smile creased his lips as I finished and took my bows. I saw him whisper to a mutual friend, and immediately they crossed the floor just coming alive with dancing couples. Then I met Sergeant John Phillips, radio man, Communications Section, Headquarters Company, Thirty First Infantry.

I cannot recall what I said to him. "Claire, keep your head," I cautioned myself, "He is too wonderful. He will never notice you."

"May I have this dance?" asked the sergeant, interrupting my daydreams.

He not only had that dance, but every succeeding one until I begged off from sheer fatigue. As the evening waned, he asked if he might see me home. The night was warm. The taxi driver took the long way (and did not hurry) as we rode along acacia and palm-bordered Dewey Boulevard, enjoying the sea breeze.

My escort did most of the talking. He told me about his former work; about his family in far-off California. "Mom's terrific," he rattled on, "You would love her." He had been in the army for three years; one to go. "I've done all right," he continued, "The army is okay, but an enlisted man can only get so far; then he's stymied." He chattered about the cattle ranches back in the mid-west where he had grown up. "I believe that's the life, Claire." (It was 'Claire' and 'Phil' by this, time.) "What do you think?"

I couldn't think because Phil was holding my hand.

"I don't know," I answered weakly.

I wondered if he would kiss me goodnight. He did, just once; then asked if he could call on me on the morrow. Thus romance was born, and Phil came to lunch the next day. Ours was a real case of true love at first sight.

Louise and Phil hit it off at once. Sometimes we would drop in at her apartment for one of her impromptu parties. If I had occasional shopping to do, Phil would suggest, "Why not give Lolita the day off? I will take care of Dian." He did, and I don't know which one of them had the most fun.

In doleful retrospect, I know now that for a while we lived in a fool's paradise... dancing, swimming, movies and horseback rides. Phil was free of all duties after one p. m. until reveille the next morning. So we shared portions of our fleeting, glorious days together, and evenings Phil took me to work; then waited to escort me home.

I experienced my first practice blackout, while singing at the Alcazar Club, about the middle of October. The sirens sounded their keening wail at nine, and the attendants bustled around drawing the heavy curtains. A deafening roar of planes over the city blended with the din from army trucks equipped with loud speakers, dashing through the streets and calling on offenders to dim their lights. The uproarious cacophony caused the musicians in the orchestra to waver, and then quit. Several officious air-raid wardens made a noisy entrance and strode importantly through the room. I gained the impression that they were more anxious to exhibit their regalia and authority, than to inspect our security precautions.

The din subsided gradually. Within a few minutes, the music resounding merrily and the evening's entertainment went on as usual. At ten, the "all-clear" sounded, and the curtains were pulled back to let the cool evening air flow in. At this time, this make-believe was a novel experience. Next day, the newspapers reported that all had gone well, and to expect another blackout the same day and hour of the next month.

Phil now talked continuously about our marriage. Sometimes he referred to it in the future tense as though we were back in the States. Then he began to mention it as though it were an already existing state of affairs.

"Why don't you give in and marry the man?" Louise prompted. "Why in the world should you wait? I've never seen two people more in love."

"Well, for one thing, I'm older than Phil," I parried.

"Yes," Phil chimed in mockingly, "She's old enough to be my mother, but I like mothers."

"Claire always was a ninny," Louise laughed. "But just give her a deadline, and after that I'll put in my bid."

"Don't rush me, you two conspirators," I admonished, and then abruptly changed the subject.

I had made one mistake; it seemed like good sense to wait until Phil received his discharge. Then if we still felt the same, it was back to the States, a big family wedding, the dreamed-of ranch, and "live happily ever after."

In our blissful state, Phil and I virtually ignored the ominous portents which confronted us at every turn. By November, the blackouts became more frequent, and unheralded. The newspaper advised all who could to build air-raid shelters, giving specific instructions how to construct them and telling where the materials could be obtained.

I recall that Phil frequently spoke in a somewhat worried tone about the young recruits arriving from the States. "I don't know what kind of sketchy basic training they are giving those kids," he lamented. "No kidding, Claire, it's just pitiful. Most of those Johns don't know the difference between right face and right shoulder arms."

One evening toward the end of November, we were playing bridge with some of our friends, at Louise's apartment. I was not in the game, choosing to play the radio softly in the corner, and attending to the needs of the players... drinks, ashtrays, et cetera. The sirens suddenly commenced their banshee-like wailing. Louise stopped long enough to put up the blackout curtains and dim the lights. I had been listening to a radio program from the States, but now I tuned in on the local broadcast just in time to hear the commentator say, "Stand by for an important announcement!"

The bridge players froze in their seats.

"Maybe this is not a practice," Louise suggested in a hushed voice. "Perhaps it's the real thing." Wop laughed. "Aw, go on!" he reassured her, "No chance or they wouldn't have given me a twelve hour pass."

The air was dead for several minutes as we sat tense and expectant. Then the announcer came in again, "This blackout will last until morning. Not one hour as before. Remember! ALL NIGHT! Pass this word along, as some do not have radios. ALL NIGHT BLACKOUT!" He kept repeating the caution monotonously until I switched off the radio.

The party broke up immediately as Wop had to go to Cavite; Phil to his barracks in the Walled City, and both figured that they would have some difficulty in reaching their stations. Phil and I walked home slowly in the ebony darkness, stopping at every corner to get our bearings. Even then we were lost in the murk, and Phil climbed up a street sign to check our whereabouts. When we finally arrived home, Phil suddenly drew me close to him.

"Claire, darling," he pleaded. "You'll have to marry me soon. Please say that you will."

"All right, Christmas," I promised impulsively.

"Christmas!" he echoed. As he kissed me there in the gloom and stillness, it seemed that we were the only two people in the world.

We began to tick off the days. December second was my birthday, and Phil gave me a blue coupe for a present.

"Honey," he told me. "It's second-hand, but in A-1 shape, and I had it painted."

We celebrated my natal day and our engagement with a gay party at the newly-opened Jai Alai Club. Here was a sight for the gods. Temperamental Basques with claw-shaped wicker paddles strapped on their right arms, running back and forth on a large court as they batted a small, resilient ball against a high brick wall. Facing them, a cross-section of the local strata of society. On the top floor, oblivious to the sport, men in uniforms and women in dinner gowns, drank at a swank bar or danced slowly to the music of a softly playing orchestra. On the next level, small tradesmen and their social equals sat at bare tables as they drank and watched the swiftly darting players. Dropping down to the next platform, one found the laboring class seated on benches. Then on the ground floor, the "vagabundos"... bums to you... betting four to the peso ticket, while bookmakers with ever twitching fingers cavorted in front of them like clowns.

A few more days passed happily and swiftly. I was sleeping late on the morning of December eighth when Lolita knocked quietly at my door. I heard her but pretended that I did not. The girl tip-toed in, and tapped me gently on the shoulder saying, "Senora, excuse me, please, but there is a war. What shall I do?"

I was accustomed to Lolita's many devices for arousing me, so I petulantly told her, "Go away and let me sleep. Call me when it's over."

"Madre de Dios!" she wailed. "Senora, I speak truth! There is a war!"

As if to confirm her statement, the excited shouts of myriad news-vendors crashed into my consciousness "Extra! Read all about it! Pearl Harbor bombed by the Japanese!"

"Mother of God!" I repeated softly. "Lolita, you did speak the truth!"

CHAPTER II

The Tumult and the Shooting Starts. War!

SO THIS WAS IT. I hastily arose and looked apprehensively out of the window. Everything seemed calm. A few natives were gathered in the street around one of their ilk who was reading a newspaper aloud, amplifying his words with many gestures. An army car with two soldier occupants came speeding down the street. A Filipino urchin darted in front of it, and the automobile swayed drunkenly as the driver swerved to avoid hitting him. The other soldier turned and shook his fist at the boy, who replied in kind with a pert flip of thumb to nostrils.

I heard Dian playing in the patio and called her in. With trembling hands, Lolita placed my breakfast of toast and coffee before me, the cup and saucer rattling on the tray.

"Don't be nervous," I told her.

"I'm not nervous, Senora. Senor Phillips come soon and save us."

My very thought. Phil will come soon... and then suddenly there was an imperative knock at the door. My soldier stood there in full battle dress... pack, gas mask, tin hat on his back, canteen, mess kit and a .45 automatic hooked to his belt.

Phil kissed me quickly. I could see that he was tense with a sort of controlled excitement. Lolita and Dian, stood closely behind me, all eyes for our warrior.

"What shall we do?" I asked him.

"Get a cab, honey. Go to the bank. Draw out all of your money. Have it changed at the Army YMCA into American currency."

"Why?"

"Because if the Philippines fall, their money will be worthless."

"I can't leave Dian that long. Suppose something should happen which would keep me from getting back here?"

"Take Dian and Lolita with you. They can stay in the cab while you attend to things. Try to buy medical supplies. Here's a list of them that I made up last night. Go to the grocers and buy enough canned goods to fill your largest suitcase. Have the car serviced; fill it with gas and oil. Park it here!"

I started making rapid notes on the back of a magazine.

"All right, Phil. Anything else?"

"Yes. Pack another bag with changes of clothing for you and Dian. Not your good things... only slacks, walking shoes and such."

"Are we going away?" I queried.

"Could be," he told me. "Have all these things packed. Be ready to move out fast just in case. See?"

With that admonition, Phil gave me a bear hug and opened the door. "I'm high-tailing it for the barracks," he called back. "After you've attended to all those things, for God's sake stay here until you hear from me."

I sent Lolita for the taxi. Ordinarily she could get one inside of ten minutes, but it seemed like hours before she came back. She told me that she had searched for a long time before she found a taxi; then had to charter it for three hours, at five pesos an hour.

As we drove through the streets, I noted people rushing about frantically in all directions, bumping into each other comically, and then hurrying on. When we reached the bank, it resembled a mad-house. After standing in line patiently for forty five minutes, I abandoned the idea of being polite, and pushed my way through like everyone else. The same procedure at the YMCA, but this time I just wormed my way through the clamoring throng without even a pretense of waiting. Next the drug store, where Phil's list was filled... quinine, aspirin, sulfa, iodine, gauze and tape. At the first grocery store I discovered that a new rule was in effect, "only one can of each kind." We visited five stores before we acquired enough to fill the suitcase... corned beef, salmon, sardines, beans, fruit and a ten pound can of dried milk for Dian.

The garage that I used was only a block from my apartment. After the cab had brought us and our purchases home, I had the driver drop me there. The indolent mechanic had not touched the car and it took a bribe to spur him into action. He finally pronounced the coupe in good shape, and filled it with gas and oil. I drove it to the apartment house and parked it in front of the building as Phil had advised.

I telephoned Louise before starting to pack.

"You've heard the news, I suppose?" I inquired.

"Yes, hours ago," she answered hysterically. "What are you going to do?"

I told her about Phil's suggestions and ideas.

"Oh, I don't think that there will be any need to go far from Manila," she said. "I heard on the radio that reinforcements are already on the way here. If I do leave, I shall go to Antipolo."

"Why there?"

"Everyone is going there... to the Shrine of Peace. The Japs wouldn't dare touch that."

"My dear," I counselled, "You're a good Catholic. The Japs are not. They will bomb the Virgin Mary's Shrine just as quickly as they will Corregidor."

I heard Louise gasp, "Oh, I never thought of that."

We made mutual promises to call each other later; then hung up.

I had no radio, and remembered that Senora Lopez, a friendly neighbor of mine, had two of them. I went to her apartment to borrow one, and lingered for just a brief chat. She showed me how she had arranged double mattresses under her bed.

"When the bombing starts, I'll make the children crawl in between," she commented. "It will keep them safe from shrapnel."

I could not eat, but saw to it that Dian and Lolita did. Maria had not returned and I had a premonition that I would never see her again. I had no qualms that Lolita would desert, as we needed each other. Her husband was away and her parents were in northern Luzon. I felt certain that she would cling to me.

About four o'clock, Phil telephoned. "We're moving out to Fort McKinley in a few hours. Try to drive here at once, I can't get away, and we must talk."

We all piled into my blue coupe, and drove through the snarled traffic to Phil's barracks in the Walled City. He was waiting at the gate, and took us to the NCO lunchroom. We ordered coffee, which became cold while we talked unceasingly, trying to plan for all eventualities. When we left Phil, it was with the understanding that we were not to leave the apartment again until he came for us.

We waved a farewell as the whole outfit piled on to waiting trucks. One soldier, Smiley, who had been in the guardhouse for being AWOL, climbed in among the others, laughing and kidding, "They had to let me out to fight this war for 'em." There were other men I knew. Harold Spooner with his wide grin, Cruikshank with his tough bark, and Webb, he of the worried look. I smiled at these men, but my eyes were on Phil until the truck disappeared from view.

I drove back to the apartment to wait.

The expected bombing started at midnight. It would be futile to describe the nameless horrors that race through the brain of a woman who has never been subjected to this ordeal. The drone of hostile planes overhead, the caterwauling of air raid sirens, the distant blasts of anti-aircraft batteries, and the vague tremor accompanying the crum-m-p of far-off bombs dropping on their objectives, produce an unholy dissonance that numbs one's nervous system.

I stowed Dian under my bed, inside a doubled mattress, propping up one corner for air. Then I sat trembling on the edge of the bed, alternately thinking and praying until daylight. The child slept peacefully until six, when she awakened and made it known that she was hungry. Lolita soon came with breakfast for both of us.

"Please, Senora," she begged, "Try to eat today. You did not eat a thing yesterday."

I made an effort, but the food stuck in my throat.

I did not dare leave the apartment, because of my promise to Phil. When I attempted to send Lolita out to shop for current needs, she demurred, "No, Senora, I no understand. I not know what to buy."

"Don't you want to go," I queried sharply. "Or are you frightened?"

"Please, Senora, yes," she wailed. "No make me leave you."

"I don't want you to leave me," I comforted. "Come on, let's do some more packing."

Shortly before noon, the telephone tinkled. It was Mona, quite cheerful, and apparently carefree.

"It looks like we will all be big heroines soon," she rattled on. "We'll probably be thrown in a concentration camp, but that will only last for a month or two. The Americans are on the way to rescue us."

"Do you really want to be here in Manila when, as, and if the Japs take it over?" I interrupted.

"Why not," she responded gaily, "I can't see myself hiding in a dirty old cave at Antipolo, like Louise plans to do. I'll just stay put and be interned. Think of the headlines in the papers 'Beautiful red-head rescued by handsome Yank!' Oh, boy!"

"Well, I have Dian to think of, and a cave no matter how dirty, sounds better to me than Japs."

"But it will all be over in three months," Mona insisted.

"Or in twenty years!" I snorted, and hung up, with a bang.

At that moment the distant thudding of ack-ack guns made me aware that something was amiss. Looking out of the window, I saw some of my adult neighbors standing in the street, gazing skywards. Cautioning Lolita to remain inside with them, I rushed out to join them. A dog-fight was in progress over Cavite, about ten miles away. Five American fighter planes were valiantly giving battle to about twenty Jap aircraft, clearly marked by the red balls on their wings. I was both elated and surprised to see any of our planes in the air as the radio had foolishly bleated out the night before that virtually all of our planes had been destroyed on the ground.

People in the streets began shouting and screaming, as they watched the unequal contest, much in the manner of fans disporting themselves at a baseball game. The air raid sirens unexpectedly commenced their belated wailing, adding to the existing state of terror. Cavite broke into flames as Jap bombs hit the oil storage tanks. A large column of smoke and flame shot high into the air, then dispersed cloud-like over the surrounding terrain. The fight lasted for two hours, before our badly out-numbered planes had to run for it, and all was momentarily quiet.

I returned to my apartment to find Dian napping, with her teddy bear hugged tightly in her arms. Lolita reported that the noise of the bombing and the shrilling of the sirens had made the baby cry, but that she had eventually lulled the child to sleep.

While I had been outside, Lolita had packed the canned goods in the big suitcase. In the other one, I placed two pairs of slacks, three skirts, two sweaters, underwear, and Dian's things. Before closing the case, on an impulse, I added a new, midnight blue cocktail dress studded with gold nail heads. Lolita, efficient, but much more quiet than usual, tied extra white uniforms and her other belongings into a big kerchief.

My prized possessions went into a big trunk that I knew must be left behind. My best clothes, two civilian suits belonging to Phil, three photograph albums, two gold spoons that had been my great-grandmother's property, Dian's gold locket and chain, seven bottles of imported perfume, and a small camera. I locked the trunk, and tied the key, along with my watch and rings in a handkerchief which I tucked into my bra.

At eight p. m., an irate air warden knocked on the door. Our one light was too bright, and visible from the bathroom window. We had no flashlight nor candles, and I felt sure that I could not stand another hideous night in total darkness. After searching frenziedly for something black, I finally thought of my mascara; then worked for three hours with a small brush, blackening the window.

At midnight the bombardment started again, and continued until dawn. I lay in bed, sleeplessly, with terrifying fantasies racing through my mind, until I heard Lolita stirring about six-thirty. She brought me breakfast, but it was the same old story. I could chew, but not swallow. The faithful girl finally persuaded me to drink some warm milk, and eventually outraged nature asserted itself. I was dead to the world until two that afternoon when Lolita gently aroused me, saying that there had been another dog-fight and bombing. Not in Manila; the Japs were over Fort McKinley. Instantly, I was wide awake.

"What's that about Fort McKinley?"

"Senora, while you sleep, I listen to radio. It say McKinley Field was getting the worst of it. Es muy malo!"

We stared at each other intently.

"Isn't that where Senor Phillips is?" Lolita whispered.

"Yes. Maybe that's why he hasn't come for us."

"Maybe we should look for him, Senora."

I nodded assent. Taking Dian, we climbed into the car, and headed for Fort McKinley, dodging in and out of the traffic recklessly. A Filipino sentry halted us at the city limits. "Official business," I told him, "Very official." I could not have bluffed an American like that, but this man let us pass.

At the gates of Fort McKinley, we were stopped by a young Filipino sentry.

"My husband is an army officer stationed here," I deceived. "He expects me."

We drove on unhindered. I stepped on the gas as we passed the barracks and headquarters buildings, as I was neither in a position nor mood to be stopped for further questioning. The reservation was approximately five miles in circumference, and I looked around energetically for some signs of the

Headquarters Company. The car stalled, and this mishap gave a sentry an opportunity to ask our business, before I could start moving again. He stated that he was certain that the Headquarters Company had moved out during the night. Not appeased by this information, I drove around the post once more, and again the car balked. This time a passing tank pulled us out of a rut and pushed us onto the main road until the obstinate engine coughed its way back into being.

"Sister, if I was you," the driver advised gruffly, "I'd go gettahell away from here and beat it home. It's liable to get plenty rough here most any time. Your old man will look for you when he has time."

Suddenly my heart was in my throat. Suppose Phil had come to look for us? I started back for Manila, foot pressed to the floorboard. Half way there, all hades unexpectedly broke loose behind us. The Japs were over Fort McKinley again with about fifty planes, delivering a knock-out punch with high explosive bombs. The concussion was so terrific that it almost knocked the car off the road. The wheel shimmied in my hands, and it was all that I could do to keep us upright and moving.

Back home, there was no sign of Phil, and I was happy that my hare-brained dash to Fort McKinley had not caused us to miss him.

I tried to call Louise, but the telephone was dead. As night fell, the streets were empty. We seemed to be living in a vacuum; a steadily menacing and tightening vacuum. I murmured something to Lolita about privacy and letters to write. Once in my room with the door closed, I threw myself on the bed and gave vent to my hitherto repressed feelings, stifling my sobs in the pillow.

The sound of a truck stopping outside, snapped me out of it. I listened eagerly in the darkness. There was a sound of hurried steps, and then a familiar knock. I reached the door before Lolita. Clad in a torn uniform, Phil stood in the dim light, red-eyed, mud-caked, his face sprouting a heavy growth of beard.

"Hello, sweetheart," he said gently, with a wan smile, "I did come back for you."

Suddenly I was in his arms, laughing and crying all at once.

After I had calmed down Phil let me know that his company had moved to Bataan, and he had gone AWOL to come and get me.

"We're going to dig in on Bataan, and let the Japs take Manila," he reported. "Unless our troops are all out of here, the Nips won't consent to treating it as an open city."

Phil bathed, shaved, and changed uniforms, while I prepared a meal for him. I was so elated that I raised my voice in song as I worked. As he ate, I ran upstairs and returned the radio to Senora Lopez. Soon thereafter, we were all stowed in the car and ready to leave.

"Those headlights!" Phil remarked suddenly. "I forgot all about them. We're sure to be stopped with no blackout lights!"

He ran back into the apartment, and returned with the first serviceable object he had found; my new coral satin housecoat which I had absent-mindedly left on the bed. This garment was a prized possession made for my trousseau, but I did not protest. Phil tore it in half, covered the headlights; then we started.

It was a moon-less night, and the city was in complete darkness. The streets were jammed with traffic, mostly army, and Phil drove at a snail's pace. We passed several cars wrecked in collisions, with volubly profane G.I.'s clustered around them.

We finally drove out of the city, and reached the open highway. We moved much faster now, but every three or four miles we slowed down as we were challenged by American or Filipino sentries. Each time Phil sang out "United States Army! Official business!" When the soldiers heard his voice and noticed his uniform, they stepped aside and permitted us to pass.

After a while, I demanded sleepily, "Where are we going, darling?"

Phil patted my arm.

"Quien sabe? Who knows? Away from Manila, anyhow... I wouldn't leave you there unless you had a gun with two bullets in it... one for you... the other for Dian."

Dian stirred in my arms at mention of her name.

"Mama!" she prattled softly. "Dada!"

In the rumble seat behind, Lolita, wrapped in a blanket, slept, trusting us to find a haven.

CHAPTER III

Father Gonzales Ties a Midnight Knot

AT TWO IN THE MORNING, we crossed a stone bridge over a small river that flowed past the small barrio of Pilar.

"You can stop here for the night," Phil advised. "My company is only about three miles farther up in the hills."

Then he leaned over and awakened Lolita.

"You can speak their lingo here," he ordered. "Go to that big house and see if they have room for the three of you."

Lolita went to the door and tapped lightly, but as we waited, there was no response. Then Phil impatiently jumped out of the car and pounded on the door. A light appeared and the door opened. I heard Lolita speaking in the local dialect, gesturing all the while in our direction. Finally they both came back, and Phil informed me that for one peso a day, we could stay as long as we wished. Phil unpacked the bags, got us settled, and I laid Dian, still sleeping, on the bed.

"I'm going to drive Senor Phil to his company," I told Lolita. "I'll only be gone for a few minutes. You're not afraid, are you?"

"Oh, no Senora," she answered. "Not anymore. It's so nice and quiet here."

The tropical moon was out now and its beams turned the beautiful white hibiscus flowers to silver, as we drove along. The scent of night-blooming cereus permeated the air with its cloying fragrance. We turned up a narrow mountain road, and Phil soon stopped the car, with the comment, "The camp is just a few hundred feet up there."

We sat together silently with his arms around me for a few minutes.

"You know, darling," he blurted suddenly, "I should have hit you over the head, caveman style, back in Manila, and dragged you to the altar. If anything happens to me now..."

"Nothing will," I interrupted.

"No, of course not. Just the same, I would feel much better and fight much harder if you and Dian were really mine. I want to talk with Chaplain Taylor about it. Can I?"

"Of course, you can. Only no more AWOL or Captain Packard will put you in the guardhouse."

"What guardhouse," chuckled Phil. "It's a date then, with the chaplain."

"It's a date," I agreed, solemnly.

He turned the car around, and got out. When I glanced back hastily after driving off, Phil was still standing there watching me.

At seven the next morning, a chattering, like a flock of magpies, outside my window, awakened me. Still clad in my slacks and shirt... I had only removed my shoes... I crossed to the window. Below me, at the town pump, Pilar's civic activities were well under way. The pump stood on a cement platform about four feet square, and several women were soaping their dampened clothes on this platform, beating them clean with paddles. These lavanderias were conducting a brisk conversation with another woman who was busily engaged in cleaning and washing a chicken. In the center of the stage, Dian clad in her birthday suit was laughing and splashing, while Lolita scrubbed her and chimed in now and then in the staccato gossip.

"Good morning," I called, and all eyes turned up to my window.

"Ah, senora," Lolita informed me, "Buenas dias! I was telling these ladies how Senor Phillips saved us all the way from Manila."

Despite Dian's protests she was dried and dressed. We prepared breakfast in the clay pots on the brick oven, as I belatedly remembered that I had left behind all of my enameled kitchenware.

Viewed by daylight, Pilar proved to be little more than a wide spot in the road. It had a city hall of sorts, in the plaza, and here was housed the mayor's office, a police station and a post office. However, the town pump with the only pure water for miles around, was the real heart of the place.

With breakfast over, Lolita took our washing to the pump, including Phil's torn, muddy uniform. I toiled over a letter to my folks back home. What to say? I did want to tell my Mother and Dad the truth, but somehow I did not want them to worry too much. When the letter was finished, I sent Lolita off to the post office with it, and started to unpack our meager belongings.

Two hours ticked away, and I began to worry about Lolita. I invaded the gathering at the town pump to inquire if they had seen her. None of the native women spoke much English, but one of them pointed to a little boy clutching a scrap of paper.

I beckoned to him, feeling that it was a note intended for me, and my guess was correct. I chuckled as I read it. "Senora, please come to the policia and get me. They think I am a Japanese... Your sad maid, Lolita."

Waving at the friendly, curious women, I put Dian and the native boy into the car, and drove as he directed to the Philippine Constabulary headquarters. There I found poor Lolita in tears. "They think I'm a Jap, and won't let me come back," she sobbed.

I told the officers who I was; that I had this maid for a long time (stretching the truth a bit) and that I was certain she was not Japanese, but Filipino. They conferred, and finally decided, "If you will vouch for her, we will release her to you. However, she has the eyes of a Jap." This was true, and on the way back, I teased Lolita about it. She admitted that there was Jap blood two or three generations back in her family, but begged me not to tell anyone. I promised never to mention the matter again.

As we returned to our temporary abode, I saw an army truck in the yard. Two soldiers were busily engaged in filling cans with water. Could it be...? Yes, it was...

"Oh, Phil," I called out, "I'm so glad to see you. How in the world..."

"This, honey, in case you don't recognize it," he explained, "is punishment. As I expected, the Old Man gave me a week's K.P. [Kitchen Patrol] for going AWOL. I have to come down here, twice daily for a week. Isn't that awful?"

"Awful," I agreed laughingly. "Give the Old Man a big hug for me, will you."

After this short visit, when Phil arrived for the "water detail," [fetching water for his camp] I always had food ready for him. Lolita had washed, pressed and mended his old uniform, and it looked almost new. He was beyond a shadow of a doubt, the best dressed and best fed soldier on Bataan. Our services seemed to please him, so I suggested that he bring some of his outfit in to eat, and also let us do their washing.

From then on, every morning, Lolita and I were the busiest *lavendarias* at the town pump. Our afternoon chore was cooking. I kept cigarettes on hand, and converted our two small rooms into an improvised canteen. Soldiers were in and out of them all day long; sometimes until midnight. A few insisted that I take an I.O.U. for their purchases, as pay-day was then two months overdue. I accepted the I.O.U.'s to salve their feelings, and then tore them up afterwards.

Evenings, Phil came down from camp with some of his pals for a late dinner and drink. The latter consisted of native beer, or gin, with sarsaparilla. There was no ice, but none complained because of a lack of it. The fried chicken and salads that Lolita toiled over, were popular, as the men were living entirely on field rations. As I became better acquainted with the villagers, they too helped, but this intimacy brought new responsibilities.

All local schools had been closed since the Pearl Harbor disaster. One day a delegation of children called on me, and asked if I would teach them a few hours per day. I started with fifteen pupils, and ended with fifty; thirty children and twenty adults. I taught English and arithmetic, or we did exercises and sang; now and then I told them stories. My only trouble was in persuading my scholars to go home.

I was glad to have this diversion, as it kept me from worrying. The calm and quiet, after the holocaust of Manila, gave me a feeling of comparative safety. We heard distant bombing, and occasionally witnessed dog-fights in the distant skies. Troops on foot, trucks and tanks, were constantly moving past in both directions.

Late one afternoon, I noticed a motorcyclist slow down and look back, annoyed, at some sort of wire that his machine had picked up, and which had snapped suddenly. He speeded up, and disappeared in the gathering dusk.

I wondered about that wire, until finally, I went out and found, as I had suspected, that it was a field telephone line. "Well," I reasoned, "I can't make it any worse, and it won't electrocute me." Using a knife, I scraped the insulation from the two broken ends and twisted the wires together, as I had seen Phil do it. I was very pleased when he arrived that evening, inspected my repair job, and pronounced it well done.

The family with whom we were staying owned a radio. At night we listened to the San Francisco broadcasts, and the theme was always the same, "Hang on to Bataan! Help is on its way from the United States! A large convoy has already started. Hang on to Bataan!"*

Phil drove up one day, as I was sending Lolita to the post office with a letter to my mother.

"Where are you sending that letter?" he asked.

I told him, and he laughed heartily.

"Honey, don't you know that all mail to the United States has stopped?" he chuckled.

Naturally, I abandoned that futile activity.

A day or so later, I noticed that my coupe was missing. No one, not even the police, could give me any information.

On December twentieth, about nine in the evening, an army truck stopped at the pump, and Phil jumped off, his arms full of packages. He came up the steps, three at a time, dropped the parcels, and hugged me.

"Well, we're going to have a nice Christmas," he exulted. "Even if I do K. P. the rest of my life."

"Where in the world have you been?" I gasped.

"To Manila; Christmas shopping. The coupe broke down three or four miles back, and I had to hitch a ride the rest of the way. Look! It's not really right, but I knew what a big kid you are. Let's open our Christmas presents now."

We did. He had brought me a dull, blue kid evening bag, fitted with lipstick and compact. For Dian, a doll in a pink voile dress and bonnet, and for Lolita, shoes that fitted perfectly.

"A fine thing," I chided. "How am I to buy you a present?"

"Oh, I've taken care of that," Phil explained, exhibiting a bottle of real Cuban rum. "Here's your present to me. By the way, you will have to go and get the car." He gave me instructions for locating it.

Retrieving the coupe was a rugged task. I arose at seven, then stood on the road until a native cart came along. I told the driver "Balanga" which was the next barrio, two miles distant. When I arrived there, I tried to hire a car at the one garage the place boasted. "No," they told me. "Sorry. We have no car, and if we did, there is no gas. The army is taking it all."

I noticed an army truck parked in front of a small cantina, peeked inside, and saw two engineer G.I.'s drinking warm beer. I recognized one of them as a patron of my "canteen." When I told him about my troubles, he said they were going my way, and would gladly give me a lift.

When we found the abandoned car, it had a flat tire. The engineers changed tires for me, before they drove on. I started back to Pilar, and after one mile had been gained, the engine died. An hour later, another army truck came along and I halted it. The driver got me started again. I drove another mile, and once more the engine failed me. After a long interval of sitting, a Philippine army truck rescued me, and towed me to Balanga. There, after much bickering and bargaining, I managed to buy a new tire and battery.

I arrived home exhausted, took time for a bite of food, and then hurried upstairs for a much needed siesta. An hour later, a persistent tapping at my window aroused me. Outside in a tree top, a native boy, one of my pupils, was staring in at me. Below, as I glanced out, sat the rest of my class, patiently waiting. I waved and smiled at them; then explained that we would have a fiesta until after Christmas, the same as the big schools.

The next day a truck driver brought a message from Phil that he was stuck with patrol duty; to please bring food and come up to meet him that evening. The messenger explained just how far and where I should drive. When I arrived at the appointed spot, a strange soldier met me. He took the food, letting me know that Phil could not get away, but would unfailingly meet me at the same place on the next evening... Christmas eve... at midnight. I drove back to Pilar with a bad case of the "Bataan Blues."

On the morning of the twenty-fourth, Lolita, Dian and I arose early. We drove to Balanga, and made extensive purchases in the big market place in preparation for a huge Christmas dinner. Of course, there were no turkeys but we did find several nice fat roasting hens. We drove back in high spirits, with the car full of provisions, and went to work at once to prepare for the big event. All day long, an unusually heavy volume of army traffic passed through Pilar, going toward Mariveles. The dust was so thick that I was forced to close our windows.

Christmas Eve! I found myself thrilled and excited as a schoolgirl at the prospect of my midnight rendezvous. I bathed, and made a really elaborate toilette, complete with makeup and nail polish. I donned the new blue dress as a surprise for my darling, and this was one of the few times I had been out of slacks since the war began.

Lolita had prepared several neat packages of sandwiches for me to take along. I stopped by Dian's bed to give her a glimpse of her mother all dressed up. She, of course, wanted to go and see "Dada" also, but settled for her favorite lullaby; "My Melancholy Baby." I sat by her until she slept, then tip-toed into the next room to listen to the "Voice of Freedom;" the United States Army re-broadcast from Corregidor. It condensed itself to the same monoto-nous plea, "You must hold on in Bataan! We are rushing reinforcements to you. A convoy is on its way. Hold! Hold!"

Time to start at last. As my car slowly climbed the narrow mountain road, I watched for the turn-off a few yards from the encampment. It was very dark, and I did not dare use my lights as I crept cautiously around the sharp curves. The final turn, and there was Phil waiting. A number of men were with him, and a wave of disappointment swept over me, as I had counted on our being alone on this, our first Christmas Eve.

"Bless you for keeping our date," Phil whispered as he folded me close in his arms, "for a Christmas wedding. Remember?"

"A wedding?" I stammered, "Oh, Phil, how...?" I searched the faces of the men behind him, "Is Chaplain Taylor... ?"

"Not the chaplain," Phil broke in. "He was needed at the field hospital. It's Father Gonzales from the village. One of the boys went down for him. Is that all right, darling?"

"Of course," I agreed. "It's wonderful. Look! I'm all dolled up in a wedding dress."

Phil beckoned to a short Filipino priest, who detached himself from the little group and confronted us, his face wreathed in a smile.

"This is the bride, padre," Phil asserted, drawing my hand through his arm. "Shall we go up now and have the knot tied?"

"One little moment please, Senor Phillips," the priest interposed. "I must ask the young lady for the information for my record."

"Sure, father, go ahead. The boys and I will get the refreshments out of the car."

After telling the priest what he wanted to know about my age and place of birth, he asked, "You have been baptized in the Faith, my daugh-ter?"

"I've been baptized, Father, but not in the Catholic faith. Does that mat-ter? And has Sergeant Phillips told you of my former marriage?"

"Yes, my child. However, this is war, and my only concern is whether you truly desire at this time to enter into a true and lifelong union?"

"Oh, yes, father, I wish it with all my heart."

"Then God will bless it and you."

Phil came up as we finished talking, and inquired, "All set, padre?"

The rest of the wedding party greeted us. Buck, an old "retread" ser-geant led the way to a little knoll where Phil's friends had cleared a small space. The men formed a semicircle as we reached it. Father Gonzales took his place on a high spot behind an improvised altar made of a fallen log covered with moss and white flowers. From somewhere a beautiful bouquet of white hibiscus dropped into my hands. A myriad number of fire-flies flitted around us. It seemed like a pleasant dream. I glanced proudly at my tall, handsome groom there beside me, looking strong and proud.

"In nomine Patri et Filio, et Spiritu Sancto," intoned the priest, and ... suddenly, it was over. Phil and I kissed as though we were engaging in a novel experience.

I tried to show the guests my wedding ring, which Phil had bought in Manila on his last trip, but they all insisted on kissing the bride until Phil laughingly objected "Say, who do you think married this girl?"

Eager and impatient hands ripped open the packages of sandwiches. As we sat down, I whispered to Phil that I hoped there was enough food to go around. It didn't quite, but we tried to see that every guest had something. Our health was drunk with great gusto in an ice-less punch made of native lemon juice and water, spiked with Phil's Christmas rum.

An obliging friend had taken Phil's patrol duty, and now there was barely time for him to drive me to Pilar. This was to be our last ride in the coupe, as we had agreed to turn it over to the army which had need of everything on wheels, due to bombing losses. Phil let me know that he could borrow it, if I needed it. "After the war they will give us a nice new one," he commented. "Maybe..."

We thanked Father Gonzales, said goodbye to our guests, and then Sergeant and Mrs. Phillips started slowly down the mountain, planning the next day's Christmas party. Phil did not expect to be on patrol duty, and he hoped to bring along as many of his friends as possible. All of them were heartily sick of their restricted diet of canned salmon and rice, and he was delighted when I told him of the feast that Lolita and I had in prospect. He gave me to understand that I could expect him and the others about eight at the latest, and felt certain that he could spend the rest of the night with me.

Christmas Day passed swiftly as there were five chickens to be roasted, and a washtub full of vegetable salad to be made.

We prepared baked camotes (native potatoes) and our special treat was to be real bread and butter. At five, I stopped to bathe; then dress myself and Dian.

The traffic was really heavy now. As I glanced out from time to time, it seemed that the entire army was proceeding toward Mariveles. A few men stopped to ask for food, and their blood-shot eyes and grimy, unshaven faces evidenced their despair as they plodded on. The dismal column showed all the visible signs of defeat and retreat.

The owner of the house had graciously granted me the use of his large dining room. Lolita had gathered armfuls of flowers, and filled vases and baskets. The table looked festive; there was even ice from Balanga for our drinks. At seven-thirty, I dropped the ice into a large punch bowl of punch, put on fresh lipstick, and took up my station at the window. Trucks, tanks, marching men... an endless procession... all heading south. No Phil. No guests.

About nine, Dian and Lolita ate their Christmas dinner, and reluctantly went to bed. About ten, I recognized some men among the passing throng... the ones who had helped me with the stalled car... and called them in. They were delighted with the unexpected treat, and sorry they could give me no news of Phil's outfit. Between hurried mouthfuls they told me that everything was snafu. They only knew that they must hurry on towards Mariveles, and then probably Corregidor, to sweat it out. They would not even sit down, leaving hastily with hands full of food, and smiles on their dust-caked faces.

I stood at the window until midnight, watching and waiting. The ice had long since melted, and the fowls at the back of the stove were drying up. Suddenly, I called out at random to the next passing group, and handed them the last of our Christmas cheer. I kept on talking and laughing. They took off, and we called to each other "Good luck! Merry Christmas! Be seeing you!"

Yes, be seeing you. Only time can dim the bitter memory of when, through anguished tears, I saw many of these same boys march again.

But, on this, my wedding night, it was for another soldier that a broken-hearted war bride cried herself to sleep.

*When Japan invaded Corregidor island in the harbor gateway of the Philippines, MacArthur moved the concentration of US troops to Bataan. The imperative here to 'Hang on to Bataan,' was adhered to for four grueling months of battle. Japan invaded in December, and beginning January 7, started a siege war. American forces finally surrendered April 9, leading to the infamous Bataan Death March and, later, MacArthur's immortal words, "I shall return," the ubiquitous phrase of the War in the Pacific that was stamped on everything from army rations to cigarette packs.

CHAPTER IV

Bombs, Birth and a Broken Heart

AT OUR FIRST AID STATION, I helped dress wounds, and our patients were removed to their homes by friends or relatives. The whole day passed without a word from Phil. After six that evening our radio was silenced as the town's electric current was shut off, and we were ordered to observe a complete blackout. The night passed without incident, and dawn found the entire household up and working feverishly to prepare food and first aid supplies, which were stored in the air raid shelter.

There were a few air skirmishes overhead during the early morning, but our planes were so badly outnumbered by the enemy that their pathetic attempts to give battle could hardly be called dog-fights.

At ten, a familiar blue coupe driven by a strange soldier drew up at the pump. The G. I. jumped out of the car, handed me a note, and left immediately in an army truck that had followed him.

"Pack all your things," the message read, "and drive to Hermosa. Be there at noon sharp. The first house as you enter the town has a windmill. Wait there for me. Love, Phil."

Within the hour we were on our way with all our belongings, including a hot pot of half-cooked stew. We drove past fields strewn with the charred skeletons of airplanes, and scarred by deep holes dug by bombs, or aircraft in their death plunges. Many of the burned planes seemed to be Japanese, but I sadly noted a few American aircraft which apparently had been destroyed on the ground. Ruined anti-aircraft guns, stripped of their camouflage, dotted the landscape. I tried to avert my eyes from the somber inanimate objects in olive drab surrounding these mute weapons. In this I was partially successful, but I could not ignore the horrible stench and the overpowering odor of cordite fumes which befouled the air.

When we had reached a point about half way to our destination, the menacing roar of hostile planes came suddenly from overhead. An army truck which had been following me closely, speeded up, and ran us off the road.

"Get to hell out of that car and lie down in the ditch!" the driver shouted, as he swung to the ground. "Do you want to be strafed by those blankety-blank Japs?"

Grabbing Dian, I ran for a ditch about thirty feet from the highway, and threw myself over the child to protect her. Lolita managed to crawl half way under me too. We crouched, trembling, for fifteen minutes or so, until our tormentors had angrily buzzed away.

As they left, I turned over and heard an irritable whine, which was followed instantaneously by an acute jab in my foot. My anguished wail brought the truck driver over on the run. He pulled out a small fragment of shrapnel which had cut through my shoe.

"Lady, put some iodine on that quick, if you've got any," he warned. "It might get pretty sore."

I followed his advice, and we started on, arriving at our destination a half hour late. Phil, wild-eyed and nervous, was awaiting us. The "House-by-the-Windmill" proved to be the home of Judge Rivera, a local magistrate. It was conveniently located a few hundred yards from the spot where Phil's outfit had pitched camp. The judge and his wife were kind and cordial, and he was sincerely shocked when I offered to pay for our rooms.

"Senora, it is so little to do for you Americans," he deprecated, "when you have done so much for us."

The jurist picked up Dian, carried her off to play with his two daughters who were about the same age, and the children were soon enjoying themselves. Phil was hungry, as usual. I asked permission to finish cooking our stew, while he availed himself of a hot bath in the judge's modern bathroom. My soldier joined us at the table, bathed, shaved, and wearing the clean uniform I had brought.

It seemed all too soon before Phil had to leave, but he returned at ten that night. He slept soundly, while I only catnapped, as I wanted to be sure to awaken him in time to report before dawn. After his morning kiss, I slept peacefully for several hours.

A school adjoined the judge's house, and it had been converted into an emergency dressing station. It was staffed by two army doctors, and three attendants. I noticed that the corpsmen were fully occupied in bringing in the wounded, so I offered my services which were eagerly accepted. As I started work, one of the medicos noticed my house slipper, and after examining my foot, he cautioned me to guard against infection.

I reported for duty the next morning, with my big toe badly swollen. The doctor lost no time in telling me, "I'll have to yank that toe-nail out." Noting my responsive grimace, he added, "Sorry, but it must be done, or you may lose the whole toe. I might as well tell you now that it's going to hurt like hell."

He did and it did.

"If you were my patient, instead of my nurse, I would order you to stay off that foot for a week," he commented as he bandaged the toe.

"Oh, I'll be all right, doctor," I assured him.

"Well, take it easy," he answered, "and I'll redress it every day as long as I am here."

The work at the dressing station kept me busy all day and far into the night. I soon became accustomed to the sight of blood and the piteous moans of pain-wracked men. I was so exhausted when I finished that I went to bed and slept without any difficulty despite the crash of falling bombs. Phil took all of his meals with us, but could not stay at night as he was on the radio set from midnight to four a. m.

My real initiation as a nurse came on the second day. We had been punished by Jap planes that morning, and many Filipinos, out in the fields harvesting rice, had been wounded. Two of the attendants brought in a boy, who although able to walk, was clutching his abdomen.

"Run over next door and get a glassful of whiskey if you can," ordered one of the doctors.

I hobbled over to Judge Rivera's house, and he gave me half a tumbler of the precious fluid. I returned just as the doctor gently removed the boy's hands. I could see that the lad was cut open across the navel, and had been holding in his bloody intestines.

The room began to spin. The thought blazed into my befuddled brain that I must not faint, or the surgeons would not let me help them further. Downing the fiery liquid in a couple of gulps, I slumped into a chair.

"Damn it to hell!" one of the medicos bellowed. "Go back there pronto and get some whiskey for the patient. We have no anesthetic, and I've got to sew him up."

This rebuke brought me back to my senses, and I rushed back as fast as my crippled foot would permit, to have the tumbler refilled. Returning I gave the boy the whiskey; then gritting my teeth and closing my eyes tightly, I held one of his arms. The attendant held his other arm and legs, while his intestines were pushed back in place, and the gash stitched.

Rivera's air raid shelter was similar to the one that we had used in Pilar, although smaller. The judge saw to it that Dian and Lolita always took shelter when the Jap aircraft came over. I was, therefore, able to spend the whole day in the dressing station, taking a rest only when Phil dropped over for a chat or meal.

By this time the Japs had the air to themselves. They bombed and low-dived, strafing at will, with little or no response to their arrogant challenge. The Treasure Island radio still chanted the same monotonous refrain, "Hang on to Bataan. Help is on the way."

On December 30th, the little barrio of Oroni, two miles away, suffered a terrific bombing. As the flames became visible, everyone in Hermosa prepared to evacuate, saying our turn would come next. The dressing station folded up. The Rivera family packed up, begging me to do the same, and go with them into the nearby hills. I refused for I had not seen Phil for twenty four hours, and promised not to leave without word from him. The Riveras did not want to abandon me, and called in the village priest to persuade me to accompany them. This terrified little man wore a tin helmet, and a revolver hung from a belt which encircled his clerical robe.

"Father," I exclaimed with ill-concealed disgust. "You're a man of God. Why are you armed?"

"For my own protection if the Japs should land," he retorted stiffly.

"What about the commandment 'Thou shalt not kill'?" I tossed back at him, and ran from the room, crying.

At that moment a Jap plane zoomed low over the house, and a foolish soldier took a shot at it with his rifle. The spent bullet dropped through the roof, and landed in the floor close to me. As I stood shaking from emotion and fright, Phil walked in, pried the bullet out, and handed it to me.

"Keep this," he suggested, "Maybe it had your number on it. Now I know you will be safe."

Phil explained that his company had moved again to Roosevelt Park on the road to Olongopo. He had been on wire pickup detail all day, but seeing the fires in our direction, had changed the duty with another man to come and look for us.

"Now maybe this foolish girl will leave," the judge hinted.

"Yes, I have a plan for her," Phil agreed.

We both thanked the kindly magistrate and his wife, promising to see them after the war. We were all packed, and we were soon on our way, passing through one burning barrio after another, until we reached Dinalupihan. Several times tumbling walls missed us by a hair's breadth, and we were compelled to swerve frequently to avoid bodies lying on the road.

"On the way down, I noticed a large hacienda where I think you should stay for the time being," Phil informed me when we finally reached more quiet terrain. "It's about three miles from where we are camped."

Juan Dymson, son of the owner of the hacienda, received us cordially. Phil saw that we were made comfortable; then went to the road to catch a truck on its way back to camp, leaving my car in the yard.

The sweet lilting voice of a girl singing awakened me on New Year's Day. Despite the holiday, the daily work of the plantation went on. I rested, and played with Dian under a huge mango tree, while Lolita caught up on the washing. Juan eventually joined me for a brief palaver.

I learned that fifty Filipino laborers and their families lived in huts scattered around the plantation. Juan managed the estate, and lived with his mother and two younger sisters. His father, he related, stayed at their other hacienda two miles down the road with a younger brother.

"Dad bought that place," Juan explained nonchalantly, "for his mistress and spends most of his time there. They have a little girl three years old. Mama is rather high-strung. Things are more peaceful this way."

"I should imagine," I commented.

"If you stay with us long enough, you'll find out. Maybe someday I will tell you all about it."

Phil appeared for lunch. He had been on the radio set most of the night, and was doing more than his share. I made him take a siesta, and after that we sat under the mango tree chatting. Our tête-à-tête was interrupted by a native who came running into the yard, and up to me, shouting something, and pointing, to the highway. I called Juan to interpret. He explained that the man's wife was having a baby, and was in need of aid.

"She's in a carabao* cart down the road," he finished.

I told him that I would try to do what I could. Phil, as he was leaving, kidded, "Good luck! See you later, Dr. Phillips."

Juan drove the frantic husband and me back to his wife, whom we found lying in the cart undergoing the final phases of her labor. Too late I realized that I had brought no equipment with me, and began looking wildly around.

"What is it you need?" Juan asked.

"Scissors to cut the cord, and a stout string to tie it with," I told him.

The obstetrical problem was solved by boiling Juan's short bolo knife in a tin can over a hastily built campfire, plus the string from an empty sugar sack. The mother smiled her thanks, and the healthy looking infant cried lustily. I felt certain that none of the spectators guessed that this was the first time I had officiated as a mid-wife. As we left, the relieved father expressed his regrets to Juan that he could not pay the kind Americano nurse.

The next day I awakened to find that my reputation as a nurse had spread via the "bamboo telegraph." Several patients, rice pickers and cane cutters, who had been strafed by Jap planes were waiting for me. I took care of them as well as I could, before eating breakfast.

The bombings were once more coming constantly closer. The market place at Dinalupihan, a mile away, suffered a direct hit. Panic stricken villagers were reported to be abandoning their homes and leaving for the hills. Phil brought the worst news of all when he arrived at noon on January fourth.

"Jap troops are entering Manila today."

"How can that be?" I argued. "When did they land on Luzon?"

"The Nips have been on Luzon for several days. They landed at four different points from transports. I didn't tell you because I've been hoping that our reinforcements would arrive almost any day, and I didn't want to worry you needlessly."

"Then we will lose the islands," I said, dismayed.

Phil nodded gloomily, and called Juan out of the house. He motioned for me to go inside, and I left the two men in deep conversation while I helped prepare lunch. Juan ate hastily, and drove off at once towards Dinalupihan. I begged Phil to tell me what he and Juan had decided.

"Let's not go into that now," was all that I could draw from him. "If I am not here when the time comes, do as Juan says. I've given him full instructions."

Phil remarked that he wanted a few hours' sleep, as he had to be back at camp by nine o'clock. I made him comfortable in my room, and promised to awaken him punctually. Lolita had just finished ironing his spare uniform, as he planned to take all his belongings with him this time, leaving the coupe with me.

After a time Juan returned, and, as I was about to arouse Phil, the telephone jangled suddenly. I heard Juan answer, and after a rapid fire dialogue in Spanish, exclaim, "San Fernando! Madre de Dios!" He hung up, shouting to me "The Japs are entering San Fernando, burning, raping and looting as they advance."

"How far away is that?"

"Less than three hours' drive. We must hurry!"

I ran upstairs with things for Phil's kit. As he dressed, I noted that he changed to heavy socks and heavy army shoes, which I knew he disliked. Noting my puzzled look as I stared at his footgear, he commented "I think that I'll have plenty of walking to do from now on. Don't ask me any questions, because I won't tell you a thing."

Juan was not in sight when we came downstairs. As I drove Phil back to his company, I remained silent about the bad news; I had a woman's intuition that this parting would be the most difficult of all, and did not want to burden him with additional worries.

As we approached his camp, the road was partially blocked with sandbags, leaving room for only one car to pass. A shave-tail, who resembled a half-baked college boy, stopped us, demanding an explanation.

"This is my wife," Phil advised him. "She's taking me back to camp."

The 'shavey' glowered murderously.

"Have you forgotten how to say Sir?" he demanded.

"No, sir," replied Phil acidly.

We drove on to a point within sight of the camp.

"Here's the end of the line," I flipped to hide my heartache.

"Not for us, honey," returned Phil, "Never for us. Now listen. Juan is to take all of you to the hills tonight. You'll be safe there, and I'll come for you as soon as I can."

"Okay," I whispered, "Sir!"

Phil paused to kiss me.

"One of the reasons why I love you so much," he continued, "is because you are not a weakling. You may find it plenty tough to live on rice for a couple of months. It won't be any longer than that because the convoy from the States will be here within that time. Juan has plenty of rice, so you won't starve. Now it's time..."

I did not want to hear him utter those fateful words. I suddenly tightened my arms around his neck, and pulled his face close to mine so that he could not see the tears welling in my eyes. He loosened my clenched hands gently, kissed them, and got out of the car.

"Take it easy, darling," he soothed, "I'll be seeing you. Keep your chin up."

I looked away quickly, shifted gears, turned the car around, and started back down the road. After it had rolled for a few yards, I stopped, brushed the tears away, and turned to wave at him. There he stood... my husband... giving me all the love and reassurance at his command. His face lighted up with a smile as he motioned gaily for me to keep my chin up.

I'll be seeing you... when ?... where ?... how ?

Only the Almighty knew the answer to these questions, and I was not in His confidence.

*The carabao is a type of water-buffalo native to the Philippines, and was the ubiquitous beast of burden on the islands during the war.

CHAPTER V

A Mistress, Monkeys and a Malicious Miser

JUAN WAS BUSILY ENGAGED IN SUPERVISING the activities of several laborers who were loading a truck with large packing boxes, cooking utensils and blankets.

"Can you tell me where we are going?" I asked him.

"Yes," he replied, pointing north. "To that big hill over there."

"You mean the one with the top that looks like an ice cream cone."

"That's just how your husband described it. We agreed on that landmark so he would know where to find you."

"Can we take the truck up there?"

"No. I sent some of the boys ahead to round up carabao. We will drive the truck as high as we can in the foothills, then hide it. After that we will transfer all of the things to congas, and move on up with them."

"What is a conga?"

"They are carabao sleds. We use them quite a bit for hauling when the going is rough."

I was pleased that Phil had displayed good judgement in asking this level-headed young man to take care of us.

When I came out of the house with Lolita, Dian, and our gear, I was hobbling a little.

"I know that your foot is still bad, Mrs. Phillips, but don't worry," Juan assured, "You can ride the last part of the trip on a sled with the baby. My father will also ride as he is not well, but the rest of us will have to walk."

"What about my car?" I inquired anxiously.

Juan did not reply at once, as he stood immersed in deep thought.

"I have it," he said happily, "I'll have one of my men drive it to the other hacienda, and hide it in a cane field."

The Number One Dymson family climbed into the truck; Juan's two sisters, Perfection, eighteen, well-educated, slender and graceful, Maria of the sweet voice which had awakened me on New Year's Day... sixteen, bashful and taciturn. Two maid servants followed them, laden with bundles.

"Where is your mother?" I asked as we were about to start.

Juan's face was set and strained, as he stepped on the starter.

"Mama refuses to budge. She says that the Japs will not dare put her out of her house. I tried to carry her out forcibly, but she ran into her room, and locked the door. I've left one of the servants to look after her."

The two girls burst into tears.

"Now don't worry about Mama," Juan consoled. "When I get you all started up the mountain. I'll come back for her. We can't lose any more time now."

As we sped north on the main highway, I could not resist an impulse to glance back apprehensively in the direction from which I knew the enemy was approaching. Juan smiled at my obvious trepidation.

"I telephoned friends who live near San Fernando just before we left," he confided. "They told me it looked like the Japs were camping there for the night, so this gives us a head start. We'll make it all right."

At the Number Two Dymson hacienda, we picked up Papa Dymson, sputtering and grumbling about Juan's arrangements. Following the grumpy old man like a shadow, his careda, Ascocenia, carrying a plump three year old baby, climbed aboard. She was about thirty, quiet, submissive, and I soon gathered that her nickname was Ascing. There was also Buddy, youngest son of the old hacendado, ten years old, nice-looking and well-mannered. The Number Two sept also brought along a maid.

Our over-loaded truck bullied its way with difficulty through the maze of traffic. The road was jammed with fleeing Filipino families; the more fortunate ones, surrounded by their household goods in horse or carabao drawn wagons or carts. Others, less affluent, pushed their belongings in hand carts. Most of the women carried large bundles on their heads. Now and then a group of pedestrians, fear and panic etched on their faces, would leave the highway and start up a hill.

We eventually turned off the highway, bumped along a narrow dirt road, and through a cut cane field, finally stopping at a small creek. Many of Juan's laborers, each sitting on a hundred pound sack of rice, were waiting for us and the carabao, harnessed to sleds, were in readiness.

We debarked from the truck, and the transfer of our belongings to the congas began. This process, accompanied and stymied by much superfluous argument and chit-chat, seemed endless. It was ten o'clock before we started the long, arduous climb to the top of the "ice cream cone." There were numerous delays. We had to stop several times to let the winded carabao rest... twice harnesses broke and emergency repairs were made. Several mountain streams were crossed, and each time the sleds were unloaded and reloaded. At two a. m., tired, dirty, wet and hungry, we reached the top, and our destination, an abandoned hunter's cabin. After a hasty, cold meal of left-over rice and fried pork, we spread blankets on the floor, and slept.

I awakened at seven, to find Lolita gone from the blanket beside me. I saw that she was up and preparing coffee. As I joined her, she handed me Juan's field glasses, saying excitedly, "Look, senora!"

A most unpleasant sight greeted my eyes; red and white Nipponese flags flying over the little barrio of Dinalupihan, far below. I suddenly felt cold all over.

"We just made it," I offered weakly.

"Si, senora. God was with us."

I nodded absent-mindedly for the moment I was thinking of Phil.

The members of the Dymson family came out of the cabin, and one by one, looked at the enemy's abode through the glasses. The Japanese were no longer an intangible threat to them, but a terrifying reality. When I missed Juan and asked for him, Perfection told me that he had returned during the night for their mother, without stopping to rest.

The laborers amidst much shouting, started noisily to slash at the surrounding bamboo thickets to procure wood for a bigger and better house. Their racket was a pleasant contrast to the frightened silence in which we had prepared for our departure. At least on this rugged mountain-top, despite the accompanying inconveniences, we were breathing the air of freedom.

About nine Perfection cried out "Here they come!" Juan appeared, partially supporting his mother, while a maid servant trailed them with a large bundle balanced on her head. Lolita and I both hurried to make them comfortable, and bring them food. When their creature comforts had been attended to, we listened to Juan's account of his mother's rescue, which was not entirely devoid of certain humorous aspects.

"When I broke into her bedroom," he related gleefully, "Mama locked herself in the bathroom, and wouldn't come out. While I was trying to reason with her, the Japs bombed Dinalupihan, and one of their bombs knocked out the hacienda bridge. The house shook. Mama climbed out of the bathroom window, and slid down the drain pipe."

"It may seem funny now," Mama Dymson fumed, "but it wasn't then. I was so frightened that I never thought about the door."

"It wasn't funny up here, either," Juan went on. "With the bridge out we couldn't use the truck and had to walk all the way. Even the carabao were gone... scared into the woods by the bombing."

"Why didn't you walk to the other hacienda and get my car? You could have come part of the way in it," I suggested.

"I did think of that, and we walked down the road to get it. As we came closer I saw several Japs trying to start your car. We hid in a bamboo thicket for a while, and then I saw your car being towed toward Olongopo by a Jap truck. So you better kiss your car goodbye."

"Did you see anything of my husband's outfit," I asked hopefully.

"Yes, fortunately, his company went past just as I reached home. He sent you a note."

The little scrap of crumpled paper read:

"Dearest Wife: We're moving back toward Balanga, but you stay where you are until I come for you. I borrowed ten dollars from Juan. Please pay him for me. All my love, Phil."

I tucked the precious missive, along with my other valuables into my bra... my high-pockets.

Eighteen of us were using the hunter's cabin, with a floor space of ten by twelve feet, and I was glad when the laborers began work on the house to relieve this congestion. After idly watching them for a time, Lolita and I began to expedite the work by helping them tie up bundles of cogon grass for the roof.

All of us spent another night in the overcrowded cabin.

After a breakfast of steamed rice, sugar and carabao milk, work was resumed at six the next morning. The new structure, made without any other tools than the Filipino boys' bolos and their nimble fingers, rapidly took shape. It stood on posts two feet off the ground, to keep us safe from snakes and other creeping things. It was floored with split bamboo, and the roof extended out over the sidewalls to give us a shady outdoor dining room. A lean-to at the back served as our kitchen.

The interior consisted of two rooms; one about seven by fifteen feet for the Dymson tribe, and a smaller one about seven feet square for Dian, Lolita and me. The Dymsons had planned it for Dian and me only, and Papa Dymson disapproved highly when I insisted that Lolita be lodged with us. The other servants all slept outdoors, and he considered it out of order for me to treat my maid as one of the family. Papa D. was short on morals, but he was long on social etiquette.

At the close of that day the house was completed, even to a dining table outside, at which we ate, standing. Phil had given me his mosquito netting and a heavy army blanket. I unpacked our meager belongings and arranged them in our cramped, but private quarters.

Some of the boys left at midnight to sneak down to the hacienda, and they returned early the next morning with a large pig. All the women-folk went to work, cutting it up. Some of the meat was smoked, some was chopped into sausage and stuffed into gut-skins to dry, and the balance was pickled in vinegar.

"This will last us for two weeks if we ration it," Juan opined optimistically.

"Won't the fresh meat spoil?" I questioned.

"Not in two days," he asserted.

He was wrong. After the first day when the pork acquired a decided smell, I did not touch it, nor would I permit Dian and Lolita to do so. The others devoured it eagerly. Presently Buddy was stricken with high fever and diarrhea, and was administered the native cure of a strict rice water diet. I spoke to Juan about the danger of eating the pork, whereupon Papa Dymson interrupted irritably, "Nothing of the kind! You just consider yourself too good to eat our poor food!" and stamped from the room. I noticed with some secret satisfaction that night, he, too, was on a rice water diet. His devoted Ascing, in the corner that they occupied, waited on him, slave-like, as he remained out of circulation for several days.

Juan who had studied, but not completed, a medical course in college now constituted himself head of the health department. After the pork episode, he decreed that all drinking water and dishes be boiled.

On January tenth, a disquieting incident occurred, which resulted in my partial banishment from the camp. Our boys reported Jap patrols coming part way up our trail, and the Dymsons promptly hid their money and firearms. Papa Dymson lost no time in pointing out how dangerous it would be for his family to be caught harboring me, an American. "They might kill every one of us on account of you!" he concluded with a snarl, baring his repulsive tobacco-stained teeth.

Juan's solution was for me to hide out in a thick bamboo grove about a mile away, during the daylight hours. One of the boys, Demyon, guided me there, and brought my lunch at noon. The Dymsons thought my olive-skinned Dian would pass as part Spanish, and could remain with Lolita. I did not look with favor on this semi-exile. Sitting alone all day, listening to incessant monkey chatter, made me unbearably nervous. I passed some of the time deliberately acquiring a sun-tan, to make myself as native-looking as possible. I also started making notes about what had transpired, but soon ran out of paper.

These monotonous days became seemingly longer and longer. If I fell asleep, the mischievous simians would throw things at me, and I would awaken with a start, thinking "Japs!" When I discovered that it was only "monkey-shines," I threw things back in a tantrum. This display of temper thoroughly delighted the monkeys, who flung themselves from tree to tree in a frenzy of playful excitement.

One evening when I returned to camp, I learned that Papa Dymson, Ascing, and their little girl, had seceded from the family circle, and taken up their abode in the old hut. Juan looked graver than ever as he explained how bitterly his mother suffered with jealousy of her younger rival. He recited how Mama D. had once taken a pot-shot at Papa, wounding him slightly. The old curmudgeon had retaliated by having Mama confined in a sanitarium for a year.

The next day, I took advantage of Papa's absence by not going to my hiding place as usual. The enforced solitude and long hours of separation from Dian were really getting me down. Three days later the crusty old hacendado came storming over to the new hut.

"I'll have to move back here," he shouted, "and see that this place is run right, even if all the noise and confusion kills me."

"If you dislike noise and confusion," I snapped, "try staying in a bamboo thicket for a while. I'll trade places with you gladly."

The old boy was adamant. He asserted his authority as head man of the outfit, and I was packed off again to the bamboos and my monkey playmates. After another week of this limbo, while in the midst of a spirited argument with a couple of aggressive simians which I seemed to be losing, I made up my mind that enough was enough. When Demyon came up with my noon-day chow, I asked him about himself and his plans. Demyon was a nice-looking boy, spoke English quite well, and was only too ready to tell me of his dislike for Old Man Dymson, plus the universal resentment all of the boys felt due to the stingy rations. He made it plain that he would like to run away to his home province, but did not have sufficient food for the journey.

"He is starving all of us boys," Demyon complained. "He has the name of being the meanest old man in this province. He got all his land and money by lending money at high rates of interest to poor farmers and then squeezing them out."

"Do you know this country around here?" I quizzed. "Could you find your way to Mariveles or Corregidor?"

"I think that I could," he replied. "But why should I go there?"

I then let him know that I, too, was tired of the camp and wanted to reach the American lines; that I would pay him well if he would guide me to the American outposts. Demyon thought that if we could get enough food for the trip, that he could guide me, sticking to forest trails above the Jap lines. After making mutual promises not to mention our plans to anyone, he agreed to meet me and my little family, the next morning at six, about half a mile down the trail.

That night I whispered my plan to Lolita, and she was delighted. The girl reported that Papa Dymson had struck her that day, shouting, "You're just as stuck up as your white mistress." Then she added, "He's a mal hombre, and he hates us."

The next morning while Lolita was packing up, I managed to speak to Juan, and informed him of my intensions. He tried to dissuade me, but I cut his protest short with "I'm sorry, Juan. You have been very kind, but my mind is made up. I must try to reach my husband. All that I want to do is buy enough provisions from you to last us for three days."

"It's a crazy idea!" Juan exploded, "Your husband asked me to look after you. I'm not going to help you. I don't want your blood on my conscience. You will be caught and killed!" The sound of Juan's raised voice brought the old so-and-so to the scene. He took a different view of the matter.

"So," he roared belligerently, "We're not good enough for you!"

Then wheeling on Juan, he ordered, "Let her go! We will be well rid of the lot of them!"

Juan usually crumpled up in the face of his father's outbursts, but this time he held out for our being given some food for the journey.

"Give her a pound of rice and two cans of fish, and see that she pays for them," my erstwhile host curtly commanded, and then stalked back to the house, muttering to himself. Before Juan went for our provisions, Mama Dymson emerged tearfully from her abode.

"It's that devil of a husband of mine who is driving you out," she sobbed. "If the Japs get you, I shall never forgive myself. It will be all our fault!"

I patted her heaving shoulders tenderly, and told her not to worry; that I was certain we could make the trip safely. We started down the trail. I carried Dian and a small bag, while Lolita followed with more bags and the bedding. Demyon was at the rendezvous, and took most of our load.

After stumbling down the uneven trail for about three miles, we halted for a rest in a large sugar-cane field. Demyon cut some cane, and peeled off the bark. I had never eaten raw cane before and we all, Dian included, chewed energetically, enjoying the strange delicacy. It soon proved too tough for Dian's little teeth, and she gave up. It made the rest of us thirsty, and we drank all the water we had brought along. Demyon went in search of more, and found a spring from which we refilled our clay water jars.

When I asked Demyon about our route, he pointed to a distant range of hills, explaining, "See that long mountain. It is called 'The Sleeping Lady of Mariveles.' We must always keep it to our right as we walk south, and so we come to Mariveles and Corregidor."

The Sleeping Lady! A blunt, round mountain creates the illusion of her head, a flat plateau her neck; her hilly breasts rise and slope down to her waist. For her feet she has a small, steep hill beyond which the range drops sharply to the water. I knew that her terrestrial toes pointed to the spot, where, only a mile or so from the shore, the small island fortress of Corregidor guarded the Bay.

That was my destination, and there I hoped to find Phil.

Chapter VI

Death Passes Me By

AFTER AN HOUR'S REST AT THE FOOT OF THE MOUNTAIN, we headed south and hiked all morning without stopping.

Demyon, with the bedding and supplies in a compact roll balanced on his head, followed small trails and sometimes broke new ones, chopping the tall brush with his bolo. Lolita and I followed in single file behind our guide, alternately carrying Dian and the bags. Demyon figured that our course was parallel to the main road, but from time to time we had to change direction to detour around a hill. Our chief concern was to remain high enough in the foothills to avoid interception by the occasional Nip patrols.

I tried to give Dian the impression that we were on a sort of extended picnic. She seemed to enjoy the novelty of being on the move, and it made no difference to her who carried her. I adopted Lolita's native method, using a towel for a sling, so that the child rode comfortably on my hip. This device left my hands free to carry small bags or to aid me when climbing. Dian was cheerful and relaxed, and even took casual short naps in her improvised hammock.

We stopped for a scanty lunch. Lolita boiled enough rice over a little fire to provide each of us with a cupful, and we had some bananas picked while en route. In the late afternoon we arrived at a small mountain road, and heard someone approaching. I clapped my hand gently over Dian's mouth. We lowered ourselves into the bush as quietly as possible and waited, peering cautiously through the bamboos and wild cogon grass.

A native driving a carabao cart, with a small child riding beside him, came into view. We were so relieved that we simultaneously exploded from the undergrowth, frightening the man badly. He spoke no English, but told Demyon in Ilocano dialect that this road was safe and led to a scattered group of about twenty refugee huts beside a stream. We mounted the creaking vehicle, and Dian was delighted at the unexpected ride with another child for company.

We were able to find an empty hut at the camp, where we spent the night. Next morning while I washed Dian, myself, and some of our clothes in the stream, Lolita and Demyon went shopping. They visited every hut over a radius of half a mile. Net result: two pounds of rice and a pound of carabao meat... but no salt. After boiling the meat for two hours, it was still too tough to eat; though the broth tasted fine with boiled rice. We left the meat simmering through the night over a small fire, and finished it for our early breakfast.

Then we started our weary trek once again, up and down hill, always trying to keep our "Sleeping Lady" to the right. About noon we approached a valley and saw a large sugarcane field. We cut some cane, and we grown-ups lunched on it, saving our remaining rice for Dian. Once in the valley, we could not spot our landmark, but we forced our aching legs to trudge on. Late in the afternoon, I stumbled and fell, and did not have the energy to arise. Lolita looked startled and asked, "What is the matter? Are you ill?"

"No, child," I said wearily, "just tired and very hungry." We called Demyon back, and opened the fish, dividing it into four equal parts. What a feast... We even permitted ourselves two cups of boiled rice. As we polished off the last mouthfuls of our provisions, we all felt our spirits rise. I longed to sleep, but Demyon argued that the spot was too near the Jap lines.

We started circling the cane field, planning to camp part way up the hill beyond. At the end of the field... too near them to turn back... we came upon several men standing near a house. As we had been seen, I knew that it would not avail us to turn back. We put on a bold front, approached the dwelling, and... thank heaven... found that the men were Filipinos.

Demyon went into an animated conversation with them. I could not understand a word of the conversation, but I could tell by his excited voice and gestures that he was greatly disturbed. After five minutes, he let me have it.

"Senora," he announced suddenly, "I quit!"

"But Demyon, you can't leave me like this," I told him, and added. "Why do you want to quit?"

"Just on the other side of those trees is the main highway, patrolled by Japs," he said, pointing to a clump of trees only fifty feet away. "The men here say the Japs sometimes come to this house. We would have to cross that road to get to Mariveles and it's too risky. I quit!"

"Now, Demyon," I soothed, my heart in my shoes, "you knew we would have to cross the Jap lines when you took this job. All that we have to do now is to hide for a while and then slip across the read tonight. If I'm not afraid why should you be?"

Demyon's answer was, "I quit."

I begged, scolded, offered him double the amount of money agreed upon, and at last he broke in, "We may be caught while we're talking here. I'll take you back up the hill. Then I quit."

We cut straight through the cane which was from five to eight feet tall, and came upon another small trail leading upwards. After following this for two miles, we arrived at a plantation, owned by the Mayor of Dinalupihan. I went in to ask for shelter and told the mayor's wife where we were headed. When I mentioned the fact that we had left Dymson's camp two days before, she burst out laughing.

"Dymson!" she chuckled. "Why they're only a mile from here. You must have been walking in a circle for two days."

My inclination was to sit down and have a good cry. However, night was coming on and there was work to do getting settled in the little hut the woman had placed at our disposal.

While Lolita and I arranged the bedding and mosquito net, I noticed a man standing in the road, silently watching us. After a while I told Demyon to get rid of the fellow. This resulted in fifteen minutes conversation between the two, at the end of which Demyon reported, "I didn't want to hurt the man's feelings, so I didn't exactly tell him to leave."

"Well?" I prompted.

"He says he has a bigger and better hut back in the woods and invited us to come and stay with his family for a while. I think it would be safer there."

This sounded like good sense, so I smiled at the man, told Demyon to extend our thanks, and we packed up and followed him. The trail to his camp was narrow and well camouflaged. I kept thinking as we progressed that we had made a good move, until our journey ended at the abode of the filthiest, most disreputable-looking natives I had ever seen. The man's wife, four children, and his aged mother and father were crowded into a fetid three-sided hut about six feet deep by twelve long. By dint of considerable hospitable pushing and squeezing, they managed to uncover sufficient floor space at one end to accommodate Dian, Lolita and me. Before long everyone except myself was sound asleep. My plan about worrying manana, native style, had collapsed.

The next morning my host suggested that if I had some money, there was rice and meat to be bought. "For everyone," he added meaningfully. I gave Lolita ten dollars, American currency, and told her to take Demyon, follow our host, and buy all the food they could carry. I still had a very small piece of soap. While they were gone, I bathed Dian and washed our dirty things in a small stream nearby.

The shoppers came back triumphantly after several hours, with five pounds of carabao meat, a half sack of unhusked rice, and ... best of all... a cup of precious salt. We were all very elated. Demyon cut the meat in thin strips and stretched it in the hot sun to dry. He told me that it would dry enough that night to prevent it from spoiling, and we could dry it more the next day.

I noticed that Lolita was acting strangely, and seemed to be very nervous. I finally called her away from the hut, pretending there was something I wanted her to do for me.

"Lolita," I whispered, "What's the matter?"

"Oh, senora, I thought I would never get a chance to tell you this." The girl was almost sobbing. "These people don't know I am Ilocano. They spoke in that dialect this morning. The women told her husband about the ten dollars you gave me, and he said 'She is a rich American. Papatayen me no maturog.' That means, 'We will kill her when she is asleep tonight; then we will get her money.' And his wife agreed."

Somehow I was not too surprised. I didn't doubt Lolita's story in the least.

"Pretend there isn't anything wrong," I cautioned. "Don't say a word to anybody. I'll take care of everything."

"Si, senora," Lolita answered in her docile childish manner.

We ate lunch and the men pounded the unhusked rice until dinner time. My witch-like hostess rolled twelve cigarettes from raw tobacco and a piece of old newspaper and gave them to me. They were strong and bitter, but after we retired I started smoking to keep awake. Every time I felt drowsy, I lighted another cigarette, and invariably either the husband or wife would inquire "Why you no sleep? You sick?"

"No," I explained. "I'm worried about my husband and can't sleep."

After the longest night I had ever passed in my life, morning came at last. I finally awakened Lolita and told her to watch so that I could doze off for an hour or so.

I was still in a daze, wondering where to turn next and how to get away from these sinister companions, when the mayor's wife sent word by a little boy for me to come to her house. I simply flew down the trail.

"I was sorry to see you get in with those people," she said, "and I took the liberty of telling some close friends of mine about you. They want you to live with them."

"Why should they want me?" I asked frankly. "I have no food and would be an extra burden to anyone."

"Senor Sobervenas does not think so," the mayor's wife assured me. "He is the friend I am speaking of. He would like to send his son to talk to you."

"This must be God's answer," I exclaimed happily. "I spent all last night asking Him for help and guidance. No, I do not like nor trust the people I am staying with." I then told my benefactor what Lolita had overheard and my long vigil.

She replied, "I'm not surprised to hear this. Don't worry. Carling Sobervenas will come to see you today."

Carling, a tall, wavy-haired man of about twenty-five years, very good-looking and obviously of Spanish ancestry, arrived at about eleven. He was clean, neat and spoke excellent English.

"My father has sent me to invite you to live with us, Mrs. Phillips," he began. "We heard from the mayor and his wife about you and your child being stranded in the hills."

I let him know that I had money, but no food; also that I had the responsibility for two servants as well as Dian. "That makes four extra mouths to feed," I finished.

"That will not matter to us," Carling insisted. "We have enough food. Father has ordered that I bring you back."

I thanked him, and we arranged to leave at four p. m.

"I have some business with the mayor and a few others near here, but I will be back to get you at that time."

I told him we would be ready, and he departed. When my host noticed that I was packing up, he told me brazenly, "I no like your leaving. I no think you should go with strangers. Maybe mayor's wife and Sobervenas family try to get your money."

"I have very little money," I advised him, "and I will gladly give it to anyone who can feed us." He shook his head angrily and walked away, sulking, to consult his wife.

It was a great relief when Carling reappeared. We started up the three miles of trail happily. The more that I talked with young Sobervenas, the more certain I became that we would be safe... even contented... with him and his family.

The last mile of our hike led almost straight up a cliff. Carling went up first when we reached the end of our journey, and Demyon handed our gear to him. Then we boosted Lolita up, and I handed Dian to her. I was the biggest problem, for Demyon pushed and Carling pulled, to hoist me. Demyon managed alone; then we all relaxed, and got our second wind.

"Surely, no Jap will ever try that," I gasped. "He would never guess that the trail continued on at the top of this cliff."

"I think you are right," Carling agreed. "We all feel quite safe up here."

Young Sobervenas told us that the little settlement composed of about twenty huts, was conducted on a cooperative basis, and with little discord. I learned that his family, in addition to his father and mother, consisted of Tessing, Carling's wife; Conching, an unmarried sister; Doming, a married brother, and Manuel, a bachelor brother. Conching, he assured me, was especially anxious to have me with them for "company."

His description of his family's daily routine sounded very pleasant and tranquil. Therefore, on our arrival, I was quite astonished to find a confused state of affairs, with everyone rushing around obviously agitated and alarmed. Inquiry disclosed that Doming's wife was about to give birth to a premature baby, and no midwife was available. I thought of the highly successful delivery in the carabao cart, drew a deep breath, and took the plunge.

"If you want to trust me," I volunteered. "I will take charge. I've done this before."

I was immediately awarded the obstetrical assignment. There were no complications, and "Doctor Phillips" soon came out from behind the sheet partition with a four-pound baby girl. I turned the infant over to Conching to wash and dress. Senora Sobervenas came in to care for the young mother, and remarked, "You must be tired and hungry. Go and eat, and I'll manage the rest."

It was now after nine. Lolita had fed Dian and they were both sleeping soundly. Food had been kept hot for me, and as I ate, the thought of finding these good people brought such a lump into my throat, that I could barely swallow. My belated dinner was interrupted by a sudden shout from Senora Sobervenas.

"Come quickly," she called. "Another baby is coming."

"Good heavens!" I cried, jumping up. "It can't be!"

I really did not know if I was equal to twins, but at ten-thirty we had brought a tiny, three-pound boy into this troubled world. I really slept that night!

At first, food was not a problem. Old Juan, the family's one remaining servant, often went down to their farm during the night, bringing back as many vegetables as he could carry, and returning before daylight disclosed him to the Japs. In addition to the essential green stuff, he also brought any meat, pork or carabao, he could buy along the way. Sometimes he was able to purchase the rich carabao milk which was badly needed for Dian, as my ten-pound can of milk powder had long been only a memory. The rice supply presented no difficulty. Boys went down at night, harvested it, and brought it to us as palay... unhusked rice. This was poured into a hollowed-out tree trunk, threshed with a pair of long sticks, and finally the kernels were poured into trays and tossed, to winnow away the chaff.

Toward the end of the month, old Juan failed to return from a nocturnal foray. We worried about him, and with reason. He came back eventually, reporting that he had been caught by the Nips and forced to work for them all day, cutting fodder for their horses. Juan vowed that he would not go down any more, and we could not expect him to take the risk, even if we did miss our fresh vegetables and meat.

More days passed rapidly. One afternoon in the early part of March, I heard the sound of three rifle shots.

"Did you hear that," I called to Senor Sobervenas. "Can the Japs be coming up here?"

"No, I don't think so," he replied. "It's probably some hungry ones shooting game."

I was dubious about the statement, as I knew by tacit agreement, everyone in the hills used traps to catch wild pigs or monkeys, and thus avoiding undue attention from the Nips.

When, a few minutes later, the sound of firing resumed, Carling advised us all to hide while he went out to reconnoiter. I had been bathing Dian. I wrapped her hurriedly in a large towel, and ran with her to hide under the house, where the other members of the household had sought refuge. The sound of the fusillade indicated that the scene of combat was moving in our direction. A few minutes later Carling came running back and scrambled into our covert. A number of men bore down on the house, and were seemingly in and out of it, shouting and shooting before they moved off. The combatants were apparently beset with their own difficulties as they made no attempt to molest us.

"It's all over now. You can come out," Papa Sobervenas advised after quiet had descended.

A strange Filipino boy, gasping and moaning, lay wounded outside the door of the hut. Noting his obvious distress, Tessing and I started forward to help him.

"Leave him alone," ordered Senor Sobervenas. "He's one of the bandits."

I did not know what had taken place, and despite my host's admonition, begged the men to do something for the pain-wracked youngster. They lifted the boy to a table in the yard, and found a bullet lodged in his arm, and a bullet hole in his shoulder. After much heated discussion, it was finally decided to send him down to the Jap hospital in Dinalupihan, as he was in apparent need of immediate surgical attention. So several men, under Carling's supervision, placed the casualty on an improvised stretcher, and took him down the trail.

When Carling returned, he gave us the facts. Four armed and masked bandits had gone into a hut a couple of miles above us and tied the women and children with rope. The men living in the hut were absent at the time, and the robbers waited in ambush for their return. Then they held them up and demanded their money, but finding none, beat the men, and tied them up also. The aggrieved men finally freed themselves, and started in search of the ladrones [Lit. 'thieves'] whom they found hiding in a hut. One of the bandits opened fire on his pursuers with an old Spanish rifle, and a chase ensued that covered much territory. It ended with the sudden demise of three of the desperadoes and the wounding of the boy.

It seemed like we always had worries of some sort, and now a plague of flies added to our sanitation problem. The natives, ignorant of the ever-present danger attendant upon promiscuity, would not use the latrines, nor take proper care of them. Malaria, dysentery, and finally typhoid was the inevitable result. Our food supply had diminished and was now limited to rice, salt and a small amount of sugar-cane. When the salt gave out, we pressed the juice from the cane (which the men filched from the lowlands at night) and boiled it into a syrup to season the rice. All too soon, our small store of rice was exhausted, and the attempts of the men to buy meat or game were fruitless.

We had two deaths in our camp. In each instance when the disease struck, the patient was so weak from hunger that he did not have sufficient strength to combat the malady.

Hearing that food was plentiful in a settlement on another hill, ten men from our camp left to investigate, while we waited anxiously for two days.

They came back laden with fresh meat, various kinds of vegetables, salt, and a week's supply of rice. They also brought soap which we had long been without, as well as three sacks of bananas; an almost forgotten luxury. Elated by their successful foraging the venturers planned on another trip for more provisions.

The men had remained an additional night in Meite, a barrio on the other hill, to listen to a broadcast on a forbidden radio, owned by the village priest of Dinalupihan, Father Cabaginis. At the mention of their beloved padre, there were happy murmurs among the women-folk who had been uncertain as to his fate. As to the news it was "Hang on to Bataan! Help will arrive soon!"

"Is that all?" I inquired with obvious disappointment.

"No," Manuel reported, "Here is some good news that will make you very happy," and then he let me know that the good priest had taken in three American soldiers, concealing them from the slant-eyes, and feeding them. I suddenly came alive again.

"Do you know any of their names?"

Manuel's face fell.

"Oh, Mrs. Phillips, I'm so sorry. We forgot to ask."

"What did they look like?" I persisted, "Was any one of them very tall... very nice-looking?"

The best description that I could get out of the boys was that the Americanos were all thin; one had a red beard, and one lay down all the time and seemed to be sick.

"The next time you go, I want to go with you," I asserted.

"That would be far too dangerous, my child," Papa Sobervenas protested, and his sons agreed with him.

"I must find out if one of the soldiers is Phil," I kept insisting, until Senora Sobervenas came to my aid. So it was finally agreed that I could go on the next trip, and, for the next few days I was so excited that I scarcely noticed my hunger.

My shoes were almost worn out. I knew that they would not hold together for such a long trip so I canvassed the colony, trying to find a pair to buy. All the women had very small feet, and of course, the men's shoes were too big. I finally found a pair of sneakers which I could get into nicely by cutting out the toes. Now I was all set, but still had to acquire a good tan. I laid in the sun for hours so that I would look as dark as the natives in case we were stopped by the Japs. My routine was to hike a mile or so from the camp, clear a spot in the tall cogon grass, strip to my panties and bra, and then simmer. This soon made me even darker than the natives.

Six men made the trip this time. I dressed like them as much as I could, hiding my hair under an old rice sack, worn as the men did theirs, half of it turned inside like a pointed hood. We left camp at sundown, and it was dark when we arrived at the foot of the hill, where we must cross the Jap-patrolled highway. Hiding in a cane field, we watched one patrol pass out of sight and hearing. Then we dashed silently across the road into the tall sugar-cane on the other side. After a few minutes of quiet vigil, we continued up the hill to the barrio of Meite, reaching it shortly after midnight. The trip was about fifteen miles and we had made good time.

Father Cabaginis, a short, stocky, friendly man, aged about thirty-five years, greeted us warmly. He summoned a guide to take me to a friendly woman's house to spend the rest of the night. At six, my guide called for me and conducted me to a wild banana grove. My heart started beating like a trip hammer.

The grove was far too big for me to start searching it for jittery fugitives, but I knew that I was well out of earshot of the Nips.

"Hello! Hello," I sang out. "Does anyone here speak English?"

"Lady, what do you think I'm doing? Whistling Dixie?" came an unexpected response, almost at my elbow.

An emaciated soldier with friendly, twinkling grey eyes and a neat Vandyke beard, materialized from behind a tree trunk. I gazed at him, speechless at the moment.

"Say, are you really an American woman?" he demanded. "Or am I seeing things again?"

CHAPTER VII

Corporal Boone Suggests a Plan of Battle

"I'M AN AMERICAN," I ASSURED HIM. "My name is Claire Phillips."

"All that I can say is that I'm more than pleased to meet you," the soldier shot back, extending a lean hand. "John Boone, Corporal, Company D, Thirty-First Infantry. That's me!"

"At ease," I quipped, clasping hands.

We looked at each other curiously. The soldier was slim, and slightly taller than I. His uniform, although not tattered as one would expect it to be under the circumstances, was obviously made for a larger man. He leaned his rifle against a tree trunk, and motioned to a folded blanket spread on the ground.

"Won't you sit down?" he invited.

"Thanks, I will," I accepted, and dropped down on a corner of it.

I brought out a package of native cigarettes, and he took one with obvious relish. He lighted mine, then his, and I sensed that this social amenity was the prelude to a flood of questions.

"Hold everything, corporal," I burst forth. "Let me talk first if you don't mind. Do you by any chance happen to know Sergeant John Phillips, Headquarters Company, Thirty-First Infantry?"

Boone drew in the welcome smoke deeply, and exhaled slowly before he answered.

"Phillips?...Phillips?.. .No, I'm sorry. Your husband?"

I nodded.

"I have met some of the men in that outfit," he continued. "Know many of them by sight, but wouldn't know all their names. What does he look like?"

"Tall, dark and handsome," was my description. "No kidding, he's all of that. Phil is not the hard-boiled kind; everybody likes him."

"Including you, I gather," the non-com joshed.

"Yes, you're right," I told him. "I saw him last at Roosevelt Park near Olongopo, about six weeks ago. I know that he's trying to get back to me. I came down here thinking and hoping..."

"Sure, I know," Boone cut in. "It's tough, but don't worry. He will get back; just be patient."

Then I turned to a new trend of thought.

"I was told that there are two other soldiers here with you. Who are they? Perhaps they would know something."

"I'll call them. I told them that I would if everything was okay."

"If everything was okay," I repeated, puzzled by his comment.

"Well," the corporal explained, "the fact is that these two boys have been pretty sick. Mramor still is... malaria... and Henderson," he touched his fore-head, "hasn't been quite right upstairs lately. It sort of gets to you, living like this, but I guess you know about that sort of thing."

Boone whistled twice in a subdued tone. Very soon there was a slight thrashing farther off in the grove, and presently two gaunt, ragged G. I.'s came up and saluted as the corporal introduced them.

"You had me worried," Mramor ranted, "talking so damn long. We thought maybe the lady was a Jap. Why didn't you signal sooner?"

"Maybe we're lucky he signaled at all," put in Henderson, and began to laugh in a manner that verged on hysteria.

"Take it easy," Boone told them curtly. "This lady wants news of her hus-band," and he repeated to them my description of Phil, stating his outfit.

His effort was fruitless, for although both men belonged to Phil's regi-ment, they could not place him. I noticed their eyes fastened on our cigarettes, so I passed the smokes around. The two soldiers accepted them eagerly. Hen-derson, lighting up with a shaky hand, looked around anxiously and whispered "You don't reckon the Nips could see the smoke, do you?"

"Oh, for Pete's sake!" the corporal tossed at him disgustedly. "It's all right! Relax!"

While his companions sprawled on their backs, blissfully puffing their cig-arettes, Boone brought me up to date on their experiences after being separated from their outfit during the fighting on Mount Samat. Then he let me know how Father Cabaginis had found Henderson a month before, deliri-ous from malaria, and trying vainly to ease his hunger with sugarcane. The padre had brought Henderson up closer to his house, made a shelter for him in the bamboo grove, and sent meals to him regularly. Boone and Mramor had learned about Henderson through some natives they had met, and were thus able to join him.

The time passed rapidly as we chatted. Boone, suddenly glancing at the sun directly overhead, commented, "it's lunch time." As if by prearrangement, several native women entered the grove, bringing bowls of chicken boiled with native squash, and generous servings of rice. With broad smiles, they also presented us with dessert in the form of bananas boiled in cane juice.

After we had eaten, we resumed our palaver. The corporal related how he and Mramor had been out on a food detail, and returned to the spot where they had left their company only to find it taken over by the Japs.

It was quite obvious that Boone was the only one of the trio who was fit, alert and capable. Henderson lay silently, and alternated periods of smoking with one of shaking with malarial chills. Mramor, too nervous to sit still very long, wandered about investigating every minor sound. I could see that both of them leaned on Boone with child-like faith.

It was nearly dusk when I left my newly-found friends regretfully, promising to return for a visit in a week's time. Despite the fact that Boone and I had not arrived at any decision (as I wanted to go to Corregidor and he wanted to await the American offensive) I left somewhat strengthened by the encounter.

The Sobervenas boys were waiting for me at the priest's house. There we listened eagerly to his radio and learned that "MacArthur is on the offensive." This sounded good, but I was beginning to have my doubts. So we told the father goodbye, filled our head-gear... the rice-sack hoods... with bananas and meat, and started back. It was a hard trip. Finally my load seemed to become heavier with every step, and I was thankful to drop on my blanket when we arrived back in camp at three a. m.

It was breakfast in bed for me. My limbs were so sore and stiff that I could not get up until Lolita had rubbed them for a time. My big toes, protruding from the sneakers, were swollen and cut from the sharp rocks I had encountered during the rugged nocturnal journey. Everybody fussed over me and gave me advice. After I had soaked my aching feet in hot water and exercised sufficiently to work off the stiffness, I was eager for another trip down. It seemed very important for me to get back quickly and talk to Boone about the possibility of joining forces and making our way to Corregidor.

One week later, when we left on the second trip, only the three Sobervenas boys went with me. We followed the same routine as before. Father Cabaginis was waiting for us when we arrived at his house near midnight. We had a good dinner, a long talk, and then listened to the radio. I heard the disheartening news that Singapore had surrendered. Once again I snatched a few hours of sleep at the home of the hospitable Filipino hostess. A boy knocked on the door at six, saying that Corporal Boone had sent him. I left immediately with my guide, picking bananas along the way for breakfast.

The three soldiers were waiting for me on the same spot where we had previously met. Although I was thrilled to see them again, I demanded a trifle peevishly, "What's the idea of getting me up in the middle of the night?"

"What do you mean, 'the middle of the night'?" laughed Boone, "I've been waiting for you for over an hour. I have a terrific idea that won't keep."

"I have an idea, too," I replied, and started right in to expound it. "What do you think the chances are for all of us to get to Mariveles and Corregidor?"

"Well, I sure ought to get to a hospital," Henderson complained, pulling the corner of a blanket around his shaking shoulders.

"Aw, go on. They wouldn't put you in the hospital. They throw awols in the guard house," taunted Mramor.

"Buddy, it would be the nut-house for you," Henderson snapped back at his tormentor. "Anyhow, I'm not awol. I got lost and you know it."

"That's your story," persisted Mramor. "But you all can count me out. I don't care if I ever get back to the Army. Leave me in the big, wide open spaces with nothing to do all day but wait for a sweet little babe like Tessa to bring me three squares a day."

At the end of this outburst he rolled over on his stomach and regarded me fixedly. "Do you think I ought to marry the girl?" he asked suddenly.

"Shut up, Mramor!" ordered Boone. "If you don't know your own mind, don't bother others for advice." He turned to me, speaking quickly and very earnestly, his lean hands locked around his knees. "There's nothing I would like more, Mrs. Phillips, than to get back to the American side, but I'm damned if I know how it can be done. I've tried so many times."

"Maybe you didn't have a good guide," I suggested.

"Guide!" he snorted. "Listen! I told you I was out on food detail just before the Mount Samat fracas that washed us up. There were two men with me. We holed up for a few days; then a Filipino boy came along and told us he could get us back through Subic on the China Sea Coast. Said he knew the trail well and had the Japs spotted since he made the trip twice. We took a chance on him and followed. He took us on the damndest roughest trip we were ever on, and one night as we were crossing a small stream my buddies whispered 'Freeze.' They had crossed and I was in the middle, balancing on a stone with one foot in the air. I froze, just like a statue. Japs were patrolling just on the other side, but they didn't see us. We started back and our guide said 'I know another way.' We followed and wound up at almost the same place. This time the Nips spotted us. The guide ran shouting to the Japs, and my two buddies were shot, but I got away. I know now that he was working for the skibbies and got two pesos a head for every soldier he turned over to them...and still does. That was the first try. Do you want to hear some more about guides?"

"Go ahead," I prompted. "Just because one guide was no good, that doesn't mean they're all bad."

"Okay," Boone agreed, "So we did find a good guide, and he took us through the very tops of the hills. This one was a Negrito, and those babies know trails that no one else can ever find. He said that Bagac on the west coast was back in American hands. The place had been the scene of many battles. One week the Japs had the town; next week the Americans had driven them out; then the Nips got it back again and so on. This was one of the times it was supposed to be held by our men. Finally he brought us down into a valley where a battle had taken place a couple of weeks before. Dead men and horses were strewn all over the field. The stench was so bad we had to wet our handkerchiefs and cover our noses to get through. Wild dogs and vultures had been at the bodies and we couldn't tell a Jap from an American or Filipino. We looked for dog-tags or other identification, but couldn't find anything."

He stopped and blew his nose vigorously.

"Hell, I can still smell that horrible stench when I talk about it. Mramor couldn't take it. He got sick."

Mramor, chewing grass blades and playing some sort of game with little sticks, said nothing, and Boone gave me a significant look.

"The Negrito took us to the edge of Bagac all right, and then we saw the Japs had it again. We had to run for it and when we looked for the Negrito, he was gone. It took us three weeks to find our way back here."

"Well, I guess it's no use asking you to try it again," I remarked, "Especially with a white woman and a child along."

"You're right," the corporal agreed, "But I have another idea. This one would work."

"Shoot!" tersed Henderson unexpectedly, and Boone started in again.

"It's this: I've been all over these hills. There are hundreds of Filipino and American soldiers lost and starving, but still with a burning yen to fight Japs. I believe that I could gather them together into an effective guerilla band."

"Why don't you?" I queried.

"Only one reason... supplies. If I had a good contact in Manila to smuggle food, clothes and medicine up here, it would work. Furthermore, that contact in Manila could be you!"

"Me?" I gasped.

We regarded each other silently for a few moments.

"How could I get to Manila in the first place?" I asked suddenly, "And once there, how would I keep out of the internment camp? All foreigners must register according to the radio. What cock-and-bull story would I tell the Japs?"

"Don't give me your answer now," the non-com answered. "Take your time and think it over."

As I listened fascinated, he explained rapidly, that once assembled the arming of a band would not be a serious problem. They could take rifles from dead Japs. As for ammunition, they could find out where it was hidden and capture it by surprise raids.

"We could keep the Nips so worried right here in Bataan," he said excitedly, "they wouldn't have time to fight anywhere else. We wouldn't stand and give battle, but kill them off one by one."

Henderson had wandered off, muttering to himself, but Mramor's feverish eyes glowed brightly as he listened intently to the dynamic corporal's plan. As he expounded his views, the vision in his mind became plain as daylight to me. I knew that the "bamboo telegraph" made rumors travel fast in the hills. Once there was a gathering place where forlorn, desperate men could assemble for food and companionship, a resistance force would be born. A leader and equipment was all that was needed to weld these angry and determined men into an effective weapon against the enemy. I did not have the slightest doubt that Boone was such a leader. Every inch of his close-knit muscular body showed coordination, and his grimly set jaws indicated tenacity of purpose. He reminded me of a greyhound, straining at a leash.

I wanted to fit in with Boone's scheme of things, but I thought of my promise to Phil to await him in the hills. I began to think of ways of getting to Manila, darken my skin, live with Filipino friends and pretend to be one of them. That path would lead me hopelessly away from the chance of the hoped-for rendezvous with Phil. Sensing my conflicting emotions, Boone begged me to keep on considering his plan, and to come back again when I could.

As we shook hands, I asked him "What will you be doing next?"

"The same thing that I've been doing for the past month," he advised, "contacting men all over these hills, and telling them to stand by until I send for them. I have been moving around from Subic Bay, north to Iba, and along the China Sea, and there are more hills to be covered."

I heard Carling calling me, so I wished "Well, good luck!" and broke away. We started homeward.

When we neared the high road, the three boys and I had to hide for a long time in the cane field, for enemy trucks were passing at frequent intervals. We finally scurried across the road, only to find, to our dismay, that the cane of the other side of the road had been cut during the day. A group of Jap soldiers riding on a truck that had just passed, sighted us in the open field, and turned their car around.

"Run for that old hut!" Doming shouted.

Fear lent wings to our feet as the whine of hastily fired bullets let us know that our enemies meant business. We rushed through the door of the shelter as the truck screeched to a grinding stop about one hundred feet away. We did not stop for a moment, but kept going and scrambled through a window at the back. The hut screened us from observation as we dived unobserved, into a bamboo thicket about fifty feet behind it.

Breathless and shaken, we watched the Nips surround the hut warily and yell for us to come out. They did not hesitate long before they applied the torch, and then ran around the structure laughing and shouting. Their action reminded me at the moment of some of the old western movie scenes depicting an Indian attack on a settler's cabin. When the flimsy hut had burned to the ground, and the "jovial" Japs had fired their last bullets into the flames and departed, we crawled on our hands and knees through the forest, for a half mile up the hill.

We had used bamboo torches on the way down, but we did not feel so brave now. With Carling breaking trail, we stumbled up through the gloom, single-file, holding each other's hands.

Behind us the sky suddenly seemed to light up, and, looking down, we saw a huge fire that brightened and rose higher as we watched. I wanted to hurry on, but Carling said "That is very near Dinalupihan. Wait for me. I must go back part way and see what it is."

We waited, huddled together, fearing for his safety, but before long he was back.

"The Japs are burning their dead," he told us. "They're piling them up and pouring petroleum over them. I've seen them do it before."

"Then all those trucks... even the one that chased us... were bringing in bodies?" I asked.

"Yes," he made answer. "I saw them being tossed in the fire."

As he spoke, a nauseating odor began to reach us, so sickening that we covered our nostrils and hurried on.

Now I knew what Boone meant by the smell of the dead.

Chapter VIII

The Death March Decides My Destiny

MY WORRIES NEVER CAME SINGLY, but seemingly in platoons. Japs, lack of food, and disease were bad enough without the inclusion of snakes and rats. The reptiles, four to fifteen feet long, and some of them thicker than a muscular arm, never entered my hut, but lurked under it. Their presence caused Lolita and I to carry Dian constantly, and she was not learning to walk.

The big mountain pack-rats were an ever-present menace. We placed the food out of their reach, but every night they ran over us in search of it. Their shrill squeaks, often sounding close to our ears, made chills run up and down my spine. I often worried through the hours of darkness about them biting Dian as she slept.

Rumor had reached us that a concentration camp had been established at old Santo Tomas University in Manila. I was fairly certain that Louise was interned there. I tried to think of some plan whereby I could get Dian into the camp, as I thought she would be safer with Louise rather than amidst the danger that surrounded us here. I finally decided that she was all I had to cheer and encourage me, so I abandoned that idea as I watched and awaited developments.

The scarcity of food again became acute. We now had no access to the farm below, but Senor Sobervenas was a pillar of optimism and resourcefulness. He and his three sons were always thinking of novel ways to replenish our food supply. Manuel killed a large snake, skinned it, and we fried the meat like steaks. It wasn't too bad. One day I failed to recognize the meat that Senora Sobervenas brought to the table, and asked what it was. Tessing started to answer, but Doming frowned at her and hastily explained "It's young carabao."

"Don't expect me to believe that," I shot back. "There are no carabao within ten miles of here, and you know it."

The senora, looking down at her plate to whiten the well-meant lie, murmured "baboy," which means "pig" in Tagalog. I smiled and shook my head, because by this time I was thoroughly familiar with the taste of either wild pig or carabao meat. After lunch, I cornered Doming.

"I've eaten the meat and it was very good," I persisted, "So I know it won't hurt me. I realize that you know what is good enough for you is certainly good enough for me. Now come across... What is it?"

"A distant relative of ours," Doming answered, smiling. "Monkey."

After that we had monkey steaks and stews whenever the boys had good hunting. Often we had no meat for a week or two at a time. Then I had to add Lolita to my other anxieties.

I had known for some time that she was pregnant and homesick for Manila. Then more worries... the lack of sanitation facilities and the promiscuity of the natives brought an ever increasing swarm of flies and rats. The only remedy that I could think of was for us to move to a new location, but when I mentioned it to the Sobervenas family the inevitable answer was "next week" or "a little later."

A chance visitor at our camp gave us detailed information about a hidden Jap ammunition dump down in Dinalupihan. He even drew a map and indicated on it just where the munitions ... tons and tons of them according to his description... were located. The next night, with Senor Sobervenas' permission, I sent one of the best boys, Pacio, across to Boone. He carried the map, hidden inside the cardboard folder of my parent's photograph, and a note from me asking what he thought could be done about destroying the dump. Pacio brought an answer stating that Boone would try to relay the map by a Negrito guide to General McArthur at Corregidor.

I kept worrying about that dump, and after a week passed, I decided to do something about it. Pacio, two other boys, and I made a careful plan and went down the mountain at midnight. I stopped and waited about a mile above the town while the boys went on carrying kerosene-soaked torches. After giving them ample time to reach their destination, I started a brush fire and kept it going to attract the Nips' attention. When they noticed it, and I saw their distant figures running in my direction, I scrambled higher into the bush and hid. Meanwhile, the three boys had circled the town, crept up and tossed their suddenly-lighted torches into the huts where the ammunition was hidden.

I happily noted the flames shoot up. The boys had barely arrived back at our meeting place when the first explosions smote our ears. We ran as though our enemies were in close pursuit, taking a long detour back to camp to hide our trail.

We arrived home triumphantly about four in the morning, breathless and shaking with fright.

Viewed by daylight the barrio was a mass of flames and momentarily free of Japs, who had scurried to the outskirts for safety amidst the deafening noise of the explosions which continued throughout the night. I certainly hoped that John Boone and the others, over on the opposite hill, were enjoying the spectacle as much as we were.

St. Patrick's Day did not bring an end to the snakes, but it did mark the success of the Nips in finally extinguishing the fire. There were two or three small explosions that day, and then the smoke gradually subsided.

An alarming epidemic of malaria now swept over our little colony, with the results that I averaged only four or five hours sleep a night, as I helped Senor Sobervenas with the worst cases. It became my duty for the first time to prepare a body for burial. After the first few minutes of repugnance and fear, I managed to control my feelings. I had known the deceased slightly... a widow with three small children. She had been kind and generous, and I told myself severely that I had no right to shrink from the task, since no one else volunteered for it. It was the least and last service I could render her and somehow I made out.

After this initial experience, taking care of the dead became a routine chore which I did mechanically. By this time, people were dying at the rate of one per day. Our losses, however, were minor when contrasted with the Japs below us. Almost daily, with the aid of field glasses, we watched them continue to stack and burn the dead brought in from the battlefield. High above them as we were, the revolting stench frequently reached us.

By the end of March we had three cases of malaria in our hut... Doming, Manuel and Conching. I realized with dismay that my mendicants were down to the last aspirin and the next-to-last quinine capsule, which I had been reserving, in case of need, for Dian.

Papa Sobervenas and I alternated in keeping watch over the three invalids. In the early part of April they were all up, and the boys regained their strength rapidly. Conching had a relapse and was forced to return to bed, and at the same time, Carling's baby was stricken. We had long been planning to send someone to Manila for medicine. Now spurred by the suffering of his baby, Carling decided to make the trip. With a boldness born of desperation, he reported to the Japanese commandant in Dinalupihan, begged and received a pass to go to Manila on a Jap army truck. This permission was not so difficult to obtain, as it was the Nip policy to induce refugees to return and till their land, so that the Japs could reap the benefit of the crops.

At the end of an anxious week of waiting, Carling's baby died. Tessing hysterically insisted that the child could not be buried until its father had returned. According to the local custom, a traditional wake for the little mite followed. Day and night a crowd of sympathizing friends milled in and out of the hut, alternately praying and singing. On the third day the poor little body had to be interred, but the wake... intended to console the bereaved... continued unabated.

On the eighth day of the vigil the young father returned with two sacks filled with medicine and food. His grief for his first-born was pitiful to witness. It was deepened by his sullen anger at the cruel enemy responsible for the delay, as the Nips had refused him a return pass. He had been obliged to return secretly across the bay by banca... a small sailing craft made by hollowing out a tree trunk... and then walk back sixty miles over the hills. He finally decided that he and Tessing would return on foot, and by banca to Manila, without the benefit of Japanese aid or permission. Doming did not wish to go to Manila to live, but decided to accompany Carling and Tessing, so that he could bring us more food and medicine.

The Sobervenas baby's death had, of course, doubled my alarm with regard to Dian. Moreover, Lolita was expecting her child in a month, and I was anxious to get her back to her husband's relatives. As the family conference progressed, I screwed up my courage, and asked if they would consider taking Lolita and Dian along with them. Without hesitation, Carling replied:

"I would be glad to take them if you know of some place in the city where they could stay."

I informed them I was sure my old friends, Judge Mamerto Roxas and his family would take them in. Carling had told me that the Japanese had made few changes in the city's municipal administration, so I felt fairly certain he would find the family intact.

"Would you like to go with us?" Carling queried suddenly.

I appreciated the gallantry contained in his invitation, because I realized full well that he knew the presence of a white woman would endanger the party immeasurably. I thanked him profusely for the risk he was willing to assume, saying that I would manage the trip somehow later. Preparations were made and the day came for the little expedition to get under way. Lolita, who had been patient and uncomplaining for so long, was in high spirits at the prospect of having her baby in the city with her husband's family to care for her. Her spirits rose as she thought there might even be a possibility of a reunion with her husband. Demyon went along to help carry bags, delighted at the opportunity to see a big city for the first time in his life. It was quite a bad moment for me when I kissed Dian goodbye, and I softened the sorrow of parting by kidding Demyon about the danger to be encountered when he met up with city slickers.

The next day, partly to keep from thinking of Dian and worrying too much about the little Manila-bound group, I exerted my best efforts to persuade the remainder of the family to move. After much palaver, we decided to transfer our possessions to another site about four miles down the hill.

It was a great relief to live again in surroundings free from flies and other pests. It took us two days to effect the change and, after the last trip, I sat down to rest on a log. I was not perspiring despite the heat, and casually asked Senor Sobervenas if he thought my condition was unusual.

"You better let me take your temperature," he suggested gravely.

"I'm all right, but go ahead," I joked. "I know you want to show off the new thermometer Carling brought back."

As I sat with the thermometer in my mouth, a terrific chill seized me, so I arose and hastily wrapped myself in a blanket. When Papa S. read the thermometer, he told me to get into bed at once. I took it from him and saw that it registered 105 degrees. My turn, so long dreaded, had come.

Blankets were quickly laid on the new floor, and I was glad when they covered me with three mere, even though it was 90 degrees in the shade. My benefactor administered hot water and the quinine capsule I had hoarded for Dian. The chills soon stopped, my temperature came down to 102 degrees and I fell asleep.

I awakened to find Senor Sobervenas holding my hand, while his good wife was trying to force a bitter hot drink through my lips.

"Hello", I greeted them, "What goes on here? Is it morning?"

I looked at the lady's kindly face, down which tears were streaming.

"Oh, my child," she sobbed. "I thought we were going to lose you."

"Lose me," I echoed. "I've had a good night. I feel much better this morning, only a little weak."

"Senora, you've been out of your head for a week," my host replied, "and last night we thought you had stopped breathing."

Then I suddenly recalled a number of strange dreams in which I seemed to be dashing through dense, burning forests with Boone's guerrillas, always getting lost and inevitably winding up at the same place, where Japs leered at us through the bushes. I realized these were the nightmares of delirium.

"What is this awful stuff you're giving me?" I asked.

"Caro mio, we had no more quinine. We couldn't get any, although we sent all over the hills for it. This is wild fern tea, made from a plant said to contain quinine in small quantities. It has kept you alive," Mama S. assured. "Doming will be back from Manila any day now, and he will be sure to bring quinine."

I sank down on the blankets, weak, but comfortable, although I could not go back to sleep. After a minute the unusual calm began to bother me. I struggled to a sitting position, and called "I don't hear any machine guns or cannonading. Is the war over?"

There was silence for a moment, as my eyes moved slowly from one sad face to the next. Papa Sobervenas always assumed the difficult tasks, and he reluctantly told me, "Last night, while you were delirious, Bataan fell, Corregidor is still holding. If you listen closely you may still hear their big guns."

"What is the date?" I inquired.

"April tenth," Senora Sobervenas replied. "Yesterday is a day that we will long remember."

"Yes," I agreed, "but somehow I think the Japanese will remember it longer. They must have lost thousands of men before capturing Bataan."

I became stronger gradually, with recurrent chills and fever coming at longer intervals. I started to walk about and eat the same food as the others, only to return to bed for a week and a diet of watery rice.

Doming returned on about the twentieth of April, bringing a good supply of medicine and some food. Dian had stood the trip well, he reported, and was comfortably installed in the Roxas home. He brought me a letter from the judge in which he strenuously disapproved of my return to the capital. "It would be a very risky thing for you to try to reach here. Dian will be well cared for, so do not worry about her." At the moment I considered that good advice superfluous, as my recurring periods of weakness made me realize that I would not be able to withstand the rigors of a trip over the hills.

On May first, I awakened with the same eerie feeling I had experienced when I emerged from my delirium. The world was much too silent. I lay in suspense and listened for the distant rumble of the big guns on Corregidor. I strained my ears and could only hear the chirping of crickets, cooing of wild doves, and the incessant chatter of monkeys. Finally I called to Manuel.

"Tell me," I asked, "do you think Corregidor has fallen?"

He turned his face away and did not answer. I caught him by the arm.

"You must tell me, Manuel," I pleaded. "What do you think? What do the others think?"

"Yes," he told me, looking away unhappily, "it happened early this morning."

The sun suddenly seemed to cease shining. I gazed, stunned, at the surrounding landscape, unseeing. Then thoughts began to race through my benumbed brain "What about Phil?" "Is he safe?" "Has he surrendered with all the rest?" Then exercising my feminine prerogative, I buried my face in the musty blankets and cried quietly for a long spell.

Pacio came back from Meite, in the latter part of the next afternoon.

"An Igorotte guide has just come over from Mariveles," he informed excitedly. "He says the Japs are marching all the American soldiers this way."

"Then we'll be able to see them from our lookout with the field glasses," Manuel advised.

"Yes," chimed in Doming "if they're taking them north, say to Manila or Cabanatuan. I heard when I was in Manila that the Japs have a big field for prisoners wired off at Cabanatuan."*

"How long will it take them to reach here?" I inquired.

"Depends on how fast they march," Senor Sobervenas replied, "I would say, sometime late tomorrow night."

Sleep was out of the question that night. I remained quiet in my blankets, to conserve my strength for the climb to the lookout. The next day the boys took turns going up to watch. Papa S. told me over and ever again "Take it easy. The boys will let you know in time."

At five o'clock, Pacio came on the run and shouted, "Senora! I think they're coming!"

Helped by two of the boys, I climbed slowly to the lockout and took the field glasses. I focused them on a dark mass resembling a large herd of cattle, far down the road, which slowly took shape as it drew nearer. I could now discern tall figures in the straggling middle lines, with smaller ones running along on both sides of them. Every now and then a little man would strike a tall one with the butt of his rifle, or kick him. Some of the tall men seemed to be holding up their comrades, and I saw a score of men stagger by, carrying their mates in obviously improvised litters. Occasionally a man would drop then one of his little tormentors would run a bayonet through him and kick his body from the road.

There was no reason for me to disillusion myself. I realized full well the inhumane treatment that was being meted out by these merciless orientals to the brave remnants of our surrendered army. It galled me to think that the sons of men who had fought at Gettysburg, San Juan Hill, and the Argonne, were being subjected to these sadistic outrages because the indifferent politicians back in Washington had failed them. "Hold on to Bataan! A big convoy is on the way! Hold! Hold!" These false and hypocritical words recurred to me, again and again. The pain and horror of it all, and my inability to lift a hand to help our men, made my heart ache.

Then it flashed through my mind that maybe Phil was among these poor devils being herded to their doom. I handed over the glasses, and sank down in the grass, sobbing, but not for long. The distant crack of a shot brought me to my feet quickly. I snatched the binoculars, dashed the tears from my brimming eyes, and tried to make out what was happening.

As the picture became more distinct, I saw a milling mass of our men bunching together and ducking their heads to escape the blows rained upon them by the butts of Jap-wielded rifles. Unable to control my emotions I handed the glasses to Pacio and sobbed, "Try to tell me what it's all about."

I waited tensely as he looked steadily for a time and then reported, "There's a water hole near the road. The Americanos are trying to get to it for a drink, but the Japs won't let them. Now they are marching on again."

I motioned to him for the glasses and as I looked through them, saw an American spring from the road into the bush. Several shots were fired at him, but I did not see any signs of pursuit.

I could not stand any more, and made my way somehow unassisted back to the hut. I lay there on the floor in the dark, thinking... thinking. 'What can I do? What can I do?' The vision of those unfortunates who had fallen along the roadside haunted me. "Suppose some of them were not dead... only badly wounded? Maybe Phil... ?"

Finally I could stand this inactivity no longer. I walked over to where some of the men were talking around the fire, and called Pacio aside.

"Do you think you could get some of the boys to go down to the road with us?" I asked. "There may be some wounded men down there."

"My three cousins will go with us, and maybe others," he responded promptly. "Shall I get them, senora?"

"Not now," I cautioned. "Meet me behind the hut in about two hours. The old folks will be asleep then, and won't try to stop me."

"Si, senora. I know that you are looking for your husband. If he is there, we will find him."

Going down the hill was not difficult, despite my weakness. It was probably near midnight when we discovered the first body sprawled in an ungainly posture near the road. I looked for a dog tag or other means of identification, but there was none. The boys tenderly lifted the corpse, carried him back a short distance into the brush, and buried him near a big tree. Then with one accord, we knelt, and I said a short prayer for our unknown soldier.

Half a mile farther down the road we found another body, and performed the same short burial service for him. Then we moved on to the vicinity of the water hole, where there were three American dead; all without identification. When they had been interred, I found that I could not take another step. Pacio looked at me in a worried manner.

"I think it is time you go back, senora," he warned.

"I'm thinking of the man we saw fall and roll off the road," I remonstrated. "We must look for him. He may be only wounded."

"You go back, senora. I'll get more boys and we'll scout all over for him. Now my cousins take you back. You'll be sick again."

The boys were compelled to half carry me up the hill, as my fever had returned, and I was too weak to put one foot before the other. Finally the boys cut two bamboo poles, made a stretcher with their coats and shirts, and carried me the rest of the way. It was rough going for them, but we made it at four in the morning. I crept into bed without awakening anyone, and passed out cold.

My undue exertions had brought on another relapse, and the rest of May I was up and down with malaria. By early June, I felt better and took short walks to try to build up my strength. We now had ample food as many people had moved back to Dinalupihan, and friends sent supplies up to us. I was keenly aware that the Sobervenas family wanted to return to their farm. The Nips had adopted a policy of friendliness toward the natives, and were freely issuing passes to encourage evacuees to return home and grow crops. I realized that my presence alone was holding this well-disposed family in the hills.

One afternoon, while trying to take a siesta, but really doing my daily stint of worrying, the priest from Meite, Father Cabaginis, came in and sat beside me.

"My daughter," he began, "there is something you should know."

"Bad news, father?" I asked him hastily.

The priest smiled and patted my hand. "Not too bad...not too good," he temporized.

"I'm ready to hear it."

"Your husband is now a prisoner of the Japanese. I've seen him in Dinalupihan."

Phil! So near! I begged the father to tell me everything he knew.

"I was walking near Captain Muri's office," he related, "when some members of a Japanese patrol brought in three American soldiers. I've been watching ever since you described your husband to me, and one of these men was, as you said, very tall and medium dark, with fine eyes. I went over as close as I dared and heard some of the questioning. When asked to give their names to Captain Muri, one of them said 'Phillips.' He asked Captain Muri to allow him to look for his wife and child in the hills, and there was quite a discussion about this. The captain said if he could tell them where you were hiding, guards would be sent for you, but Phillips must remain in the town prison. Your husband begged the captain to let him go with the guards, but when this was not permitted, he directed them far away to the hills up near Olongopo. This made me believe that he had a good idea of where you really are, and that he purposely misdirected them."

"Where is he now, father?"

"They have him in the guardhouse in town."

"How does he look? Is he well, do you think, and not too thin?"

"He looks well... and this will please you... I managed to get near and whisper that you are safe with friends of mine. How he smiled at that! Now I plan to keep watch over him, and will let you know if he is moved."

"Oh, father!" I cried out, "I must see him! I must go down to him now."

The priest smiled sagely and said nothing. I realized the folly of my remarks a moment after I had spoken, for I knew that Phil would not want me to come out of hiding and give myself up to the Japs after all we had done to avoid that eventuality.

"Can I send him food?" I asked suddenly.

"Not now," he advised. "We don't want to draw any special attention to him. Try not to worry. I'll be back soon again," and with that he was off on his little white pony, his long cassock gathered up and tucked into his trouser pockets.

During that week that followed, it required all my self-control to keep from going down to the outskirts of the barrio on the chance that I might get just one glimpse of Phil. It seemed at times that if I could do just that, it would not matter what happened to me afterwards. I managed to stick it out, and at the end of the week Father Cabaginis came again.

"Last night they moved your husband to San Fernando. A boy that I can trust is trailing them and will let me know what happens next. In any case, the boy will bring back regular reports."

My spirits sank to a low ebb. Phil was already farther from me!

"Did you manage to speak to him again, Father?"

"Yes, I finally asked permission to do so, but we were never left alone together. He told me that before he was captured, someone he called 'the old man' had given him leave to try and find you. He said that he had been traveling in the hills with two other men for almost a month, looking for you. I also learned that the day before he was captured, he had been told you were sick with malaria. As he said that he gestured with three fingers, by which I think he meant he was within three miles of you when the Japanese patrol intercepted him."

"Have they been cruel to him, father? Has he suffered much?"

"I don't think so. He's been at work, taking care of their horses."

"What do you think he wants me to do? If I only knew that."

"I tried my best to let him know you are safe and recovering and I think he understood. I am sure that he is happy you are not in the hands of the Japanese."

"He need not worry about that," I cried. "I will never give up and be interned. I'll die in the hills before I do that!"

After exacting a promise from me to do nothing rash or foolish, the little padre mounted his pony and was off again, promising to relay more news to me when it came.

Five days later, a boy arrived to tell me that Phil and many other Americans had been loaded on a truck the night before at San Fernando, and sent toward Manila; probably to Cabanatuan or Bilibid Prison.

This was the last straw! Now all my doubts had vanished, and the miserably long days of watching and waiting were over. The time for action had arrived, and I knew that I must send a boy posthaste with a note to John Boone:

"I'm going to Manila as soon as possible. Phil has been taken and sent there. The moment that I am settled, I will send you word. You know that I want to help. Long live the guerrillas!"

*The Japanese prison for American POWs situated near Cabanatuan City was the final destination for survivors of the notorious Bataan Death March.

CHAPTER IX

Dorothy Fuentes is Born

CARLING RETURNED FROM MANILA NEAR THE END OF JUNE.

"I've tried my best to get a pass for you, Mrs. Phillips," he deplored. "But everyone is afraid to help an American. All of my friends said that sooner or later you will be caught and sent to Santo Tomas. Maybe you better not try it."

"Carling, don't you see that I must go to Manila? How can I stay here in the hills now? The ones that I love most in this sad world, my child and my husband, are in Manila. Please help me."

"I knew that you would say exactly what you did. However everyone, even Father, made me feel that it was my duty to warn you. Well, now I've done my duty. Give me a little time to perfect my plan, then we will start."

"Carling, I'm very grateful. We won't fail. I feel it."

We shook hands; he left camp immediately and was gone all that day and evening. After I had retired, I heard Carling's low whistle, and slipped out to meet him.

"All set, Mrs. Phillips," he whispered. "I've sent boys ahead to take care of things, and I think it will be fairly safe. We will start at four tomorrow morning. Let us tell the family that I have a pass for you from the Jap captain in Dinalupihan; then they won't worry."

After snatching a few hours' sleep, I packed the scanty possessions that I could take with me, and divided my remaining belongings among the generous Sobervenas family. Carling forbade my having on my person any object that would disclose my identity in case I was caught and searched. So my most precious articles: my passport, Phil's army papers, our marriage certificate, and the "bullet with my number on it" were left in the keeping of Conching.

Carling and I made our way down the hill by torchlight. He told me that he had advised Boone of our intentions and the guerrilla chief had promised to have Negrito guides waiting for us at a designated spot. We crossed the Jap-patrolled highway without incident, arrived at the rendezvous, and waited patiently. Finally I became anxious and suggested to Carling that our savage friends had failed us.

"Don't be alarmed," he cautioned. "They are peculiar people and are probably hiding in the woods watching us. They want to make sure that we are the right ones, hence their caution. Just be patient, and they will appear in due time." As we watched expectantly, Carling told me a few things about the primeval men we awaited. The Negritos, he said, hunt and raise vegetables, high in the hills, seldom visiting even the smallest barrio. They barter, and do not have the faintest conception of the use or value of money. They are expert hunters, make their own mountain trails, and conceal them so well that they can be found only with the greatest difficulty. Their dialect is similar to Tagalog as spoken in Manila, and they have some slight understanding of that idiom.

Probably an hour later, although it seemed like a week, I heard the bamboo moving and a gentle rustling in the cogon grass around us. Then a score or more of small, scowling diminutive black men erupted suddenly into the clearing where we sat, and surrounded us.

I screamed, and started to arise.

"Sit still!" Carling ordered, almost curtly.

I gazed at the sullen face of the aborigines, and was not reassured by the sight of their glistening white teeth, which had been filed to points. Four of them were partly clad in civilized garb, but the remainder wore G-Strings and little else, save quivers of arrows and hunting bows on their backs.

As the natives approached us warily, Carling spoke to them in their tongue. Their leader mumbled a reply. Then Carling talked again, and wide grins spread over their primitive faces. One of them walked up to me, and extended his hand. I looked anxiously to Carling for guidance.

"They know we are all right," he reassured. "Shake hands with him. Some G. I. probably taught him that."

I was frightened, but smiled bravely, and took the small, claw-like paw. The native pumped my hand up and down vigorously at least a dozen times, before I managed to withdraw it from his greasy grasp. Carling went into a huddle with six of the Negritos while the remainder of the band squatted on the ground around me in a close circle, and stared unblinkingly. This surveillance made me nervous, and for lack of something else to do, I opened my battered purse. This was a mistake, for they moved in still closer, and literally snatched purse and contents from me. My excited protests attracted Carling's attention. He (as I learned later) told the head man that I was frightened, and asked him to tell his followers to leave me alone. The Negritos restored everything promptly, but returned to the unceasing scrutiny which lasted over an hour, and did not help the state of my jangled nerves.

We finally took leave of the band, in company with four of their number who were to be our guides. The Negritos took our baggage, and we started a long, weary climb uphill. My legs seemed about to burst after a while, as we stopped briefly at the foot of a steep cliff which one of the aborigines scaled. He let down a vine rope, and one by one, we were hauled up to a small plateau. We rested for the balance of the day, and started on at dusk, down the reverse slope of the hill.

The men lighted bamboo torches as we continued the descent. My leg muscles were so stiff by now that I could barely place one foot in front of the other. The guides noticed my condition; one of them took my hand and pulled, while another gave me a friendly push intermittently. When I complained, Carling replied that we had to cover much ground before dawn, and the natives were only trying to be helpful.

By two a. m. we neared the Jap lines, and the torches were doused. The bush through which we moved was very dense, and we were compelled to hold hands to maintain close contact in the darkness. We moved at a snail's pace until dawn; then hid in a small cave. We could not cook, and ate pre-cooked cold food, after which we slept while the natives took turns standing guard.

When I awakened and looked at my watch, it was two p. m. My leg muscles were sore and almost knotted; I rubbed them with coconut oil which one of our guides gave me. Two hours later we ate again; then waited for another hour until one of the Negritos returned from a scouting trip and told us that it was safe to move on. We climbed over and descended a small hill, arriving at a small stream near midnight. Carling warned me to be very quiet as we were near the barrio of Oroni, and there were many Jap patrols in our vicinity.

The natives slipped silently into the water, after which Carling and I removed our shoes, and waded downstream near the water's edge. The aborigines moved like wraiths, but we civilized beings were unable to proceed as quietly as we would have liked to, due to the brush and wild bamboo which fringed the bank. We arrived and halted at a spot where tremendous boulders blocked the stream; almost damming it. At this point, we climbed out and waited for almost an hour while one of the Negritos reconnoitered, and returned to report that all was well. We then started ahead warily and were glided to a banca hidden in the underbrush.

This tiny craft was launched without delay, and one of the natives clambered in with us, while his three comrades waved a farewell and disappeared silently into the bush. We hoisted our small sail and were soon scudding over the choppy waters of Manila Bay. Carling stated that we were behind schedule, could not cross the Bay before dawn, and would therefore soon have to hide. We spotted a small island, landed, pulled the banca out of the water, and concealed it in a bamboo thicket. I slept until mid-afternoon while the men alternated in standing watch. As we sighted no Jap patrols in the Bay, we ventured a small fire, and cooked some dried fish and rice. Then while the Negrito kept a vigil, Carling and I explored the island and found it to be uninhabited. We picked coconuts and bananas, taking them with us.

After sundown, we launched the banca and set sail. Near midnight we sighted some object moving not far from us. We lowered our white sail to avoid attracting attention and started to drift. Then the indistinct shape moved closer, and we heard the rhythm of paddles dipping in the water. Carling covered me with a spare sail, and then piled the bananas and coconuts atop of me. As the strange craft came nearer, Carling whispered that it was manned by Filipinos.

I heard the other boat come alongside and there was much staccato conversation for fifteen minutes or so, before we hoisted our sails and moved off. I remained in my hiding place for some minutes longer to make sure that we were well out of sight. Carling told me that our unwelcome visitors were Hukbalahaps... radical Filipino partisans who were assisting the Japs to patrol the Bay. He had finally convinced them that we were only engaged in transporting bananas and coconuts to Manila.

We arrived on the Manila side of the Bay near a small barrio, known as Haguni. Carling thought that it was not safe for me to be seen here as the place was known to be full of "Huks" in the pay of the Japs. We sailed past the village and up a small stream where we landed, beached the banca, and hid. Then Carling strolled into the settlement, and while the Negrito kept watch, I slept. When I awakened at noon, Carling had returned and was now sleeping. I went to the water's edge, washed, and changed clothes much to the alarm of our guide who impatiently called "Siggy! Siggy!" Knowing the risk attendant on my ablutions, I heeded the native's demand to hurry.

After Carling awakened, the Negrito let him know that he was returning to Oroni, and thence to his home in the hills. After the man's departure, Carling told me that while in Haguni he had made arrangements with a dependable Filipino who owned a truck, and had a Jap license to carry produce to Manila.

It was nearly seven p. m. when we struck out for the outskirts of Haguni and found the truck waiting for us on a side road. I climbed in the back, and dozens of charcoal sacks were piled around and over me, with bananas and coconuts atop of them. Alas, my washing at the stream that morning was in vain. Carling climbed in with the driver and we drove off. We stopped in Haguni to pick up a few more passengers, and show the driver's permit to the Jap. We remained there fully a half hour, and I literally held my breath as Nip sentries walked around the truck and poked the charcoal bags with bayonets and sabers. We finally drove off with several more Filipinos sitting in front and a few on the back of the truck.

It was a rough and bumpy ride, and I suffered great discomfort in my stifling covert. Again and again, we were stopped at every small settlement or barrio. The routine never varied... a shouted Nip command to halt..."Tomare!"... the inspection of the driver's pass... and Jap sentries walking around the truck, prodding the bags with their bayonets. I knew full well that a sneeze or cough at such peril-filled moments would have been disastrous, and my lungs ached from the charcoal dust and frequent periods of holding my breath.

We reached Manila at nine-thirty p. m. and the truck discharged its surplus passengers. The driver took us up a dark street near Carling's house, and we unloaded. As I emerged from my hiding place, both of the men laughed heartily. I looked at myself, and realized that I had given them good cause for mirth for I was black from head to foot with charcoal dust and perspiration. Carling hailed a passing carromata, and we drove to his home as we thought the hour was too late for me to go elsewhere without exciting suspicion. Tessing was waiting anxiously, and she greeted me with a smile, while tears of happiness coursed down her cheeks.

During the past months in the hills, my purposeful sun tanning had made me as dark-skinned as many Filipinos. For that reason, no one considered it risky for me to drive with Carling to the Roxas home in one of the open carromatas. However, I still felt a bit timid and wore dark glasses borrowed from Tessing, plus a hood which almost covered my face. Once at my haven, we all permitted ourselves the indulgence of a few joyous tears, save Dian. She did not recognize me, and would not have anything to do with me; I was sufficiently rewarded by the knowledge that she was well and happy.

Judge Roxas lost no time in summoning his family physician to give me a physical check.

"Yes, you still have malaria," the doctor announced. "It shows in your blood test. You also have traces of scurvy, but you can get rid of it by eating plenty of fresh fruit and vegetables."

The medico started at once to give me a course of quinine injections. The Roxas family were so hospitable that it seemed wonderful once more just to be alive. When my hosts discovered that my funds were almost exhausted, they insisted on taking care of my medical expenses. Not only that, but they made it plain that they wanted me to remain with them indefinitely, making only one stipulation... that I should not leave the house. They had not encountered any trouble with the Japanese, and it was natural that they did not care to face the dire consequence that confronted them if they were caught harboring an American guest.

I asked the judge if we could listen to the States on his radio to learn what progress, if any, our side was making.

"It's forbidden now, you know," he told me solemnly, "to listen to American broadcasts. The Japanese have threatened to shoot anyone caught in the act. In fact, we have all been ordered to turn in our radios to them to be reconditioned, so that we can only get Manila with them. I'm about to send mine in. Nevertheless, we will listen just once and see what we can hear. I'm certain that it won't be much."

The Roxas residence was built away from the street, and in midst of spacious grounds. Despite this, we turned the set down low and sent a boy out to make certain that we were not being spied upon. After all these precautions it was a disappointment when we were only able to bring in snatches of music and news, broken by static. The jurist explained that the Japs were purposely jamming the wavelengths to ruin any reception of "foreign propaganda."

After seven months of using a blanket on a hard floor, my first few moments in a real bed seemed heavenly. I had even slept on the floor the night before at Carling's house, as he only had one small bed for himself and Tessing. It was not long, however, before I started twisting and turning, in vain efforts to get comfortable. It took all my will power to remain in bed and not move down to the floor.

At breakfast Dian began to place me. I felt refreshed and began to think of some way to get in touch with Phil. I could not remain a virtual prisoner, even though assured of comfort and safety. With my dark skin, I felt certain that I could pass for either Spanish or Italian. The latter seemed preferable since that ear-marked me as a national or an Axis ally. There were few Italians in Manila, and I realized that while I did not speak their language, neither did many Japanese.

I telephoned an acquaintance of Phil's and mine... a young Spaniard who was an accomplished linguist and had worked at one time in the Italian Consulate. When he called on me, I presented my problem to him... how could I, an American, circulate freely in Manila?

"How do you think I can help?" my visitor inquired, looking exceedingly surprised.

"By making out some false Italian papers for me," I suggested bluntly.

He was far from happy about this proposal. After much discussion he finally thought of a Filipino printer who could be trusted to make up the necessary forms at his direction, after which he would fill them in.

A week later, my reluctant accomplice reappeared with the precious papers, duly made out to Dorothy Fuentes, born in the Philippines of Neapolitan parents, long deceased. Emboldened by the possession of this spurious safeguard, I went out to find Madame Fanchon, the dressmaker, whom Louise and I had patronized. This seamstress, as I suspected, proved to be a fountainhead of news. I learned that Louise and Mona were confined in Santo Tomas, and were none too happy because of lack of food and other creature comforts.

After laying in a supply of food and cigarettes, I called at the gates of the old university during the brief hours allowed to leave packages. Warned not to wave or signal to our friends, I stood in line with other visitors while American internees (trusties) searched the bags we carried for notes and weapons. Japanese guards were just behind the trusties watching their every move. I saw Louise standing in back of the fence and smiled at her, remembering in time to make no gesture. A delighted smile crept across her face. Then I caught sight of Mona nearby, strangely bereft of dimples, charm and makeup, looking sorrowful and sulky.

Upon returning to the Roxas home, I found the judge very disturbed over my venturing out, even with my "authentic" papers.

"Claire," he warned me soberly, "I shall have to do something very unpleasant for me, because as you know the Japanese have issued a manifesto that anyone harboring an American or British national will be shot as well as his whole family. I shall have to write to Colonel Ohta, Head of the Japanese Military Police, telling him that you are with us. Of course, I shall offer to act as your guarantor. In that way, we are all protected."

"You are perfectly right," I agreed, "and remember to stress my Italian ancestry, as well as my Philippine citizenship."

The letter was duly sent. Out of deference to the family's anxiety, I remained quietly at home until the answer arrived a week later. It stated that the judge was to bring me to Ohta's office and sign for me there. On the way to Fort Santiago, my host impressed upon me that I was to say as little as possible and leave the talking to him.

The judge explained to Ohta, through an interpreter, that I had been stricken with malaria while visiting friends in Bataan and had just returned. My papers (he lied gracefully) had been destroyed in the bombings there. Ohta asked the jurist if I would be staying in his house and had adequate means of support. Judge Roxas replied that I would be a member of his household and have no need to work. Colonel Ohta was very suave and pleasant throughout the interview, and let us know that Philippine women nationals were not expected to cooperate with their Nipponese "liberators" except in one way. "Here it comes," I thought, and crossed the fingers of my left hand, out of sight in my skirt pocket. Would I promise not to do anything to help the enemy? Keeping my fingers firmly crossed, and making a mental reservation as to the identity of said "enemy," I promised, and the papers were signed. It seemed as if hours had passed, but a parting glance at the clock over Ohta's shoulder disclosed that the whole transaction had taken place in less than thirty minutes.

The Roxas household was overjoyed by our news, and even Dian waxed enthusiastic and made up to me. Judge Roxas cautioned me to be extremely careful. He warned that in spite of the Jap police official's apparent civility, the possibility existed I would be closely watched, and any false move promptly reported to him. I reminded myself, over and over again, that the loss of my freedom through some indiscreet word or act would cut off all hope of either locating Phil, or helping Boone. I forced myself for a whole month to remain inactive, eating fruit and vegetables, exercising to build up strength, and carefully refraining from making any move that would disclose my all-consuming desire to aid the American cause. I left the house only once a week to carry food to Louise and Mona. The judge agreed that this would cause no comment as we girls were old friends, obviously bound together by a common tie of "Italian" ancestry. Hundreds of Filipino nationals kept me company in the long line outside the university's big double gate; visible proof that they had not forgotten their American friends.

At the end of this period of inaction, realizing that Lolita's baby was due, I went to the home of her husband's family. There I learned it had arrived; that mother and child were doing well, and still in the hospital. I visited her there and we had a joyous reunion. Lolita looked well and was bursting with pride in her healthy, though tiny new-born boy. Her plan was to leave as soon as she could for her mother's home in northern Luzon. She felt sure her husband would be able to visit her there. We bade each other an affectionate farewell and... supreme sacrifice... I left her my good suitcase, one of a set of three in blue leather, imported from Hong Kong, that I had bought to use on my honeymoon. Lolita had used the bag in the hills and needed it now for diapers.

On the way home I stopped at the Dakota Apartments and found Senora Lopez, my erstwhile Spanish neighbor from whom I had borrowed the radio during those first black hours. She and her family had come through the Jap bombings safely. They had not been disturbed by the occupation, other than by the routine door-by-door checkup made by the Nip civil administration. Senora Lopez asked me about Phil and Dian.

Upon inquiry, she told me she had requested the manager to move my trunk to the apartment house storeroom.

"Senorita Del Rosario," she confessed, "seemed a little annoyed about it. It struck me that she was planning to take it away with her. Everything else of yours disappeared during the looting period, I'm sorry to say."

I remembered Senorita Del Rosario, the thin, well-tailored, not-so-young spinster whose impassive, carefully made-up face appeared at my door promptly on the first day of the month.

"Take it away with her?" I repeated. "Isn't she managing the apartments anymore?"

"Caramba! No!" Senora Lopez vociferated. "Haven't you heard? She is the big shot now," and went on to explain that the lady in question had been educated in Japan and could speak, read and write their language, almost as well as a native of that country. I learned that she was employed as an interpreter at Fort Santiago, living on the purloined fat of the land, and lording it over all her former acquaintances. I suddenly shuddered as the thought occurred to me that she may have been present in Colonel Ohta's office when I was called in for that interview.

"Interpreters must be worth a dime a dozen in this city," I cut in. "How does it happen that Del Rosario got to the head of the class?"

"Because she was once presented to the Empress of Japan," my friend elucidated. "You really have to be someone to rate that. In Japan it's a rare honor conferred upon those women who have distinguished themselves in the service of the Empire. I guess that you know how Japanese usually regard women, so she probably stood high in their good graces."

I found my trunk as I had left it, locked and packed, and took it home in a carromata. There I found the judge's sister and sister-in-law energetically making nurses' uniforms. They explained that the school conducted by the Malate Church had been converted into a charity hospital under the guidance of Father Lolar, an energetic Irish priest. It accommodated sick Filipino soldiers, currently being released by the Japanese from O'Donnell Prison Camp. The Roxas household was responding to an urgent call for nurses.

I borrowed their patterns and promptly turned myself out two uniforms. The three of us reported for duty on the following Monday at the newly-named Remedios Hospital. As unpaid volunteers we could up for as much time as we wished, so I enrolled for three and a half days per week. Without delay, we were all given a rapid and comprehensive practical course in all phases of nursing care and first aid. In a short time, two of us had full charge of a ward of twenty patients.

My nursing duties brought me in contact with Ramon Amusatague, a young broker, who was the leading canvasser of a group which sought funds for the upkeep of the hospital. There was something magnetic about this fair-skinned Spaniard, whose reddish hair and grey eyes belied his ancestry. His obvious sincerity and enthusiasm gave me the confidence to tell him of my growing anxiety over Phil, and I found a sympathetic listener. He offered to see a possible contact, the Filipino nurse of a Dr. Wattress, an American oculist confined in Bilibid. She was permitted to visit the prison at intervals to assist the doctor with his work. Ramon gave the nurse Phil's name and description, and she agreed to take a verbal message to him.

"We should have an answer within a week," Amusatague reported. "If not we'll just keep on trying."

While awaiting results, I covered most of the better residential sections, asking for donations of beds, sheets, towels, dishes or money, and made use of the opportunity to slip in a word for Boone's hungry, ragged guerrillas. I told the Filipino and Spanish families I visited, that someday they might owe much to these heroic, unconquered men in the hills. I pictured them as I had seen them, living like hunted animals, trying to keep body and soul together, until fresh American forces arrived. "They don't ask much; only food and clothing, so they can keep on fighting the enemy." I begged. My indiscreet, well-meant efforts were a distinct failure. Many a door was slammed in my face. Other people, more courteous, curtly informed me that I must be out of my mind to meddle with such dynamite at this time. Not one peso could I extract from these cautious ones, and my dejection became more pronounced with the passing of each fruitless day.

I met another tireless worker at the Remedios Hospital ... Dr. Romeo Atienza. This happy-go-lucky little medical man was an unsung hero of Bataan, for he dashed in there after its fall to attend the sick. After the Death March, both he and his wife went to work at Camp O'Donnell, the first established there ... smuggling in extra food and medicine to them... that the Japs finally sent him away. Undaunted, the two Atienzas went to work with the Philippine Red Cross and at Remedios.

Dr. Atienza checked with friends at Camp O'Donnell, and was able to tell me that a Phillips, who seemed to answer my description, had been there for one day only and was then transferred to Cabanatuan. The doctor promised to get in there at some time in the near future, and see what he could find out. Ramon heard from the nurse "No John Phillips at Bilibid." All signs seemed to indicate that Phil was confined at Cabanatuan, but the end of August arrived without any progress being made to contact any of the captives there.

My funds were getting low, and I decided not to impose any longer on the hospitality of Judge Roxas. I made inquiries and found a singing spot open at a popular night club run by a German Jewess, Ana Fey. I decided to return to my old occupation and, after expressing my gratitude many times, Dian and I moved back to my old apartment house. I engaged a gentle Chinese amah for Dian... one Ah Ho about sixty, short, fat, with snapping black eyes and scanty hair skewered into a determined knot atop her head. Pressa, a neat appearing native girl, agreed to market and cook for me.

Ana Fey, a tiny, doll-like little person with platinum blond hair and baby blue eyes, was a clever business woman and a good entertainer. She had formerly owned and conducted a dancing school, and could execute the dancing of many nations; specializing in Spanish numbers, many of which she had picked up in Spain. Her place was patronized exclusively by moneyed Japanese, and I soon learned that she was under the "protection" of a husky, six-foot (yes, they have them) Jap newspaper man, to whom she was indebted for many special privileges. Her paramour was Horiuchi, one of the ace reporters for the "Asahi Shimbun," a local Nip sheet.

There is only one adequate adjective to describe the state of my mind the first night on my new job... jittery. Singing by request was by far the least nerve-wracking end of the business. Much of my time, I found, was supposed to be spent moving among the guests, sitting at their tables, drinking and chattering with them. After a few nights, I lost some of the eerie feeling of being confined in a cage of man-eating tigers, and achieved some degree of nonchalant indifference. Noting that I was learning the ropes, Ana began assigning me the job of buttering up important customers.

One night she told me to spend some time at the table of Masamoto, a dapper, youngish officer who had come in alone. He swallowed both the drinks and large doses of flattery that I handed him; before long he was regaling me with an account of his duties as an official at Santo Tomas.

"Oh," I commented helpfully, "how can you enjoy life, constantly surrounded by those awful Americans?"

"They are not so bad," my vis-a-vis responded with a knowing grin, "Dere some very nice radies there. Radies, pretty rike you."

"Yes, I admitted with apparent reluctance, "the ladies are all right. In fact, I have two friends there."

Then I told him about Louise, "Italian" like myself, who had "unfortunately" been born in the United States. I described Mona as unhappily half-American but, of course, in mind and heart, entirely Spanish. The gullible Nip rose to my bait.

"I rike meet your friends very much," he confided, "Next time you come Santo Tomas, I arrange rittre tark for us, yes?"

"A little talk? Can you do that?" I quizzed with seeming awe, "I thought that all visiting with prisoners was forbidden."

"To me noding forbidden," my companion boasted, "Gate guards must do as I say. You come next Sunday morning at ten thirty. I ret you in, myserf."

"But," I protested genuinely surprised, "that is the hour when the gates are closed."

"Hai!" Masamoto agreed, "But you forget it is my guards who crose gate. It is for you to be rast visitor we admit. I be rooking for you, cara mia!"

"A rivedici!" I replied, combining the informal Italian farewell with the prescribed, humble Nipponese bow.

The most talented entertainer at Ana Fey's club was a diminutive well-educated Filipino girl, Fely Corcurea, who could sing some Japanese songs, and was a remarkably versatile dancer. I was drawn to her from the first, sensing that she was an ardent patriot. My judgment was later confirmed, when she confided in me, speaking with obvious emotion of her relatives fighting in the Philippine Army.

When Fely heard about my small success that evening she was happy over the prospect of my gaining admittance to the camp to visit my friends. "Maybe you could slip a note to them to give to Fahny's father," she suggested, "He's interned there, and neither Fahny nor her mother have been able to get a word in to him all these months." Fahny was our clever negro mestiza dancer, very dark, but beautiful in an exotic way, witty, spunky, big-hearted, and like Fely, thoroughly patriotic.

The following Sunday my visit to Santo Tomas went according to plan. Masamoto san, standing just inside the gate, looked very stern and official. When he spied me he smiled broadly, gestured for me to enter, and directed me to his office, as the gates were closed.

"Dis is present," the Nip official commented as he joined me. "Now give me your friends names and I hope the radies enjoy yourserves."

In a short time, Louise and Mona arrived, followed by a tall, handsome American who was not admitted to the sacred precincts. Masamoto saluted in a courteous manner, and took his leave, remarking, "You may have fifteen minutes for your rittre tark. Do not mind de guard. He understands no Engrish."

As Louise hugged and kissed me, she whispered "Be careful! There may be a microphone in the room."

"Who is the good-looking man following you around?" I began, by way of conversation.

"Oh, that's Louise's latest," Mona answered for her.

"My latest and my last," asserted Louise, laughing and blushing. "I wish that you could meet Bob. He's a mining engineer and really terrific."

"Want to know something? He even does her cooking and washing for her," Mona supplied. "He's nuts about her."

"Oh, no, he isn't," Louise protested, "It's just that he likes me and has no other friends. I'm the one who is nuts about him."

"Say," I broke in, "I must bring in more food now that you are three."

"You must not rob yourself," Louise returned promptly, and then whispered, "We know it's not too easy on the outside either these days."

I told the girls where I was working, and added a few choice hypocritical compliments for Masamoto just in case our conversation, or a summary of it, would reach him through a hidden "mike" or the supposedly stupid guard.

"Yes, Masamoto is the nicest Japanese officer we have ever met," Louise agreed, taking the cue, "He's always pleasant to us, smiles, and asks if he can be helpful. He has given passes to several sick Americans so they could go out for hospital care."

The guard at the door had turned his back to us. Mona suddenly drew me as far as possible across the room, and whispered in a pleading tone "For goodness sake, try to get me out of here. After all. I'm not like Louise. The old commandant is away in Japan. I don't think you realize that your friend Masamoto is now acting commandant. If you could arrange for him to see me alone, I think I could manage it. Tell him I'll be very grateful... tell him anything you like... only get me out of here, please."

"I'll try," I promised, and just then Masamoto returned, saying that our time was up. When we thanked him for his courtesy, he remarked affably, "You may come again next Sunday to see friends."

On Masamoto's next visit to the club, he was more cordial than ever. He told me of his early life, and ambitions to study in the United States, and how he had graduated from Northwestern University, "But you," he finished, "not being an American don't know where that is."

"How I envy you all your travels," I sighed, "Imagine living one's whole life here in the Islands."

"Never mind," he consoled, giving my hand a pat, "some time some good friend of yours must take you traveling to America... after we conquer country."

He reached for my hand again and I moved back out of reach, smiling, and informed him very confidentially, "You must understand. I have a husband on another island who is looking after our hacienda there. He is apt to visit me unexpectedly, and he does not like for me to be too friendly with the patrons here. But, tell me, what did you think of my pretty friends at Santo Tomas?"

"Very nice," he conceded, "especiarry de smarr redhead."

"I thought you would like Mona," I continued, "Of course, she is half American, but we never think of her like that. Her father was Spanish, and a very distinguished man." That last touch was added for my companion's benefit, because the Japanese are always impressed by exalted family connections.

"I know what you want," Masamoto informed, "Your red-headed friend... you rike her out on a pass. You have come to right man."

"Not on a pass; permanently."

"Dat another matter. Friend must renounce her American rights and have two prominent Spanish or Firupino peopre sign as her guarantors; arso job assured her."

"There would be no trouble about that," I assured him, and to my surprise he handed me a form advising, "Have dis signed and den come see me at my office."

A few days later I brought the signed papers back to Mona's benefactor. She was sent for, and duly renounced her mother's country and all its works. It gave me quite a let-down and a feeling of deep disgust to hear her glibly repeating the words.

Mona took the whole procedure very nonchalantly, and walked out of the office, once more a free woman. The commandant motioned for me to stay behind and closed the door. Thanks seemed to be the order of the day, but Masamoto anticipated my action by interposing, "Yes, you right. A big man can do much for pretty rady. Now what is pretty rady going to do for big man?"

He went on to suggest that I must be very lonely with my husband so far away, and volunteered himself to act as a substitute. I listened quietly, then hastily assured him that I was not lonely at all, having a daughter to care for. The impromptu discussion was concluded when I issued a cordial invitation for him to see us both at Ana Fey's club. After a few moments reflection, the Japanese bowed, and I was permitted to join Mona outside the gate.

"Well, you're rescued all right," I remarked caustically, "Sorry that it couldn't have been by the handsome Yank you pictured last year. Remember?"

Mona flashed her cute little smile, dimples again in evidence, and assured me that she would never forget my kindness.

My newly liberated friend was just as timid as I had been at the prospect of entertaining our "distinguished" enemies. I worried about her at first, but my fears soon dissipated. On her third night at Ana Fey's she met a Japanese mining man, who, like Masamoto, was an alumnus of Northwestern University.

"Back there they all call me George," he stated in perfect English, and "George" he became. Unlike his fellow alumnus, George did not convert the "i" to "r", and he was able to pronounce "th" without transposing it to a "d."

George indiscreetly let us know that he was born in California, and had both American and Japanese citizenship papers. "If the Americans come back, I will destroy my Japanese documents, but while the Japanese are here, I just hide my American ones," he said, laughing. "I don't know who is going to win, but whoever it is, I wish they would hurry up and do it. I'm in a hurry to get back to New York."

George was distinctly on the prowl. He had plenty of money, and made it known that he was in need of some clever girl to find an apartment and furnish it for him. Mona threw herself into this task, even finding him a cook-housekeeper to look after his needs, laundry included. I told myself that perhaps this unwonted activity came under the head of war-time indiscretion, but when Mona handed Ana Fey her resignation, I inquired sternly like a maiden aunt, "What next?"

"You won't have to take care of me," Mona answered blithely, "George has an extra room and..."

"Mona, you can't do that," I almost screamed at her, "Maybe you don't realize it, but can't you see people will know you're living with a Jap."

"At least I'll be living. George has the best of everything. You can't imagine what the food was like at Santo Tomas. Ugh!"

"Food! Is it really that important? After the war you know what they will say."

"Who will say?" Mona mimicked, with a shrug of her pretty shoulders. "After all I'm only half American."

"Yes, and that's stretching it!" I spat in disgust.

I was happy to be rid of her, and went back to my duties at the hospital. While there I had been checking with Dr. Atienza, but he reported no success in obtaining a pass to Cabanatuan. Betty Wright, one of the volunteer nurses, heard us talking.

"I can promise you anything that you write will get in," she volunteered. "Don't ask me how I accomplish it, but I have a means of slipping notes in there to Bill Dooley, my fiancé, and I hear from him once or twice a month. You must have heard about him. He was a lieutenant in your husband's company."

I sat down without delay, and filled the tiny sheet she gave me with some of the love and longing that filled my heart.

"How soon can I get it in, and when can I expect an answer?" I asked expectantly.

"Take it easy," she replied, "You may have to wait a month."

A month! That seemed like an eternity. I had found that the best way to make time pass rapidly was to keep my mind occupied. More sick Filipinos began to flood into our hospital, and I worked longer and harder hours there, starting at eight in the morning and not leaving until six. Then I went home to take supper with Dian, and spent an hour with her before reporting to Ana's.

The month finally passed, and an answer came to Betty from her Bill. There was nothing for me.

"Bill is doing everything possible to trace your husband," she comforted, and then with a slight change of tone added, "Listen, Claire, if the news isn't so good, you must not take it too hard."

I could get nothing more out of her.

A sudden horrible thought flashed through my mind. Could it be that Phil was... Oh, no, no... I must not think morbid things like that. I remembered my husband's parting admonition "Keep your chin up!" and that made me all the more determined to run down every possible clue until my quest met with success.

CHAPTER X

Club Tsubaki Opens Its Doors

FOR SOME REASON, MY CONSTANT HEARTACHE and yearning for Phil did not interfere with my success at Ana Fey's. In retrospect, it seems that to escape the ever-present concealed pain and apprehension, I prodded myself into a show of vivacity that stood me in good stead. It gave me a thrill to be so easily accepted in my new role as I made the rounds of the tables between my singing numbers. The sensation was akin to walking at the bottom of the sea in a diver's suit with the dangerous alien element in the guise of sharks and octopuses. I was getting away with it, but still had to learn a few harsh lessons.

My employer was a stunning dresser, a smooth talker, and a strong believer in portable assets, for her small person was always ablaze with diamond jewelry. "You're doing okay, Dot," she encouraged on the first night of my second week, "Take a couple of encores if you like, on your next number."

I did just that, and then accepted an invitation to join four Japanese civilians at a table. I was barely seated when one of them demanded ice. As I turned to call a waiter, he shouted, "No... you!" emphasizing his demand by a heavy spank on my stern. I turned on him furiously, whereupon he touched my stockingless leg with the end of his burning cigarette, snarling "In Japan women wait on men." I was mad enough, before the sudden pain added insult to injury. Unable to control myself, I slapped him hard on the side of his scowling monkey face.

It constitutes a crowning insult for a Nip to be struck by a mere woman, and it took the combined efforts of his three companions to keep the outraged skibby from tearing me apart then and there. As he frothed and fumed, his friends reminded him of his dignity and persuaded him to wait while the matter of my proper punishment was discussed by all of them. As the place was too public, they decided to take me to a back room to mete out their own peculiar brand of justice.

I looked pleadingly at Ana Fey, but her metallic blue eyes reflected nothing but complete indifference to my fate. With a shrug, she strolled languidly to the far end of the room, sending Fahny and Fely about some business as she passed them.

I had no other option but to follow the Japs from the room.

First, came a lecture, lasting half an hour, on the proper conduct of a female in Japanese-held territory. "Regardless of being an Italian," I was told, "as long as I was in Japanese-occupied country, I must learn to act like a

Japanese woman, that is, humble, and as a servant." I was commanded to bow very low and apologize, which I did, thinking that would be the end of the affair. I was wrong... that was just the windup.

Now my "friend" started to pitch. Standing, according to his orders, with my hands behind me, I closed my eyes and took the rain of stinging blows that followed on my face and body, until I slumped partly conscious to the floor. A few kicks terminated this disciplinary and educational conference.

I learned afterward that Ana had ordered the orchestra to play very loudly to smother any outcries from me, and had, herself, stood guard at the door to prevent any interruption of our parley.

While in the dressing room, bathing my bleeding lip and repairing my make-up, orders came from Ana to return to the floor. The parties of the first part put in a brief "save-face" appearance, and when they departed, I was permitted to go home.

I wakened the next morning, stiff, and literally black and blue from head to foot. As I inspected my bruised body in the mirror, I made an important decision. The thought occurred to me that since I could expect no protection from my employer, I would be as well, or better off, running my own place. I had sized up Ana Fey and found her lacking. I figured that I could do as well as she... possibly better... and then I had an over-powering desire to obtain money for the American cause. I had not failed to observe how freely the Japanese sometimes talked, particularly when alcohol stimulated their tongues. In my own club, I thought, it would be possible to gather valuable bits of information from the enemy to send to Boone. I, too, had been aware that Ana's business had been falling off, due to her absorption in her "great romance."

When my bruises were not so much in evidence I returned to work at Ana's, almost enthusiastically because of the newly-hatched plan in my mind. It seemed as if Fely read my thoughts, for the first time we happened to be alone together, she suggested, "Miss Dorothy, you should have your own club. If you did, Fahny and I would both come to work for you."

"It's a deal," I told the tiny Filipino, "but keep it under your hat until I work out the details."

On consulting Fahny, I learned that she was also keen to join the new venture. The girls' eagerness gave me confidence. They were Ana's two star entertainers, and I knew that if they left and followed me, so would most of Ana's customers. My next move was to sound out some potential backers, and the result was disheartening.

Help came most unexpectedly. I casually invited Fely to lunch with me after we finished a routine practice of some new numbers, and she suggested Chan's Restaurant near the waterfront... Phil and I had often eaten the Chinaman's delicious food. He greeted me politely, but without any sign of recognition. I was puzzled for a moment, until I noticed a group of Japs sitting nearby. When we finished, I told Fely I would see her later, and remained at my table drinking tea until the Nips left. When the door closed behind them, Chan appeared before me with a broad smile.

"Missy Phil," he whispered "what you do here in this sad Manila, and where Mr. Phil?"

"Oh, Chan, I want to talk with you," I told him. He motioned me to a booth at the back. I poured the story of my flight from the city and my many adventures into his sympathetic ears; I informed him of Phil's capture and my anxiety.

"Those Japanese devils," the celestial kept repeating. It seemed wonderful to talk at last with someone who had known Phil. Encouraged by the old man's kindness, I told him of my burning desire to launch my own business venture. I made no bones about the fact that my main objective was to raise funds for Boone's guerrillas and to alleviate the suffering of our prisoners, rotting, like Phil, in Japanese hell-holes.

The Chinaman listened attentively to my plans, and at the end commented gravely, "O-klay... I helpee. How you likee biggee place on next corner for your club? Too biggee?"

"No, Chan," I exclaimed, "I want a big place. It must be the best place in town because we must make lots and lots of money. It must be a number one place, fixed up better than Ana Fey's or any other, so that everyone will hear about it and want to see it."

"How muchee money you got, Missy Phil?" Chan asked suddenly.

I placed my entire capital on the table before him; two diamond rings, a watch and two hundred dollars in American currency.

"Chan," I pleaded, "you have occupation money. Take this as security and lend me enough to pay two months' rent on the corner place and put it in shape."

"O-klay. Can do." Chan agreed, sweeping up my collateral with one wide paw. "Come tomollow for chow... same time. Then I have money."

"You're a prince," I told him, adding, "Don't spend those American dollars. I'll be getting them back one of these days."

I went directly from Chan's to inspect the place he had suggested and saw at a glance that it was ideal for my purposes. The well-situated two story building was easily visible from the waterfront. A wide stairway led past the lower floor, which was occupied by small shops, to the second floor which consisted of a big studio room with other small rooms adjoining it. The premises had formerly been used as a dancing school, and in my mind's eye, I could see that a bit of remodeling would glamorize the spot.

Fely was overjoyed at the result of my interview with Chan. We told her sister Flora, and Fahny and all of us decided to begin a discreet publicity campaign on behalf of the new enterprise. We confided the news to a few of our best customers, as a top secret. This, of course, made the tidings spread like wild fire, and many of Ana's patrons were highly amused at what they thought a good joke on her. Very lovelorn, she had been neglecting them and the club more and more ... sometimes not putting in an appearance the whole evening ... and one thing the Nips demanded was personal attention.

One of my ardent fans, Mr. Hochima, a wealthy mining man, had visited Ana's place frequently, apparently just to hear me sing. He contributed the name for the new place... Club Tsubaki. The gist of what he advised was this: "Tsubaki is Japanese for camelia. The camelia flower is not only a favorite in Japan, but also carries the significance of 'hard to get.' Also be sure to have your sign read 'Club' as well. In Japan 'Club' means exclusive, and that name outside will frighten the lowly people so they dare not enter." Realizing that this well-meant advice was good, I resolved to follow Hochima's suggestions faithfully... my new place would be as high-hat and snobbish as possible. I had cards printed for distribution, through Hochima and others of his ilk, to "the best people" only.

Chan loaned me the money as he had promised. I rented the place, and as I signed the lease... noted the date... October first. A poignant recollection of the gay, carefree October of the year before, flashed through my mind. This month held a date to be commemorated, and I resolved then to open the club on October 15th... that was the day when I had first met Phil. All of us are perhaps a trifle superstitious and to me, at that moment, I deemed that my decision would bring good luck.

After removing a few partitions to give the studio room an even more spacious look, I had a painter cover all the wall surfaces with a coat of white cream paint. Fely and I managed the hangings in a manner that was almost professional. I had been fortunate enough to find a quantity of pale orchid satin, slightly sun-streaked, and consequently a bargain, at a Hindu-operated store. We converted this material into showy long drapes for all the windows, and had enough left over to provide a curtain to conceal the entertainer's floor show entrance. I went overboard on indirect lighting and installed a baby spotlight. There were no regular tables as I did not plan to serve food, except such special orders which could be sent over from Chan's restaurant. Instead I lined the walls with comfortable low-slung rattan settees and occasional portable armchairs. In front of the settees, low cocktail tables provided space for drinks and ashtrays. The whole effect was that of a luxurious lounge, rather than of a restaurant or cocktail bar.

Following a suggestion made by Hochima, who pointed out that some patrons might be willing to pay extra for privacy, I had two private booths installed on one side of the entrance. At the same time the entrance hall at the top of the wide stairway was also furnished with a large settee, tables and chairs, making it a comfortable meeting place for our customers.

Fely, Flora, Fahny, along with another popular hostess, Judy Geronimo, formed the nucleus of the club's personnel. Little Fely, whose dancing and singing was admired by many, had quite a following of her own. She numbered among her followers the famous composer, Hajime Ichikawa, who was at the moment conducting the symphony orchestra at Manila's Metropolitan theatre. Ichikawa was sincerely in love with Fely and wanted to marry her. She handled the matter cleverly, keeping him at arm's length without hurting his feelings. Due to his friendship and coaching, she added a number of Japanese songs to her repertoire.

Fahny could be depended upon to supply everything that Fely and I lacked. She was an eccentric dancer, highly appreciated by our more jaded patrons who relished the sensational and grotesque. She was eager to earn money to send to her father, a physician, now seriously ill in Santo Tomas. Her two sisters, Anna and Lily, joined us, and introduced David, a dancing waiter. In turn, he produced his sister, a clever pianist. Fely found the rest of the orchestra for me... Filipinos who specialized in Hawaiian music. Our five piece orchestra gave us a decided edge over Ana's music, provided by her one weary ivory thumper.

Carling returned from a trip to the hills where he had gone to visit his parents, bringing along my precious papers and the spent bullet. He sent these to me by Pacio, who immediately clamored for a job as a waiter. I was happy to take him on, knowing that he could double as a carrier to the guerrillas. We managed to get four more waiters, including the ubiquitous Demyon. Judy begged me to take on her eighteen-year old brother, Memerto, as bartender. I thought that the Number One bar man should be thoroughly experienced, and engaged a well-known master of drink mixing; but Memerto was employed as second boy.

On Fely's advice, I applied for the club license through a friend of hers at the city hall, who, after we had paid over two hundred and fifty pesos, expedited the filling out of all the required papers. Then Fely took me to the beer company where I had to get the very essential beer permit from the Japs. I could not open without it, as beer was the main beverage that the Nips drank. Fely introduced me to Kisimoto, a big, fat jovial slant-eye, the president of the brewery, whom she had met at Ana's place. After holding my hand for a half hour, while I listened patiently to his inanities, he finally gave me the permit.

There was, of course, the usual last minute hurry and bustle, but the Tsubaki Club had its formal opening as scheduled. On that night the Nipponese elite deserted Ana Fey's and other night spots, crowding our staircase. I received them at the head of the stairway, clad in a new clinging, halter-necked white evening gown. All my hostesses had new dresses, copied from year-old fashion books; the only ones available. Our waiters were all in spotless white coats, pants and shoes. A bowl of peanuts was on every table, and we served hors d'oeuvres consisting of crackers spread with hard-to-get Australian cheese or corned beef. These "delicacies" were contributed by some of our friends who followed the established Nipponese custom of presenting gifts to a new enterprise.

The club's original well-wisher Mr. Hochima, arrived with a party of mining men, which included Ichikawa, Fely's smiling admirer, a Mr. Mitsui of the well-known family, and George Terada, a graduate of Columbia University, small and fat, who spoke good English. Among the Japanese artists, in addition to Ichikawa, we were honored by the movie star Kawazu, Hiraoka, the famous xylophonist, and Mujamoto, perhaps Japan's greatest limner. Colonel Saito, rotund head of the Department of Propaganda arrived, followed by five doctors from the Stotsenberg Army Hospital. The medicos soon were in a gay mood, and importuned the girls to give them dancing lessons. By ten o'clock we were turning prospective patrons away.

Our floor show opened with the Filipino rice-planting dance. Girls in native costume strode in barefooted, carrying flat woven trays. With a musical accompaniment, they simulated the planting of rice... hands becoming tired from working in the mud... then its harvesting and husking, shaking the trays, throwing the imaginary grains in the air, and blowing away the chaff. The dance wound up with a final tossing away of the trays, while the dancers went into a joyous fiesta celebration. This number became our most popular specialty.

A Siamese Temple dance followed, featuring Fahny and David. She was strikingly costumed in gold brassiere and panties, with a trailing purple, taffeta skirt. Her head dress was a copy of the one worn by Hedy Lamarr when doing the temple dance in a movie called Tropical Lady, and not a bad duplication considering the circumstances. David had strips of gold material wound around his slender body, and had increased his height by means of a tall, black Hindu turban. He advanced with consummate dignity to place an incense burner at Fahny's feet as she stood motionless, posed on a black pedestal. The scent of the incense brought the ebony statue to life, and as the tempo increased, dusky worshippers sprang from the shadows and joined the mad dance. As the performance continued with weird steps and contortions, I noted that our visitors were open-mouthed and attentive.

After a typical Igorrote wedding dance, David bounded back on the floor in a fantastic new number, done in complete darkness. He carried two flaming torches, and was only wearing a G-string and a headgear of turkey feathers. Our orchestra accompanied his unpredictable leaps and bounds, more or less, with "Rhapsody in Blue."

When midnight arrived there was no doubt about the success of the Club Tsubaki. All the varied parts of my little machine were running smoothly, and compliments showered down on me from the delighted patrons. Our achievement was reflected in my full cash box and the unfeigned gaiety of each member of my staff.

Ramon Amusatague dropped by the next day about noon, to congratulate me. He had seen the story of our auspicious opening in the newspaper.

"I've thought of another way to get word into Cabanatuan ...through Father Buttenbruck," he suddenly remarked in the course of our conversation. "He is a German priest, who has a permanent pass from the Japanese, permitting him to engage in charitable work."

"Do you think he will take in a note for me?" I asked hopefully.

"No. He will not take that risk. He says that he is always searched upon entering and leaving the prison, but he will make an inquiry for you. Here is his address. There is no need to worry about him. He's a real Christian and no Nazi."

Soon after Ramon left, I called a carromata, and drove to the priest's house. I told him frankly that I was seeking word of my husband in Cabanatuan.

"I would like to help you," he said. "As you know, I dare not take in a note, but if you can think of any word or song... something your husband might recognize... I could slip it in with a package. Then he might find a way to answer you." "May I send a bag of clothes and food in?"

"Get together a few articles that you think your husband will find useful and place them in a small shopping bag. Put the message in the bottom. I will hand the bag over to the American officer in charge, and try to give him your husband's name as I do. I'll be making the trip a week from today."

I thanked Father Buttenbruck and hurried back to town where I bought shoes, pants, socks, a shirt, toothbrush and paste, quinine, aspirin, and a few cans of food. All the way home I cudgeled my brain to think of a word or phrase that Phil would surely know was mine. Then I remembered a night just a year back... "I don't want to set the world on fire"... that was it; he could not forget that song.

A week later, I went again to Father Buttenbruck's house, with the shopping bag made up as he had directed.

"It's been so long," I told this good man. "Please ask anyone that you can about Sergeant John V. Phillips."

"I will do my best, my child."

"Thank you, father. I don't know how to express my gratitude."

"There is no need for that. We are all doing our best and God will repay us in His way. Good-bye and God bless you!" Driving home, my spirits soared, as I thought that now I should certainly learn something worthwhile. Finally I could sit still no longer, and dismissing the carromata at the Luneta Park, I started to walk home.

A Japanese army truck was halted near the park's entrance, and near it two men were resting on the grass. As I approached closer, I noted that one was a Jap soldier; the other an American prisoner of war. I was wondering whether I dared break the stringent Jap regulation and speak to the

American. At that moment I caught sight of Dian and her amah entering the park. I called and Dian ran to me. I picked her up, and moved toward the two men. I smiled at the Jap who responded by sitting up, and motioning for me to approach.

"I rike baby very much," he announced, and started talking to Dian.

Holding her over one shoulder toward the Nip, I spoke quietly behind her, to the American, in a low tone.

"Do you know Sergeant John Phillips?"

"You are Mrs. Phillips?"

I nodded.

"Betty told me about you," the prisoner continued. "I'm sorry. Phillips died last July in Cabanatuan."

I shook my head violently in negation.

"It's true," he whispered bluntly, "I'm Joe Rizzo, sergeant from your husband's outfit. Take it easy!"

I stumbled away, my eyes blinded with tears. Fely noticed that something was amiss as I entered the club. When I told her of what I had heard, she consoled "Wait until you get an official report. Don't give up hope."

"I won't, Fely," I responded weakly.

I had remembered there were at least three men named Phillips in the Thirty-First Infantry. Rizzo might be mistaken, but then he said he belonged to my husband's outfit.

I smiled bravely at Fely, then went into a small side room and gave vent to my emotions, using a handkerchief to muffle my sobs.

Success and possible failure had all been mine within one short week.

CHAPTER XI

Guerrillas Minus Guns

FELY HAD A NATURAL TALENT FOR LEARNING LANGUAGES RAPIDLY. She had managed to acquire a smattering of Japanese and we decided that she should take advantage of the Japanese offer of a free daily lesson of one hour's duration. Within a short space of time she was not only able to speak and understand Japanese fairly well, but had begun to learn how to read and write the hiragana and katakana alphabets. We kept her accomplishment a secret from our patrons, thus making her more valuable than ever as an eavesdropper.

Business was good but not sensational through the weeks that followed our opening. The venture had four thousand pesos of unpaid indebtedness against it, and my first objective was to liquidate these obligations. It was my goal to get real results by the first of the year, and we all began to build up interest in the special attractions we expected to offer during the holiday season. We worked hard on a new floor show, and sent engraved invitations to our best guests saying that we would be happy and honored to reserve a table for them on Christmas Night or one of the special evenings following. The result was a gratifying number of reservations, and we knew we had nothing to worry about on that score.

Exactly two weeks from the day I had visited Father Buttenbruck, he telephoned me. Ignoring my request for information, he asked if I could come to see him soon. When I answered affirmatively, he said he would await me in his study. As I entered, the compassionate look on the good man's face and the paternal gesture with which he motioned me to a chair beside him, made me aware that the news I was about to hear was not good.

I can no longer recall his soothing words, but do remember that he showed me the list of deaths in Cabanatuan for the month of July. Through a blur of tears I read the name of Sergeant John V. Phillips among them, date... July 27th, 1942 ... causes... malaria and dysentery. I even recognized the Army serial number ending with thirteen, a little detail we had joked about.

Any woman who has lost her loved one under such tragic circumstances will understand my emotions... emptiness... anger... bitterness... and pity for my poor, gallant husband who had perished so needlessly after heaven knows how much suffering and despair. If only, I could have reached him by so much as one note... one word...

My private Gethsemane lasted three nights and days. During this time I remained in my room and took things to make me sleep... and forget. Fely and the others carried on for me, explaining that Madame was suffering with a miserable headache. They couldn't say heartache. Finally Dian's anxious little query, "Mama well, now?" could no longer be ignored. I realized that I must go on living... for her.

Then a note from Cabanatuan reached me through Betty, signed by a prisoner... Frank L. Tiffany, Chaplain. It verified the facts I had learned from the priest and added another cause of Phil's death... malnutrition. After expressing sympathy, the chaplain closed with, "But I beg of you not to forget the ones that are left. They are dying by the hundreds." A thought flashed in my mind. Men who had known Phil and served with him... men, like Phil, waiting, enduring... hoping. That was my answer. I must help them, and to do so the Club Tsubaki must go on... and there was always Boone and his tattered band.

I told Betty what I had in mind, and begged her to trust me with the name of her Cabanatuan contact. She finally disclosed his identity... an American sergeant, Joe Rizzo, who drove for the Japanese guards.

"Rizzo!" I exclaimed, "Why I met Rizzo in the Luneta and talked with him. I wouldn't believe what he told me. Come to think of it, he mentioned your name. I should have guessed."

Betty's eyes were moist as she answered, "I didn't want to believe it either. I hoped that it was a false rumor. On the other hand, I did want you to be prepared."

That little talk brought on more bad days. I missed Louise badly, and found the need of talking to some sympathetic friend who had known Phil. I found myself dreading the approach of Christmas Eve... our first wedding anniversary. I wanted to pass it without brooding too much about the memory of that one wonderful star-lit night in Bataan. I decided to ask the staff to an early dinner on Christmas Eve. They were all delighted, and all came bringing gifts. I made a little speech, taking them even more completely into my confidence than before. I told them about the large response to our invitations, and let them know what our hard work was all about. "We must help others," I concluded, "who are so much worse off than we are." A glance at their friendly faces reassured me that they understood.

We sang carols around our tree, a little artificial one, aglow with tiny wax candles. Everyone was as thrilled as Dian with it. She was in the seventh heaven with her first life-sized doll, a beautiful young lady dressed in pale blue taffeta, with long golden hair and eyes that open and shut. The party wound up, David lifting his arms in one of his grotesque gestures, as he led the group in a grand march singing "God Bless the Philippines," a great favorite, to the tune of "God Bless America." Perhaps the happiest face there belonged to Memerto who had realized his ambition of being promoted to number one bar boy. My original high-powered choice and I had parted company by mutual consent, at the end of the second week. During his short stay, the ambitious Memerto had watched him closely and picked up much of his technique.

The high spirits and enthusiasm generated at our little party remained at a high pitch over that entire evening. I could not help but note that the unsuspecting Japanese were infected with the unusual mood of gaiety, although they were, of course, far from guessing what had caused it. Our guests could not tear themselves away until nearly six a. m. The night's take was so good that I was able to tell my crew that another such party on New Year's Eve would see us with a surplus in the till. My prediction was correct. We repeated our program with variations; then found ourselves with sufficient funds to meet all obligations, and leave us a thousand pesos in the clear.

Pacio took off the next night with money for Boone and a request for a list of his needs. I sent a note along which read, "Our new show a sellout. You can count on regular backing. Standing by for orders and assignments," and when I thought of a name to sign to it, my habit of sticking valuables in my bra occurred to me. Thus the code name "High-Pockets" was conceived, and that's how I signed myself.

A week later Pacio returned safely with a note from the guerrilla leader who used "Compadre" as his signature, enclosing what he called a "wishing list"... food, medicines, shoes, clothing, razor blades, soap, and a "little whiskey for medicinal purposes." Boone also acknowledged my information about enemy activities, and pointed out that the most important thing that he wanted was a radio set. Pacio told me that this was to be sent up into the hills, piece by piece, using different carriers and over a period of time to avoid detection. As soon as he could get this set functioning, Boone planned on contacting other guerrilla groups on nearby islands, particularly one in Mindinao which could reach MacArthur at Darwin.

Now that our objective was clear and the means to attain it established, I began to take a renewed interest in life. Pacio remained my regular number one carrier, making any extra trips required, while the regular first-of-the-month trip was taken over by a trusted appointee of Boone's, a stout-hearted, bright-eyed young Filipino girl named Mellie who, along with her father, had joined his band.

This girl's father had been one of Boone's henchmen for some time, and she went up into the hills to visit him. At that time Boone was vainly trying to get some of the Filipino guerrillas to go down to Dinalupihan and spy on the Japs. They all feared possible recognition and refused to take a chance. With Mellie's consent Boone let the word drift in to the Nips that he had kidnapped her. A few weeks later this plucky girl went into the barrio and gave herself up, pretending that she had escaped. The Japs, at first, were suspicious of trickery, and confined her in a cell at their headquarters. In a few days they relented and allowed her to roam through the building freely, but not to go outside. As the time passed she won the Nip's friendship by cooking and sewing for them, and they no longer restrained her movements. Mellie gathered considerable information about troop movements and ammunition dumps, and then slipped off to the hills. When the slant-eyes discovered her defection they issued orders to shoot her on sight.

On reaching her father again, she courageously volunteered to act as a carrier and it was arranged that Mellie would leave Boone's camp the first day of every month, and we could expect her by the third, or at the very latest, the fifth. If she failed to arrive then, I was to send Pacio to find Boone and check. The girl had noted a number of safe places along the way in which to either hide or cache her papers, in case of trouble.

Now that I was certain that the Club Tsubaki was a success, I decided to make it my personal quarters as well. The Japanese curfew was a nuisance and some nights I had not been able to reach home. It only took a friendly carpenter a couple of weeks to convert some of the smaller rooms into a four room apartment, in the rear of the club. There was a bedroom for Dian and her Ah Ho, a combination office-bedroom for me, as well as a kitchenette-dining room and bath. It pleased me very much to have all my precious eggs in one basket. One large room next to mine was remodeled, and used as a dormitory by any of the girls who had difficulty getting home at night. Any stranded boys were always welcome to use the settees in the lounge as emergency bunks.

Boone's guerrillas now numbered about fifty Americans and about a thousand Filipinos. It was growing daily, and his wishing lists grew longer accordingly. His list of January fifteenth gave us a good laugh. In addition to the usual food, medicines, clothes and money; he wanted combs, a mirror, playing cards, books or magazines, ending up with the request for "news from home and a blonde." We sent everything except the last two items, which we explained were a little hard to get.

Business continued to flourish. We packed the visitors in every week end, and around the twentieth... Japanese pay day ... there was standing room only at the Club Tsubaki.

Betty Wright told me that she thought the best contact for sending supplies to Cabanatuan would be a Filipino girl, Naomi Flores. She explained that Naomi had gone purposely to the place in the autumn of 1942, for the express purpose of finding a way to communicate with the men buried alive there. Now, after three months, the girl was well and favorably known to the Japanese guards as a licensed fruit and vegetable pedlar, and anxious to pass along contributions from sympathizers. She promised to send Naomi to me.

"If you hear from her," she concluded, "the message will be signed 'Looter,' her code name."

One morning, Victoria, my cook, came to my office followed by a plump, smiling young woman who had some very fine fruit she wanted to show me personally. It was Looter, of course. She was about twenty-four, sweet-voiced, and had learned fair English in her brief grade-school days. I learned that she had been a beauty parlor operator before the war.

Looter explained how she had won the confidence of the Jap guards around Cabanatuan by being "stupid and hard-working." She related that, so far, she had only smuggled in money hidden in the bottom of bean bags, but was confident she could get in other articles, even large packages of food, clothing or medicine, in the future. Her main reason for the success of this venture, was that she now had access to the prisoner's detail that drove the carabao carts outside the enclosure for firewood.

When I asked how the prisoners would explain having money and clothes in their possession, she informed me that all prisoners able to work were paid so much a day by the Japs, according to their rank... privates five cents, on up to lieutenant colonels, fifty cents. All officers above that rank had been sent to Japan. I learned that the Nips, allowed some clothing to be sent in by the Swiss Red Cross, which, after selecting any choice pieces for themselves, they permitted the prisoners to buy. Our contributions, she was certain, would be indistinguishable from the Red Cross allotment.

"Does the produce supply that you sell come from Manila?" I queried.

"Yes, a friend brings it out to me by train."

"Would she be willing to take our money and notes out to you?"

"Oh, yes. You see she's part American. Her father and sisters are in Santo Tomas, and she is engaged to an American prisoner named Dempsey. She renounced her citizenship in order to be able to help them and others."

Looter went on to say that her Manila contact's name was Evangeline Neibert, who used the code name of "Sassy Suzie." It had already occurred to me that a number of people in the ever-increasing group of "guerrillas minus guns" would welcome an opportunity to send in money and badly needed medicines to Cabanatuan. I therefore arranged to have Sassy call a week later to pick up our contributions.

Sassy was an American-Filipino mestiza of about twenty-five, as alert and dependable a little heroine as her friend Looter. There was a false bottom in her shopping bag for our contraband. I sent one hundred pesos with a note to Chaplain Tiffany, telling how happy I was to be able to help his men, and asking for the names of the ten most needy ones. I signed the message "High-Pockets," knowing that he would guess my identity from its contents.

Looter told me that men were still dying in Cabanatuan as Phil had, of malaria, malnutrition and dysentery, so I called on all the doctors that I could trust to help me accumulate a supply of quinine and emetine.

Sassy came back two days later and reported that Looter was overjoyed with all the things sent. We decided that Sassy should make the six-to-eight hour trip on the dinky little train after another week. We thought that by that time Looter would have smuggled the articles in, and should have some notes out to us.

On Sassy's next visit to the club she brought letters. Chaplain Tiffany had let a number of men learn of this opportunity to send word to friends outside. Among them was a letter for Sassy from her fiancé, one for Betty from her Bill, and one for me from Chaplain Tiffany. My note began "Dear High-Pockets" and was signed "God Bless You...'Everlasting'." It read:

"It is hard to pick out the ten neediest men here, but I will do my best. Here are the names..." (followed by ten names)... Thanks so much for the medicine. We can use all we can get and also money. Among other men here who can help spread your cheer around are Father John Wilson, Lieutenant Colonel Mack and Lieutenant Colonel Schwartz. Also Chaplain Robert Taylor who tells me he met you on Bataan. These men are on other details and can reach men that I can't. Below is the name the men here have given me. They say I'll last forever. I seem to be the only one who does not get sick."

It was encouraging to know that at last we could reach the despairing men, so I arranged with Sassy for her to take regular trips every two weeks. When the next "mail" went out, ten pesos were forwarded to each of the men on Chaplain Tiffany's list, twenty pesos enclosed in cheery notes to Lieutenant Colonels Mack and Schwartz, and fifty pesos each to Father Wilson and Chaplain Taylor, asking them to divide it as they saw fit. I sent one hundred pesos to Everlasting as he was in the hospital area where the money was mostly needed. I knew that the Nips had a commissary there where fruit, eggs, milk and vegetables could be bought.

At the head of Everlasting's list of the ten most needy men was the name "Yeager," with the notation "Tuberculosis; might pull through if he had the will to live. Write him a cheery letter." I did my best to comply, even calling on Fahny and Fely to help me think up funny things to help cheer him up. I told him that I would get him anything he especially wanted, even if I had to loot a Jap warehouse to do it.

Mellie arrived after the first of the month with disheartening news. Boone wrote:

"Sorry to inform you that I was raided by the blankety-blank Japs and lost everything you sent me. Looks like we will have to start over again with supplies. I had my shoes off and lost them too. I did not lose a man, but one was wounded, so rush what you can right back. The money you sent last time we used to buy rice and we lost the rice too. Eating wild bananas and coconuts until Mellie returns. I've got quite a bunch of men together now and we are training them every day.

Held up a Jap truck the other night and got a nice mess of hand grenades, but we can't eat them, so hurry my wife back here. Yours in war,
     Compadre.
     P. S. Yes! It happened this week."

After reading this note a second time, it dawned on me that Boone had married our courageous little carrier, so I wished the bride all the happiness possible in war time, and plenty more after that.

I made a rapid estimate and, learned to my dismay, that it would take about four thousand pesos to replace the lost supplies. All of my spare funds had been sent to Cabanatuan, and the club was only taking in about four hundred pesos a night. It would take some time to accumulate the necessary funds and Boone's message stressed urgency. I glanced at my diamond ring, and decided that it must go the way of all things.

While Mellie waited, I hastened to the Remedios Hospital to see my friend Senora Mencarini, who spent several hours there every day as a volunteer nurse. This tall, good-looking Spanish woman of about forty, was the mother of three children. She and her husband, a prosperous businessman, lived in an impressive big house on Taft Avenue. I had heard recently that both were working hard to collect money for our cause, and I knew that this generous woman had converted many of her own cherished possessions into cash to help feed the sick and hungry at Santo Tomas. "Will you please sell this ring for me I asked, handing it to her, "What do you think it will bring?"

"If it's a fast sale, not over three thousand pesos. If you can wait for a week, I can probably get you five thousand. Jewelry goes up every day."

"I can't wait. It's for the guerrillas. They are in trouble and I need the money in two days at the most. Please get what you can for the ring and send the cash to the club."

"I'll bring it myself. Don't worry. You will have it." Senora Mencarini arrived at noon the next day with three thousand pesos. I thanked her profusely, and, as she was leaving, she suddenly invited, "Come to my house for lunch day after tomorrow at one o'clock."

I expressed appreciation, but began to make excuses that I was very busy, and unable to make any social engagements, only to have the lady smile cryptically. "You will have time for this," she remarked quietly, "A few people will be there whom you will enjoy meeting, and you must know."

"All right, I will be there," I accepted.

The rest of the day, Memerto, Fely, Fahny and I scoured the city getting supplies... medicine, food, and clothes. Mellie left the next morning. She would have been unable to carry the big bags without the aid of her helper, Zig-Zag, whom Boone had sent along with her. From then on, Zig-Zag either accompanied Mellie or substituted for her. He wore double-soled shoes in which he carried notes until a Japanese sentry took a fancy to his footgear. After that he hid his notes in a banana in the inside of a small cluster.

When the appointed time came, and I arrived at the Mencarini home, I greeted the people that I knew among the dozen or more guests assembled... Sassy Suzie, Ramon Amusatague, his wife Lerry, Father Lolar, Doctor and Senora Atienza. I was not presented to the others.

When we were seated at the table, Senora Mencarini told us, "Since we are all doing the same kind of work, I thought that it would be nice for us to become acquainted." Then she introduced each guest, explaining what individual action they were taking to help the American-Filipino cause. It was obvious that we were a hand-picked group, for she gave the code names of all present for use in our future dealings with each other.

She, herself, was "Boots" and her husband "Rocky." My old friend Father Lolar, was henceforth to be known as "Morning Glory." I had not realized before that Ramon and Lerry Amusatague were hand in glove with us. I now learned that they too, were gathering supplies and sending them in to Cabanatuan. Ramon, whose code name was "Sparkplug," was gathering forbidden news from the States, condensing it, and circulating it in little news sheets to keep up the morale of American sympathizers. His pretty wife, Lerry, inconsistently code-named "Screwball," college-bred like her husband, and the mother of two small boys, was busily collecting money for the cause and supporting Ramon's activities in every possible manner.

The most taciturn guest present was a tall, heavy Filipino, about thirty-five... a Senor Torres. I wondered briefly why he was not in the hills with his fighting countrymen, especially when he mentioned previous military experience, and seemed to be in good physical condition. The few remarks that he did contribute to the discussion were very much to the point. He sat next to Ramon and I gathered that they were on intimate terms. Senora Mencarini referred to him as "The Doctor," and I inferred that this was not a title, but his code name. She added with a gentle smile that he was the person to call on in case of trouble, and I found out the full meaning of this remark at a later date.

On the other side of the "Doctor," sat a rather gentle-looking youth, slender, with blonde hair and baby blue eyes, very fair for a Spaniard, and obviously well-educated. This was German (pronounced Herman). He was very elegantly turned out in old, but custom-made clothes of an unusual pattern. His sartorial inclinations were obviously responsible for his code name of "Fancy-Pants."

Next to "Fancy-Pants" was a serious-looking Spanish mestiza in her early thirties, addressed as Marie... code name "Papaya." She was apparently well to do, and volunteered to cash prisoner's personal checks and I. O. U.'s from her bank account.

A middle-aged Swiss, Charles Rigeness, who typified a business executive, sat at the foot of the table. I learned that he had been head of the Manila Gas Company at the time of occupation. He had the additional distinction of having told the Japs off when asked to collaborate and had gotten away with it. After his refusal, the Nips arrested him, but finding themselves badly in need of his services, released him after a week. After that both kept their distances; Rigeness operating his utility and the Sons of Heaven leaving him attend to his work without interference. "Swiss"... that was his code name ... was one of the leading money collectors in the group. Because of his connections he could approach the large Swiss firms for help, which none of the rest of us could do. As ardent neutrals the local Swiss were caution personified when approached by a Philippine national for financial assistance.

My hostess asked me to explain the work which Sassy and I were doing at Cabanatuan through courageous little Looter. I had discovered that both girls were facing a struggle to make both ends meet, as they were forced to earn a livelihood while carrying on their hazardous relief work. When I mentioned this, the group prevailed on Sassy to accept thirty pesos a week for expenses, and awarded the same amount to Looter.

I finished my talk by telling briefly of the real purpose behind my club, asked them to consider it their unofficial headquarters, and to use me and my staff in any way that they could at any time. As I spoke, looking from one to another of that strangely assorted group drawn together by a common cause, my heart was filled with hope and confidence that "The Time Would Come."

As we lingered over the coffee, a number of practical suggestions were made and plans laid. We were assigned army ranks like the guerrillas in the hills. My club office was to be a clearing house for donations to Cabanatuan. Anyone wishing to send things through Sassy was to telephone me and inquire "When are you sending the cookies?" If the mail was ready to go, I was to call them and state "Bring your recipes. I'm going to bake today." If mail arrived from the prison, I was to inform any of the group, inquiring, "Come and try my fresh cookies." Should anyone be arrested we would spread the word by informing the others "So-and-so went to school today."

Before separating we spent some time committing to memory the code names of the various members; also what turned out to be the inception of a communication code, a ludicrous adaptation of American slang. I also suggested the use of pig-Latin and they seized upon this with great glee, feeling that no Jap listening in could make sense out of this "language" so common to American school children. All of these precautions were designed to aid us in communicating with each other, and also serve as identification, because spurious patriots, either working their own rackets or for the Nips, were in our midst.

In spite of the group's warning, it was not long before I was taken in by one such specimen. Judy Geronimo spoke to me about a twenty-two year old American boy who was hiding out in Manila. Her family and friends had been helping "Beans" as they called him, as he would not divulge his name. I told Judy to bring him to me at the club some night after hours. The fugitive proved to be tall and good-looking, with something of Phil's build, only slighter. He told me that he was a lieutenant and his real name was Collins. I did not altogether believe the "lieutenant" part, ascribing this to a youthful desire to impress me, but he was undoubtedly an American and in distress. I urged him to go into the hills, and without disclosing the location of Boone's headquarters, gave him directions which would bring him in contact with the guerrilla outposts. I knew that they could perform a better job of investigation than I was able to, and would take him into their ranks if he proved worthy.

"Beans" seemed to agree with my plan, but insisted that it would take a little time for him to manage to get out of town. He was in need of both clothes and money, so I dug down in my trunk and gave the boy Phil's two civilian suits. A small still voice inside me protested this act, but I deemed it due to a natural reluctance to part with anything that belonged to my departed. I consoled myself with the thought that Phil would want his things used by an American soldier who needed them badly.

A few days later "Beans" came back, looking very neat in his new array, and confessed that he had gambled away the money I had given him. He seemed to think that his defection was very ludicrous, and saw no reason why I should not come across with another handout. I realized that I had a weak sister on my hands. "Don't you realize how hard money is to get," I scolded, "You claim to be an officer of the United States Army! You should know that it is needed by the guerrillas with whom you should be fighting. If you were a prisoner of war, you would appreciate the purposes for which my money is being used." In the midst of this furious tongue-lashing, he arose with a sneer on his insipid face, and left. Other pressing matters made me forget the incident temporarily, but a few days later I discovered that Collins (if that was his name) had gone from my club to Father Lolar's church with a plausible story... that he was on his way to the hills and I had sent him for a hundred pesos... which he promptly received.

This experience was of great educational value to me. I was thankful that it had cost no more than two suits of clothes and a few hundred pesos. The lad simply disappeared after this, and, at least, did not turn informer, as far as we know.

It made me think and think hard, of the very thin ice on which we were all skating, and I resolved to be much more careful in my future dealings with strangers.

Chapter XII

Under the Nipponese Heel

As time passed, we became accustomed, but not reconciled to life under the Japanese rule. It was irksome to ask their permission for everything and anything. We never knew when we saw Nips walking down the street, whether they would turn into our house. They came in any time they felt like it, asked for food and drink, and we dared not refuse them. They even made us mend and wash their clothes without pay. If they took a fancy to any article in our homes, they picked it up and walked out. We could not telephone the police and complain that it had been stolen. That would ear-mark us for undue attention, and they would not believe our story. It was plain, unadulterated open looting, but we were helpless.

Many of the former palatial homes of wealthy British and American internees were now occupied by Japs. They took works of art that they liked and sent the "souvenirs" to their homes in Japan. What they did not like, they wantonly destroyed. Many Nips were incredibly filthy; at least when on other people's property. Every house they occupied had a bathroom, but the little Sons of... say, Heaven, would repeatedly use the corner of any room they happened to be in, and then summon a native to clean up.

It was a common occurrence to hear the harsh shout "Tomare! Halt!" It might be the kenpei,* the military police asking to see our papers, or a sentry we had forgotten to bow to.

When I heard a shot ring out in the night, followed by the sound of running feet, I would peer cautiously out of the window, but I never saw anything. No one dared investigate what went on in the darkened streets of Manila between the dread hours of midnight and six a. m. These were the curfew hours, when only Nips were allowed to roam unmolested.

*The Kenpeitai or Kenpei were Japan's dreaded military police. The unit was similar to the Gestapo but was actually modeled on the French Gendarmerie of the 19th Century. By Claire's time, they had developed into a dark unit with extra-judicial powers including state sanctified torture.

Now and then I was awakened by the sounds of a convoy of trucks passing the club on the way to the piers. I would arise and sit by the window, watching old American army trucks loaded with every conceivable cargo...

food, electric refrigerators, bath tubs, radios... on their way to the piers to be loaded on ships and sent to Japan. It was maddening to watch them stripping Manila with no one to hinder their plundering activities.

Many people too, began to disappear; picked up haphazardly on the streets, or arrested in their homes or shops, by the military police. A few individuals would eventually return to relate that they had been released after being held in Fort Santiago for several months, without explanation. Some, not so fortunate, were never heard of again, and it was not an uncommon sight to glimpse bloated, headless cadavers floating in the Pasig River. The "guerrillas minus guns" made strenuous efforts to trace these unfortunates, and now and then, were successful. Many of these victims were prominent Filipinos, Spaniards, Swiss, and Chinese. Our enemy seemed to take a sadistic delight in tormenting the celestials.

Although I no longer worked there, whenever I had a spare moment, I dropped in at the Remedios Hospital to talk with the nurses or Father Lolar. On one of these visits, the priest introduced Bobby Jones... a male nurse.

"This Jonesey here is a fine broth of a lad," the father told me, "and as darling as you are, my child."

Jones, an American mestizo, said that he had some new plants to show me, and led me into the garden.

"Senorita Dorothy, is it true that you are the owner of the Tsubaki Club?" he inquired, when we were well out of hearing of anyone.

"Yes," I admitted, "that's the place where the Japanese elite meet."

"Do they ever say anything that it might help our side to know?"

"Yes, they do. Quite frequently."

"I have a radio sending set," Jones confided unexpectedly.

"What? A radio set!" I gasped, knowing that the Japs had numerous radio detectors strewn around the city, "where have you hidden it?"

"It's in my home, right across from the Japanese headquarters. They can't find it because it's right under their pudgy noses!"

"That's very dangerous," I warned, "and I think it would be suicide to try and send from there. Have you ever thought of trying to get it up to our men in the hills. They need one very badly."

Bobby said that the idea had occurred to him. I told him that I would contact Boone and work out a plan for transferring the set to him, and Jones consented. In the interim Bobby promised to pass on to me, any news from San Francisco that he managed to pick up. As I received this information, German and Ramon made numerous copies of the notes. In this manner a miniature tabloid was born that, from then on, carried true and encouraging news to the prisoners of war, internees and our Filipino sympathizers. Father Lolar distributed these news sheets to the nursing sisters and others, helping immeasurably to boost the faltering morale in the hospitals.

Many Filipinos, by this time, were not thinking of abstract right or wrong. They were growing weary of the whole gruesome business of war, and were concerned chiefly with how they and their children could be fed and clothed. They were beginning to fear that it might take many years for the Americans to return, and dreaded a future of this miserable, uncertain existence. Our news sheet did much to relieve their mental strain. The enemy managed to get possession of an occasional copy at times, and picked up a few people who were taken to Fort Santiago, questioned; then given sentences ranging from five to ten years. However, thanks to our workers' courageous silence, the Nips never learned where the paper originated.

Boone was delighted when he received a news sheet, telling of the advance of the American fleet and troops in the Pacific theater. He was anxious to get the radio set, and it was arranged to send it up to him over a period of weeks, part by part, through various carriers.

Assignments were now coming in to me from three main guerrilla groups, for in addition to Boone, Colonels Thorpe and Straughan had assembled a number of irregulars who were giving the Nips a bit of an argument and causing them to lose some sleep.

We operated in a methodical manner. After our hostesses had coaxed our high-ranking official guests into a jovial mood, either Fely or I would join the party and cajole the alcohol-befuddled Nips into talking. If they were army men, we led them on to tell about troop movements, and the conditions of roads and bridges. If naval officers, we lured them into talking about their ships. We pumped many newly arrived business men about the locations and nature of their establishments. Boone, for one, was certain, that much of the new Japanese materiel was now being manufactured in Manila.

I finally became aware that the average Nip army officer passing through Manila, never remained for more than a month. So when a new face appeared at the club, I attempted to become friendly with the newcomer and worm his destination out of him. This happened many times, but the Case of the Lonesome Captain will serve to illustrate how we operated.

I noticed that this youthful and good-looking officer came to the club nearly every night, unaccompanied, for almost a week. Finally I sat at his table and twitted him about being a lone wolf.

"Don't you know anyone in Manila?" I queried.

"So sorry, no. I come Nippon rast week. Not even knowing shoku (officers) my rentai (regiment)."

"But you will make many friends after you have been here for a while," I suggested.

"No time enough. Am onry here anoder week."

"That's too bad," I deprecated, "If you were going to be here for a while I could introduce you to many people. Maybe you will not be stationed far away, and can come to Manila often."

"No can do," the captain informed, taking the bait, "Manira too far for trip. Am going Ringayen Gurf."

"Lingayen Gulf!" I echoed, "Why should the army send you way up there, where it's quiet and peaceful?"

The Nip smiled at my assumed colossal ignorance.

"You woman; not understand war," he explained. "We Nipponese randed dat prace and found it easy to take. Beikokujin (Americans) maybe have same idea. We fortify heavy. Keeping many heitai (soldiers) dere. Now you understand?"

I shook my head in negation, and hoped that my eyes conveyed a sufficiently blank stare.

"You are a very young officer to be in charge of such an important pest," I flattered, "With your looks, you will be breaking some feminine hearts."

"You saying nice tings," he admitted, "But I onry taking five thousand heitai dere. Tinking maybe tirty tousand dere now. My men taking prace oder ones who reave."

That closes the Case of the Lonesome Captain, who influenced by liquor and flattery told me all that I wanted to know, and the intelligence was soon on its way to MacArthur via our usual channels.

It was a pleasant thrill when I heard from Boone that information we had forwarded to him was now reaching Australia by means of a radio set operated by a guerrilla group in southern Mindinao. Unfortunately the small bamboo set donated by Jones did not carry far. Then I heard that Boone had received a good sending set, that had been sneaked into Mindinao by an American submarine. Natives risking their lives, brought it over piece-meal in sail boats at night, when the Jap patrols were far more lax than in the day time. Boone lost no time in relaying information our runners brought up to him, sending to MacArthur in code. Several months passed without a response; then messages started coming in from MacArthur's new GHQ in New Guinea, and some of them were assignments for the "guerrillas minus guns" or me.

I was asked to watch for a Jap aircraft carrier which was expected to come limping into Manila Harbor. I was told when to expect it, find out where it would be repaired, how long the reconditioning would take, and send, if possible, the exact date and hour of its departure, plus its destination.

This was a job that we at the club could really get our teeth into. I started the ball rolling by giving Captain Arita, the vessel's commander, an especially warm welcome when he arrived with his staff. These naval officers, like all newcomers to the club, had to be warmed up through drinks and flattery, and reassured through more of the same, plus ingenious confidences on my part in regard to my Italian blood and sympathies. Their nauseating prattle in limited and butchered English never varied, sounding like a phonograph record with the needle stuck in the groove.

"I rove you. You rove me? You very pretty girr. You rike me?"

After several visits, Captain Arita was our pal. He was the shy, quiet type, but anyone could see that he was mad about Fely. He brought her many gifts, and was at the club every night to hear her sing. When I felt that the opportune moment had arrived, I told Fely to find out how soon the carrier would be leaving. The captain never took anything but a soft drink, or now and then one of the hostesses' cocktails upon our insistence that there was no alcohol in it.

His sobriety made us go easy on trying to pry information out of him, but as the carrier's repairs neared completion we found out that it was going directly to Singapore from Manila. On learning that its departure was impending, I invited the captain and his staff to join us in a special last-minute farewell party (at their expense).

This was no gag. I even cried real tears when he left, as I knew I was sending him to his doom. He was really a fine chap. He told us of his home and family in Japan; how he would be glad when the war was over, so he could join them. He hated war, and was quite an anomaly for the commander of a fighting craft. He was such a meek-like mouse that he only looked hurt if we said anything to offend him. He never replied to our quips, or took a swing at us like other slant-eyes were prone to do.

Yes, I cried real tears when he left, but war is war. As he and his staff departed by the big front door, my runner left by the back door on his way to Boone with a note stating that the carrier was leaving at six a. m. for Singapore and then Rabaul.

The next evening I witnessed a most unusual incident. A Jap army captain insisted upon dancing with one of the hostesses, in defiance of a proclamation long-since posted by the kenpei, forbidding this frivolity. A military policeman... and a private at that... walked into the club, crossed the floor and slapped the captain's face. I was fearful that the aftermath might be harmful to the club.

However, a friendly major with whom I was seated when the affair took place, assured me that the military policeman was within his rights and the captain had no recourse. At my insistence, the major did a bit of judicious bribing, and this terminated the episode.

About every two months there was a complete change in the personnel of our customers. Captains of carriers would be replaced by captains of battleships or submarines. Beneath this changing tide of visitors was a current of steady patrons in the guise of administration or newspaper men. The information we pried out of them was less dramatic, but often of great importance. Our stock query to newspaper men which often produced good results was, "What is it you are not going to print?"

Then the great day arrived when Boone first contacted Treasure Island... the San Francisco naval base. After that we had first-hand news for our secret tabloid. The morale in the prison camps and Santo Tomas definitely improved. It was no longer if but when the time comes.

I was pleasantly surprised one day, to find the name of my old friend Wop... Charley De Maio... on the list sent me by the chaplains at Cabanatuan. I wrote him at once, enclosing one hundred pesos, telling him to use the money to make life more endurable until "the time came." I eagerly waited for a reply from this old friend who had once shared our pleasures, and so recently had shared Phil's misery. On her next trip, Sassy brought back his reply:

"Hello High-Pockets:

When I got your letter I came to life again. Gee, it's good to know someone like you. You've done more for the boys' morale in here than you'll ever know. Let me tell you what I did with part of the money. Now don't get mad, High-Pockets, I had to do it. I donated forty-two packages of tobacco to the boys. Some of them are flat on their backs and I wish you could have seen the looks of gratitude. Please don't get mad, because it's the first money I've had to share with anyone since I was a prisoner.

Don't send me any more money. Take care of your baby and if there's any left, help out Louise. As for Mona, I guess I always expected she would act like she has. You were right to tell me.

In answer to your question about John's grave... don't worry, Pal. I won't always be here and neither will the others. When it's all over you and I will come back here and get John. I made arrangements right away with a boy who works in the cemetery to take extra care of his grave.

I repeat, I won't always be here, and when that time comes you and the baby will always have someone to call on if you are ever in need. You deserve more gold medals than all of us in here together."

Same old Wop! Big-hearted and still "afraid" that I would be "mad" because he had so generously distributed "his share." I was so happy that I shed tears of joy as I read his letter over and over. It was wonderful to know that he was alive.

The next morning I telephoned Mona, asking if she wanted to send him something. Her retort came like a dash of cold water: "I'm through with all that. What I have, I need for myself." I slammed the receiver down, furious at myself for having bothered to call her. It was the last time.

There were other letters. One from Chaplain Robert Taylor, whom I had met on Bataan, Lieutenant Colonel Mack, and a doctor, Lieutenant Colonel Schwartz, who was seeking more medicine for his charges; also a Major Levine asking for banjo strings and reeds for cornet and sax. I never learned how these instruments had been smuggled into the camp.

A notice in the newspapers stated that the Emperor of Japan, in his imperial benevolence, had sent the Philippine government a million quinine capsules.* This gift was to be distributed to all drug stores, and a ration given to all who applied.

I sent every one of my employees to procure their quota, and even made use of Dian and Ah Ho for this merciful purpose. Ramon and many others of our group also applied for their share. At the end of a week we had accumulated over ten thousand capsules which I packed, and sent to Cabanatuan.

In due time Chaplain Tiffany wrote me: "The quinine arrived okay. We can make use of all you send. I hate to be begging all the time, but I do need shorts for my church services. I am ashamed to stand in front of the men looking so ragged. Your friend Wop was so very happy to get your letter, I almost had to tie him up. We read the letter you wrote Yeager all over the hospital area and everyone got a big laugh. I hope you don't mind. It sure cheered the men up. I had to do the reading as Yeager is almost blind. I bought eggs, milk and fruit for him with the money you sent. Yeager says to tell you he would like some candy... God bless you. Everlasting."

*Quinine was essential to fight the tropical diseases – primarily malaria – that jungle-dwelling guerillas living outside with mosquitoes were especially susceptible to – as well as combat troops, in South East Asia.

The candy was forwarded when Sassy left on her next trip, but my poor efforts were in vain. My next note from the chaplain said in part, "Yeager got the candy and enjoyed it very much. He insisted I take one piece. I'm sorry he died the day after your candy and letter arrived. (It wasn't the candy, I'm sure). I should not joke about it but you need cheering up too. I know you worked hard to save him, but it was just not meant to be."

On the other side of the ledger, reports from Boone were heartening. I could not expect detailed reports of the guerrilla activities, but his carriers kept me fairly well informed of important happenings. The irregulars had managed to slip their spies into Japanese camps in the guise of workers, and these men brought them much information of local value. Then under cover of darkness, they crept down from the hills; touched off mines in roads and under bridges almost as soon as the Nips had laid them. It was notable that, almost from the beginning of their occupation, the Japs took every essential defensive precaution, despite their constant blatant propaganda that "the Americans will never return."

The guerrillas repeatedly raided Nip installations and made their getaway with surprisingly few casualties. In this manner they managed to keep themselves supplied with ammunition, and frequently captured additional weapons. It was highly essential that they be assured of a steady supply of their principal item of food... rice... and fortunately I had been able to arrange for this with the aid of faithful old Papa Sobervenas who had long since returned to his hacienda.

During one of our after-hours staff meetings, Totoy, one of my waiters told me about some information passed on to him by an aunt who lived near Pasay. At this place a converted school still known by its former swanky name of "Park Avenue," housed about a thousand prisoners, originally confined in Cabanatuan. It was reputedly, the worst hell-hole of all the Nipponese prison camps. The p.w.'s referred to it as "Devil's Island" because of the extreme brutality of the guards. Totoy reported that one guard was known as "The Wolf" because every time he started beating a prisoner, he never stopped until his victim died. This sadist had a partner in crime known as "Cherry Blossom" whose atrocities were also notorious. They were just one step ahead of their fellows who used lead saps and brass knuckles on the slightest provocation. The prisoners were dressed in pieces of; rags, many of which were barely sufficient to make a breech-cloth.

Totoy urged me to come and see the captives as they marched back and forth each day from the prison to work details. I wanted to act as quickly as possible, so in the late afternoon of the following day, Totoy took me to meet his aunt, Claring Yuma, a sturdy, little woman of about thirty, whose righteous anger and unselfishness was reflected in her plain, good face.

"Those poor men are dying like flies," she complained indignantly. "I've seen the awful food they are given; and a pig would not touch it. It's just water in which fish and rice have been boiled, with carrot tops and potato peelings thrown in. This slop is all they get; a teaspoon three times a day. It is a miracle that these men could live on that swill and still do the long hours of work demanded of them, in addition to marching ten miles a day."

She urged me to accompany her to the road down which the men would pass at six p. m., on the arduous five mile hike from Nichols Air Field. We took a carromata, and as we drove along, Claring and I discussed where we would hide to conduct our observations. It was a rule of the military police that anyone addressing, or even staring at prisoners of war, was liable to arrest. As we neared the spot, I noticed a vacant house at the junction of two roads.

I suggested that this would make a good vantage point, and Claring agreed. We dismissed the carromata, telling the driver to return for us later. We entered the house through the back door, unobserved, and waited, safely hidden behind the dusty lattice. At the sound of marching feet we stopped talking, knowing that the guards and prisoners would pass closely outside.

When I glimpsed them, my heart sank. It was almost impossible that these ragged, bearded specimens of humanity, with shaven heads and red-ringed eyes were once proud American fighting men. It was obvious that many of them were ill or desperately tired, as their comrades supported them to keep them from falling. This galling sight brought back bitter memories of the "Death March," and tears blinded me.

As Claring had related, the men's uniforms were in rags. Nine out of every ten stumbled along the uneven gravel road with cut and bleeding bare feet, and many had big festering sores on their legs. I knew at a glance that it was impossible to recognize anyone among these living dead. Their only identification was the number the Japs had printed on the big straw hats they wore or carried. As the last poor wretches, followed by the last guards turned the corner and disappeared in the twilight, I turned to Claring and assured her, "Yes, something will be done. That's a promise. If we could only find someone we can trust to let those men know we are here."

"There is someone, senora. Did you notice the Filipino worker walking with the prisoners? That is Pedro. He is a mechanic and works for the Japs because he has such a large family to feed. He hates the Japs and would gladly help us. I feel certain that we can approach with safety."

"If you trust him, I will. Tell the man that we will pay him with money and rice for his family."

My first move was to rent the house at the road junction in Claring's name, and she, with several of her relatives moved into it. Having established this base of operations, I began to ask circumspect questions. I learned that although the Philippine Red Cross sent occasional supplies to "Park Avenue," three-quarters of them were appropriated by the Japs, in complete disregard of the provisions of the Geneva Pact. The remainder could be bought by their victims if they had the money. Some individuals whom I approached for funds to carry on our work, had a way of saying "Even though you sneak in a handful of beans, what good would that do?" My stock retort to these defeatists was "Anything we send in to the boys reaches them; all of it. It's better to send a little and be sure that it gets into hands of the prisoners, than a quantity only to have it wasted or help feed the enemy."

The first note that I sent in to "Park Avenue" by Pedro read:

"To the one who gets this: I have been helping Cabanatuan and any one of you who may have been there will know me. My two helpers can be trusted. Tell me of any way that I can get help to you. Number 607, the house on the corner of Park Avenue and the National Highway is mine. Watch, and as soon as you see curtains up, drop a note near the house and I will get it. Send answer through this boy if you can. Yours in war,
    High-Pockets."

Two days later Claring brought me the first of a long stream of pathetic notes. It was signed by a Captain Muir who agreed that Pedro could be trusted with notes and money, and confirmed the fact that the Japs had a commissary in the prison where the men could buy a few things. He stated that he would be glad to distribute any money we sent in, and asked only one favor. A guard had struck him, and his glasses had been broken. He was almost blind without them and could arrange to have them replaced for fifty pesos. Could I send that to him?

I sent the requested fifty pesos, plus a hundred for the general mess fund, and asked the captain to try and send me a list of all his fellow prisoners. After almost a week had passed without a reply I started to worry. Had Pedro failed us or kept the money? Had the note and money been intercepted? Was Pedro being tortured to make him disclose the sender? I shivered at that thought. My anxiety ended when Claring came triumphantly bringing a large sheet giving the names, rank and army serial numbers of every prisoner in "Park Avenue." Captain Muir appended his thanks; his glasses were repaired. He even sent the Jap optometrist's receipt for twenty pesos; the Jap intermediary having kept the balance of the fifty.

I scanned the list to see if any familiar names appeared and found one H. Spooner listed. I wondered if this could be Phil's old buddy, and just on a chance sent him a note containing fifty pesos and a query. His reply stated in part: "Dear Friend: So you are Phil's wife. Your letter was a God-send. I had begun to think that we in here were the Forgotten Men. Thanks for the money. I sure can use it. I'll be known from here on as Sky Pilot." I sent him more money and urged him to get shoes. From then on, we conducted an extensive correspondence, during which I told him about Wop in Cabanatuan and even managed to exchange letters between them.

Claring had managed to establish friendly relations with some of the Nip guards; an essential prelude for the success of our new-hatched plan. She hired a carpenter to build a lean-to shed on the vacant lot opposite our house, and I stocked it with fruit and empty cans which still bore labels; the latter for window-dressing. We bought about three hundred bananas a day and other fruit, when it was available, placing our wares in large bags on the little counter. As the prisoners wearily stumbled past our stand, four or five of the guards (bribed by gifts of money, American watches and fountain pens) would fall out, grab the bags, and give them to the men. After the first week, however, the guards "improved" on my plan, by selling the bags to their charges for one peso each.

This forced me to send in more money. As the prisoners were paid five cents a day and up for their labor at the air field, their possession of a small amount of money would not excite too much suspicion. We soon added peanuts to our stock, knowing that the men needed them so much for their nutritious food value. We bought the goobers in one hundred pound sacks, and roasted them fresh every day. We heard that the men were anxious to get catsup, so we managed to smuggle in four cases of a Philippine-made product, which they wrote us about, stating that it made their rice-slop almost palatable.

With the thought of supplying vitamins to prevent scurvy, we bought quantities of the local lemons known as calamanci. We squeezed these and, adding two cups of sugar to each one of juice, let the mixture come to a boil to keep it from spoiling. We scoured Manila, to find little bottles for this fruit concentrate, and put them out in the morning so that the prisoners could drink the mixture with their water at noon. We asked the prisoners to throw the empty bottles into the weeds along the roadside on their way back, Claring's numerous relatives picked them up; then we washed, sterilized, and refilled them.

As often as possible, I watched the dreary procession, from a darkened room in Claring's house. The men passed so near that I could have leaned out and almost touched them. I would pick out the ten most ragged-looking men, noting their numbers from their hats, then send ten pesos with a note to each the next day. In that manner it was possible to see that all received some sort of aid.

I had noted the name, Gentry, on the list Captain Muir had sent me, and in response to my inquiry if he was the young sailor Phil and I had known, he wrote back:

Dear High-Pockets:

Yes, I'm the same Gentry you know. I met you at Louise's apartment a few times. I had about given up hope of help, even though I heard several men here talking about an angel named High-Pockets sending things in. I never dreamed you were the angel. I got shoes from a Nip guard with part of the money you sent. Been barefooted for the past year. Sure good to get shoes on my feet again. I got bananas with the rest of my money. Thanks a million. I'll try to repay you someday, somehow.

God bless you. Gentry. Gent.

It finally seemed safe to branch out. I wanted to get clothing and shoes to the men, so I wrote in and suggested a plan. We would plant articles alongside the road, near the house, for them to pick up on their return trip to the prison. Between us and the unfortunates on the inside, we finally evolved the following scheme.

The prisoners marched four abreast and a guard flanked about every tenth rank. They did not maintain a close military formation. Therefore when the first guard had turned the corner by our house, the men a few ranks behind could pick up the packages undetected. The men were to look on the telegraph pole for chalk marks, before turning the corner. We placed them fairly high because we thought that the diminutive Nips would not be apt to notice them. One "X" meant "Look in the middle of the road" and "XX" indicated "Look along the roadside." We camouflaged the packages with green banana leaves.

We could not send in enough money with Pedro, so after a time, we started rolling old, dirty notes very tight in a banana leaf placed in a small box. Then we scattered gravel over it, and stuck a few sprigs of grass on top to mark the spot. By now, the nearby natives had found out what was taking place, so we were forced to plant the money a few moments before the prisoners passed, to make certain that it got into the right hands. Claring watched for the approach of the column, and when sighted, she or I ran out to plant the gifts.

I was determined to celebrate the "Glorious Fourth" by giving hamburgers to my boys. Fely and the other hostesses sliced fifty loaves of rice bread, while the rest of us fried sixty pounds of meat patties for the thousand sandwiches we made. "Operation Hamburger" was completed by the distribution of these tasty morsels in bags, from Claring's stand.

I was watching from my vantage point, and saw the happy-for-a-moment Americans look into their bags. Captain Muir knew that I would be there, and he probably told many of his fellows, for as they passed, heads turned toward my window, and there were smiles on their gaunt faces. This sight in itself, was ample reward for our hard work.

After we had been operating for over four months, disaster struck. The guards commenced fighting among themselves over the food stand graft. The rifle-toting guards could not pick up the bags, so they made their pistol-toting colleagues alternate with them. One day, a pair of rifle carriers, sulky because of graft-less days, stopped at the stand and beat up poor Claring. The enraged prisoners watched helplessly while the Nips struck the woman again and again with their rifle butts. Cries of "Sonofabitch!" and "Bastard!" larded with other choice G.I. expletives filled the air. Finally some of the indignant men broke ranks to go to Claring's aid, only to be knocked down and mauled by other guards.

This marked the end of our food stand, but we worked harder than ever planting articles along the road. We even procured soap for the men, and this was an exceptional achievement, for it was one of the first items to be rationed, and very difficult to buy even on the black market.

Pedro had a very unique method of getting clothing and shoes to the prisoners. He would wear as many pairs of pants and shirts as we could get on him, one over the other, without appearing too conspicuous. While working with the prisoners during the day, he discarded the superfluous garments one by one at opportune moments. He also wore a pair of shoes each day when he reported for work, but came home barefooted. The only way that I can account for his success, is that the Japs were not too observant, and probably were too busy watching their charges.

We were eventually able to furnish nearly all of the prisoners with shirts. After we were not able to buy them in the stores, we used some of the club's drapes and curtains, and made them ourselves. We washed the material with strong soap, and then faded it in the sun. When the drapes gave out we removed the sheets from our beds, and cut them to pattern. Insofar as we knew, the Japs thought that these gifts came from the Philippine Red Cross.

One day as I was bringing a carriage-load of articles to the house, the column passed ahead of schedule. My carromata was in the middle of the road, and the driver promptly pulled over to one side. I promptly slid down in the back of the vehicle, making myself as inconspicuous as possible, and ostensibly averting my eyes. Fortunately, the Nips did not notice me, but some of the more observant prisoners did, as they hastily glanced at me and smiled.

There were even... I swear it... twinkles in some of those sunken, bloodshot eyes.

CHAPTER XIII

An Informer Goes to Hell

NEWS FROM ABROAD WAS ENCOURAGING, but living conditions were becoming more difficult. American canned goods, clothing and medicines had disappeared early in 1942. Now, by late 1943, we were rationed on rice, lard, sugar, matches and coconuts. We had long since been given a cloth allowance, and gas and electricity had long been stringently rationed. If we used more than we were allowed, our bill was doubled and we were fined. If we offended a second time, the utilities were shut off. So we had to be careful.

Our new monthly food quota was so small that it rarely lasted us a week, and during the balance of the month I was forced to buy on the black market at unreasonable prices. When food cannot be bought because of its scarcity, it is alarming. I had Dian and several employees looking to me for their sustenance. My staff expected me to perform the impossible, and I could not let them down.

Our desperate situation was alleviated somewhat through a contact with a Jap who frequented our club. I soon learned that he was in charge of the navy warehouse, and plenty of rice was stored there. At this time rice was selling for five hundred pesos a sack on the black market... if it was available.

I was on the look-out for this commodity at all times, not only for ourselves, but the Remedios Hospital, the guerrillas and the prisoners. For that reason, Fely and I exerted ourselves to win our patron's friendship. When he confided that his pay was small, we let him know that we would pay him one hundred pesos for each sack he could bring us. He had no idea of its black market value and demurred that this was too much.

I knew that he wanted money to spend at my club, and after a few days he accepted our offer. To allay any suspicions, I told him that part of it was for the club, and the balance for the poor, sick Filipinos in the hospital. This was partly true, but there were many Americans and British internees from Santo Tomas who were also patients there. I figured that he would not find out about that, and he never did.

Our plans were laid when he left the club. He told me that whenever he saw a chance to take the rice out, he would call me and say, "I very hot and come for a beer." For my part, I was to have boys in the alley in back of the club to unload the rice and act as lookouts. We started the next day, and I managed to get about thirty sacks, before he was apprehended ... thank God!... not in the vicinity of my club.

Our "underground group" long since coordinated, had grown and prospered, thanks to Boots and others of her determined breed. Ramon and Swiss were indefatigable in their efforts to raise funds from their fellow nationals. Our strengthened position made it possible to keep up with the demands of Boone's growing band which now numbered over three thousand men. We also aided two other guerrilla bands about five thousand strong, one in the north under Colonel Thorpe, and another in the south commanded by Colonel Straughn, a formerly retired veteran of the Spanish-American War.

These were the principal recognized groups. Others used the word "Guerrilla" for their own selfish gain. They operated more like bandits, gathering money, and living "like kings" in the hills, but never were known to attack or harass the enemy. The bona-fide guerrilla chiefs contacted each other through me, and we eventually compiled a "Black List" of those not worthy of our assistance.

I acted as an "information center" in this manner. Properly accredited carriers reported the various plans and locations of a given band to me. I made several copies of this information and relayed it to other guerrilla groups. Thus, in a short time, the activities of half a dozen or more of such bands were coordinated. If one was raided by the Japs or forced to change its position, they sent word to me immediately of their new hide-out, and I, in turn, sent the intelligence to the other groups. The various leaders also arranged meetings in the hills through me.

The support of Boone's band remained my responsibility. The other bodies each had an agent in the local underground. They often checked with me, coming in the back way, one at a time, ten or fifteen minutes apart. My visitors were disguised as peddlers, old bottle collectors, telephone repairmen, water and light meter-readers. I became nervous as the number of people "in the know" increased. It was impossible to investigate the loyalty of each as we had one with our small initial group. I had to either trust the people who were recommended to me, or rely on the "sixth sense" which all of us seemed to develop in spotting a stool pigeon planted by the Nips. The "Captain Bagley" incident was a good example of the ever growing menace which confronted us.

A strange Filipino boy arrived at my back door with a very formally worded note in English from a Captain Bagley, asking help for his guerrillas in the hills. I re-read the note while the boy waited and hastily decided that it was false, not only because of the total absence of our slang code, but for the reason that no American officer in a tight spot would use such long words.

My suspicions were further aroused by the fact that Boone had warned me never to have any traffic with any carrier, save he or she was previously identified by a carrier known to me.

I dismissed the boy angrily, shouting that I was Italian and not interested in the least in Americans or their works. As he left, at a sign from me,

Memerto followed the messenger who crossed the Luneta Park and was met by four waiting Nip military police.

When Memerto returned with the bad news, he suffered his first and only bad attack of jitters, making quite a speech about how, for my own sake and Dian's, I should drop all this perilous work. I told him that we were all in it too deep to think of quitting... too many people depended on us.

"As for Dian," I concluded, "if anything happens to me, Fely and you are to get her out of this house as fast as you can and up in the hills to Boone. Do you understand?"

This un-nerving experience made me think all the more of redoubling my efforts. I had heard some horrible tales of the painful and peculiar tortures which our enemies inflicted upon their victims, particularly when they sought information. I was fully aware of the danger that I faced, and this knowledge made me jumpy and at times, irritable.

One day, much to my astonishment, a letter came out of Cabanatuan via Looter and Sassy for Juan Elizalde. I had known this attractive, well-educated Spaniard slightly for several years. He owned a large local distillery, was part owner of the large Elizalde Shipping line, and had retained the confidence of the Japanese. I recalled that he had been a member of Mr. Hochima's party at our grand opening.

To determine his sentiments, I took the letter to Elizalde myself. It was pleasant to learn that he was whole-heartedly in favor of our cause. At the close of our conversation he offered to supply the club with all needed liquor at pre-war cost. I accepted eagerly, for it had become increasingly difficult to obtain; even empty bottles were scarce. It was a bright moment when Elizalde told me that he could furnish us with plenty of empty demijohns for the life-giving calamanci juice we were now sending in regularly to Cabanatuan prisoners.

When I tried to express my gratitude, he stopped me, saying, "If I sold the liquor at retail I would only donate the profits to the cause anyhow. Your place can't run without liquor and we can't get along without your place... so it's easier for me to make my contribution this way. I'm the one who should be thanking you."

We gained an important new worker in the person of a Mr. Monoloto, who was recommended by Lieutenant Colonel Mack in Cabanatuan. After investigating him carefully, Ramon took him into our fold, and re-named him "Mutt." Ramon was now ready to commence smuggling food into Cabanatuan by the operation of a stall in the market-place under Mutt's guidance. His regular business necessitated his commuting back and forth to Manila, bringing farm products to the city, and other merchandise back to the prison town. Mutt's suggestion was that he take along the supplies our group had gathered, as though they were his own, store them in the back of his place and "sell" them to American officers who, tinder guard, were allowed by the Japs to purchase for the men two or three times a month. Our new ally volunteered to place our notes, money, and other items into the bags intended for American hands. We adopted his plan with enthusiasm as it enabled us to reach and help a much greater number of men.

This new idea was almost defeated by its own success, for a Nip officer commented on how much money the prisoners seemed to be spending all of a sudden. A search of the barracks was ordered, but the Americans had been tipped off, and nothing was found. After a brief interval, we renewed operations on an even larger scale. We knew that the principal cause of the deaths among the prisoners was disease chiefly brought about by malnutrition, and therefore considered it of the utmost importance to augment their starvation diet.

One of the notes coming out of Cabanatuan begged someone to locate friends of the sender, in Cavite. This family, the soldier wrote, had money and would be able to help him.

Visiting Jap-held Cavite was a rather ticklish assignment but I took it on, chartering a carromata for the several hours required for the round trip. It was weird to see the enemy's flag flying from the old fort, and another from the flagstaff which rose from a tablet reading: "On this staff the American flag was hoisted for the first time over the Philippines on May 3rd, 1898 at eight a. m. by Commodore George Dewey, U.S.N." Japanese guards were watching as I read the inscription, so I shrugged my shoulders, made the required bow to them, and passed on. The Filipino family to whom the note was addressed were no longer wealthy. They said that they knew the prisoner well, but could not help him as all of their property had been confiscated. Telling them of the importance of keeping up morale, I suggested that they write him a note of greeting and cheer. I urged them not to mention their own troubles and let me enclose some money for them. This was done.

The delivery of another note took me in the vicinity of the once famous Santa Ana cabaret, where Phil and I had once danced with several thousand others on the floor reputed to be the largest in the world. I found the place surrounded by a high barbed wire fence, and turned into a stable for Jap army horses.

From time to time, I continued to visit Louise who was becoming increasingly dissatisfied with being cooped up in Santo Tomas.

"If you can be a phony Italian and walking around free as air, why can't I be one?" she asked on one of my calls. "You really haven't Italian blood and I have. I can even speak the language. Why shouldn't I be out working and helping the cause like you?"

"It's no bed of roses on the outside, either, but if you really want me to try and get you out, I will."

"How would you start?"

"I would ask one of my customers from the Japanese Administration office whom I should see; then go to him and explain your case."

"I wouldn't want you to get into any trouble over it, Claire, but I sure would like to get out of here."

"I would love to have you out but no more of this 'Claire' stuff. My name is Dot... remember?"

"That's right, Dot. I had forgotten. You see, now that they have sent Bob up to Los Banos along with all the other single men, it's terribly lonesome here."

"So, it's still Bob? This is a record for you. It must be real love this time."

"I really believe it is," Louise told me soberly.

Several Japs from the Administration happened to come into the club that night. I started the ball rolling by telling them about my good Italian friend who had been, unfortunately, born in the States, and so was in Santo Tomas, but was miserable there with all those stupid Americans.

The Nips kidded me and wanted to know if my friend was a man. When I told them she was a girl, they wanted to know if she was beautiful. Assured that she was, they told me whom to see at their office.

Taking Fely along with me to speak Japanese to the guards at the gate and ask directions, we went to the Administration Building and finally found the right office. There I explained my mission, and the English-speaking official listened politely, only interrupting a few times to ask questions.

"That quite easy, Madame Tsubaki," he told me when I had finished. "Arr your friend must do is to renounce her American rights."

I thanked him and started to leave but, as usual when dealing with Nip officialdom, there was a catch.

"By the way," he queried casually, "What is your nationarity?"

"I am of Italian blood, but I was born here on this island," I lied, holding my breath.

"Have you not read papers of rate? Dey state arr people of Itarian brood must renounce now Itary has been invaded by Americans... or go to Santo Tomas," he fairly barked at me.

"I did not know that, but I will do so at once," I told him somewhat shaken. "Where do I get the necessary papers to sign?"

"You must go to Bureau of Vitar Statistics in Nationar Assembry Buirding, and take your Firupin and Japanese Residence Certificate with you. Dey make out renouncing papers which arso incrude new Firupin citizenship."

We thanked him and left. Then Fely asked "Do you have the two certificates he mentioned?"

"Yes, thank goodness. I got them when I was still living with the Roxas family. They had one of their Filipino maids line up and pretend to be me. For those they only asked the name, age, address and nationality."

As soon as we reached home, I telephoned Judge Roxas and explained what I had to do. He told me that he had a friend in the Bureau of Vital Statistics who would take care of the matter.

"Just mention my name to him and it will all be very simple," the Judge told me.

The next day I found the jurist's friend, the papers were made out and signed before none other than Judge Roxas. I was not even asked to swear to anything, just told "Sign here." It was impossible for the Nips to thoroughly investigate the hundreds of natives conforming with the new regulations, so my compliance did not merit undue attention.

Boone had heard a broadcast from the United States which stated "We will not recognize any Japanese made laws," so I did not view this coercive measure as being of real importance. I slipped in a note telling Louise as much. The Nips had stiffened the regulations for internees so we could no longer talk together. I therefore suggested that if she agreed to the plan of changing her citizenship in Japanese eyes, to send a message saying "Need money."

On my next trip to Santo Tomas, I picked up Louise's reply at the gate! It read "Don't need money." Later, when she had a chance to explain, she said that she could not force herself to renounce her country, no matter what the circumstances.

We were all grieved and angered when the morning papers carried the headline news of Colonel Straughn's capture and execution after a summary court martial at Fort Santiago. That evening at the club, everyone was talking about the death of the American officer. I asked Nagahama, a Japanese Colonel if he had ever seen the executed man. To my horror, he grinned broadly. "See dis hand," he boasted. "Dis is hand dat used gun on him in Chinese cemetery." Then he went on to brag about what a wonderful shot he was and laughed heartily over his achievement. I had to pretend to laugh with him, but at the first opportunity, I left the room and was violently ill.

"Just a tired old man," Straughn had described himself in a note to me. Now the tired old man could have his rest... he had earned it. Although we could show no outward expression of sorrow, Colonel Straughn was not forgotten. Fahny told me that many an extra candle burned that week for the repose of his valiant soul... hers among them.

Sparkplug (Ramon) telephoned, asking, "Are you coming to church in the morning?"

"Yes," I told him, according to code. "I will be at mass, seven as usual."

At the appointed hour, I found Ramon, accompanied by Father Lolar who was looking very distressed.

"Our friend here," the priest told me unhappily, "is talking me into murder and I don't like it."

Sparkplug grinned at the good man and remarked, "Well, you run along and keep your conscience clear, Father. High-Pockets and I will finish this business." With an audible sigh of relief, the priest left us.

Almost as distressed as the Father had been, I turned to Ramon. "Did he really mean what he said," I inquired. "Do we have to..."

"Neither you nor I have to do it personally, but we must arrange for someone's exit from this world who has no right to stay in it. I'll explain it to you and... well, here... better read this first."

He handed me a torn, faded scrap of yellow paper on which I read:

Corregidor.... 1 April 1942.
Flash ....HQ U.S.A.F.F.E.
Look for Rathman... American-Filipino mestizo 5 ft. 8 in. Appearance.... American Indian; expert radio man; nervous type... bites fingernails; loves to brag... may be officer with P. I. Constabulary. Was caught once in Bataan, tampering with communications wires, but escaped. Any information about Rathman should be turned in to A.C. of S., G-2.

"Where did this come from," I asked curiously.

"The Doctor found it in Bataan in an abandoned American headquarters."

"What do you want me to do?"

"The Doctor has located this rat in the Walled City. He and the cousin he lives with are in the money, and go night-clubbing almost every night. One of the Doctor's men, who works at the Constabulary, will steer him into the Tsubaki Club within the next two nights. The guide will come to the bar and give an order for French champagne 'well-chilled.' That will be your cue to telephone the Doctor who will be waiting at my house. You can say something like 'The birthday party is starting. You better come over'."

"What happens then?"

"Torres and two gunmen will wait outside and follow Rathman. It's their worry from then on."

"I suppose that it has to be done?"

"Yes, it must be done. Rathman is not only an A-1 informer for the Japs, but has been bragging for the last few months about how he helps pound information out of the prisoners at Fort Santiago. That scoundrel has forfeited all his rights either as American or Filipino, and only belongs wherever dead Japs go. The Doctor believes that he may have recently found out something about our group, and we have to nail him before he can do any further harm."

"I see your point, Ramon, but it must not happen near the club, as we are in no position to be investigated."

Two nights later several Filipinos appeared at the club. One of them went at once to the bar and ordered French champagne "well-chilled."

I took the cue and went to the telephone in the hall.

"The guests have arrived," I informed Ramon, "for the Doctor's birthday party. Is he on his way?"

"Yes," came his quick reply, "He has started. He should be there any minute now."

I strolled back to the table where the newcomers were seated, and introduced myself. They gave me their names and we shook hands. Even if he had not made himself known, there would have been no doubt in my mind as to which was the informer. The description on the frayed yellow sheet fitted perfectly. Moreover Rathman started in at once, bragging about the beatings he had given the dumb monkeys who refused to cooperate with their "liberators."

"The stupid bastards can't seem to realize that the Japs are here to stay," he ranted.

"You said a mouthful," I 'agreed,' and kept praising his (ig)noble efforts and encouraging him to boast until... to my great relief... I saw Torres standing at the entrance. After one quick glance toward me and my companions, he turned and left, giving the impression of someone who had blundered in, looking for a friend.

The Doctor's brief appearance was, of course, the signal that I need detain Rathman no longer. Presently I excused myself, and soon afterwards Rathman and his "friends" left.

I joined a newly arrived Jap army officer at a table, and was barely seated before he commented, "Haven't I seen you somewhere before?"

"Oh, you mean before...." and that was as far as I got before a smashing blow from his fist knocked me to the floor.

"Arways you people say 'before Japanese came.' Baka! Degenerate Americans gone forever," my assailant thundered, "Onry Nipponese New order now! Remember dat!"

With this sage advice, he stormed from the room, leaving me a bit wiser, but still puzzled at the unpredictable Nip mentality. First Rathman, and then this... I turned things over to Fely and went to bed... my aching head warned me that I had enough excitement for the time being.

The following night to my alarm and amazement, my first customers were the evil Senor Rathman, still in the flesh, chattering affably with his cousin. There was no other alternative for me but to turn on the charm and join them again.

"I see that you like my place," I greeted.

"There's a special reason for our coming back tonight," Rathman half-snarled. "You may be able to solve a little mystery."

Pointing to a bullet hole in the front of his hat, which he was still wearing, he insinuated, "It looks like someone around here is gunning for me."

"That's ridiculous," I protested, "Why don't you tell me what happened?"

"When we left here last night, we walked across the Luneta. Damned if some man didn't jump out from behind some bushes and take a shot at us. Fortunately for me, some Jap soldiers were around and frightened the ladrone, so he ran away. You can bet I won't go out again without my gat," and Rathman patted his protruding abdomen which bulged even more where his concealed weapon rested.

"You had a narrow escape. That calls for some drinks," I commented.

He ordered a round and I drank with him, gradually working him into a better humor by teasing him about the big bankroll he must be carrying to attract such unpleasant attention. Before long, the mestizo was in a more jovial mood, and left, partially convinced (I hoped) that the incident was casual.

When we closed that evening, Memerto, who knew about this assignment, noted my worried look, and offered to have some of his friends take care of Rathman if the Doctor did not finish the job. I thanked him, but told him to wait developments.

A week later the cousin came in alone. When I unconcernedly inquired about Rathman, he remarked that his relative was probably away on some important business as he had not been home for several days.

"I hope that you are not worried about him," I baited.

"Not him," the cousin chuckled, drinking his beer in big gulps. "There's an hombre who can take care of himself."

I drew a big sigh of relief when I checked with Ramon in the morning, and learned that the informer had been attended to by the Doctor.

He had been "well-chilled," and I was glad of it.

Chapter XIV

Yamada Was a "White" Man

AN ASSIGNMENT CAME DOWN TO ME FROM THE HILLS: "Find out what the Jap Red Cross ship is unloading."

Our underground group had placed several trusted Filipino boys at my disposal, so now I sent two of them to get jobs on the piers, loading ships. They did this easily enough. By now the Japs apparently felt that they could trust the Filipinos, or that the natives did not have sense enough to grasp what was taking place. I could see the ship from the club windows, and knew that it had been unloading a cargo for several days.

The ship's captain visited the club virtually every night, but was very close-mouthed. He drank very little, and one bottle of beer would last him all evening. His idea of pleasure was to sip his beer and flirt with me across the table. If I left, even for a few minutes, he would send a waiter to bring me back. Finally one night the expected break came, for as I started to move to another table, he ordered, "Don't go away. You do not have me here much ronger."

Next day, I sent for the pier boys and told them, "You must break into one of the crates in the hold tonight. I must have proof of what is being loaded."

They were terrified, and told me volubly of the fate in store for them if they were caught in the act. I allayed their fears by telling them there would not be much danger, because the captain was bringing all his officers to the club for a special party I had arranged. I promised to hold them until after midnight.

When the captain and his party arrived, he almost floored me when immediately after exchanging greetings, he announced, "We can not stay rong. My ship finish loading about midnight, and we probably reave about two or three. I must stop at Manira Hotaru (hotel) for some papers too."

I seated the group and said I would start their special floor show at once. Dashing to my room, I wrote a hurried note to Boone, giving the expected time of the vessel's departure, and adding that I would have another carrier leave when I had other data. I sent Demyon off packing, and held Pacio in reserve.

I was wearing a new dress that night in the captain's honor ... a real Parisian creation, bought from a hard-up "Petain" refugee. It was powder blue and backless, sparkling all over with crystal beads which weighed down the short train, and had an enticing slit in front, right up to the knees.

As I passed the bar, I called to Memerto, "Five nice drinks for my captain." That meant "spike the drinks." My prescription was not a success. The Nips refused the drinks, complaining they tasted like spoiled beer. The floor show held the attention of the junior officers, and meanwhile I racked my brains to think of a way to make the captain linger. Then it flashed into my mind that I had read at some time, somewhere, cigarette ashes in a drink act like knock-out drops.

I smoked one cigarette after another, dropping the ashes into any glass I could reach, while my guests had their attention focused on the entertainment. The captain's glass apparently received the most of my "mickey" for presently his face turned a ghastly greenish-white. I had a waiter help me, and we half-led and half-carried him to a booth where he could lie down. Here he passed out cold at once. His breathing was very shallow and his pulse faint. I was very frightened, but sent word to his subordinates that he felt better, but wanted to stay, rest and be alone with me.

A raucous shout of laughter and some bawdy jokes greeted this announcement. I kept the floor show going incessantly until the performers were exhausted. About one o'clock the other Japs left, whispering to me to please send their captain back soon. When the place was cleared, I called Pacio and sent him to bring a carromata to the back door. I was very dubious about whether the captain was long for this world, and if not, did not want to have his carcass in the Club Tsubaki. We managed to carry the inert Nip to the carriage with some difficulty, and a twenty-peso bill helped calm the fears of the apprehensive driver.

"Just drop him near the sea wall," I instructed, and breathed a deep sigh of relief as the vehicle moved off.

My two pier workers arrived a few minutes later. They were able to make an unhurried inspection, and brought me as proof, a handful of bullets, taken from one of the crates in the ship's hold.

In one of his few lucid moments, while alone with me in the booth, the captain had mumbled something about Singapore. That could be his destination, so I wrote a note to that effect, and gave it, with the bullets, to Pacio, to rush into the hills.

When I gazed from my window the next morning, the large white converted luxury liner with its over-sized, protective red crosses, was gone.

I assumed that the captain did not miss the boat, after all.

The volume of my work was gaining, and I frequently wondered how much more I could do before something unforeseen ... and I shuddered... would put a sudden end to it all. Bilibid Prison was still a hard nut to crack. Ramon was only able to get mail, through Dr. Wattress' nurse, a few times.

She was frequently searched, and could not be blamed for preferring to take in only verbal messages.

One note that did come out through her good graces, was signed by a Jerry Stewart. It was to his wife, a Navy nurse in Santo Tomas. As she had been transferred to Los Banos, I could not deliver it. Instead, I answered the letter myself, telling Stewart that his wife was all right, and sending him thirty pesos. Later I was able to help this couple, through an American internee truck driver who was able to deliver verbal messages.

An abandoned gas station across the street had recently been occupied by a Filipino family consisting of husband, wife, and two small children. Lacking furniture of any kind, they slept on the cement floor. The wife related that they had been evicted from their home because the Nips said it was too near one of their army posts. Despite their adversity, the little family never failed to smile at me when I passed. One day the father came to my door in obvious distress.

"Senora, excuse me. I am Jose. Don't be afraid, but I have been around Americans for long time. I know you not Italian. I worked long time at Cavite for American navy. I know Americans are good people. They will come back and free us. But now my family is starving, and I won't work for Japs. Will you let me work for you?"

I told him that I had more help than I really needed at the moment, but made him take home some rice and beans; telling him I would have work for him to do later on. This white lie was necessary for I could sense that Jose was a proud, self-respecting man, and would not have accepted the food otherwise. Shortly after his visit, he injured his hand, and I was able to arrange for his entry into the Remedios Hospital for treatment. While his member was healing, Jose had an idea. If I could loan him fifty pesos, he could start a cigarette stand on the corner. I helped him, realizing that it could not be harmful to have too many friends and allies. I was grateful that this man had come to me, instead of taking the easy money that would have been his, had he turned informer. He prospered, and insisted on repaying my loan.

One noon as Dian and I were sitting down to lunch, two American prisoners drove a couple of Japanese army trucks into the empty gas station. The trucks stopped and the prisoners and their two Nip guards started to eat.

I hastily scribbled a note: "Dear Friends: How are your guards? Dare I try to help you? What camp are you in, and can you write me out a complete list of all the men there? The native, Jose, selling cigarettes on this corner is a friend of mine. If you toss a note to him, he will see that I get it. Yours in War, High-Pockets."

I folded this missive very small and tucked it underneath the matches in a box, along with fifty pesos. Then taking Dian, I crossed the street, apparently to buy cigarettes from Jose.

As I knew the Japanese liked children, I was not surprised when one of the guards came up and started to talk with Dian. I recognized him as the same one I had seen with Sergeant Rizzo, months before in the Luneta.

I asked him casually "May I buy some cigarettes, for the American prisoners?"

"Yes," he responded pleasantly, "You give. Make boys happy see pretty ota (woman)."

This unexpected permission was almost too good to be true. I handed the men the cigarettes and passed them the match box also. After a few moments of conversation with the amiable guard, I returned to the club. I watched, but could not see if the prisoners found the note before they drove away.

The following noon the same trucks and men came back again. I went out once more, but when I repeated my question to the guard, he suggested "Why buy shigarettu for prisoners? Dey prenty hungry, give food."

I could hardly believe my ears, and hastily told him, "Wait a few moments and I will go home and bring food for all of you."

This seemed to please the Jap very much, and he ordered his charges not to start eating. "Matte! Wait!"

Scurrying back into the club, I told Victoria and Fely to bring out all the cooked food we had on hand. We put it on a tray, along with six bottles of cold lemonade. I hurried to my room, put fifty pesos in a matchbox, and took everything over to the expectant men.

While the Americans ate ravenously, the other Japanese guard remarked "Anatano kuni wa nani desu ka?"

I shook my head and said one of the few Jap words I had learned, "Wakarimasen" which means "I don't understand." His companion, the friendly guard interpreted, "He say what your country?"

"I am Philippine citizen, but of Italian blood. You may call me Madame Tsubaki. What is your name?"

"Yamada," he smiled.

"Every day you come here, I will prepare food for you. Maybe spaghetti, my native dish. Do you like that?"

"Hai, okay we come... but better you have back door. My captain maybe see. He ver-ry bad man."

I pointed out to him the alley behind the club, and said I would expect them at noon tomorrow. At the appointed time, not one, but five trucks appeared! Each was manned by one American prisoner and one Nip guard. Yamada urged me to sit and eat with him and his prisoner, in the front of the truck. I climbed aboard, stating that I had eaten but would be glad to chat with them.

The American driver said that his name was Cimini. I asked him a few innocuous questions which he answered, while Yamada listened quite unconcerned. As they were leaving, I tried to slip a matchbox with money in it to Cimini, but he protested, "You don't have to do that as if you didn't want Yamada to see. He is a good friend of mine, and I don't want to offend him."

"Do you mean that I can give you the money openly?"

"Certainly, and here is the list you asked for. We are quartered at Fort McKinley."

He handed me a sheet of paper with about a hundred names on it. Emboldened by the guard's indifference, I gave the prisoner one hundred pesos and asked if he could take in some clothes to the men. Cimini spoke to Yamada in a mixture of English and Japanese, before replying, "Yamada says we must hurry now, but we could take the clothes tomorrow. Bring all you want. There are an awful lot of scarecrows in our camp." From then on I had a steady luncheon date. Every day from two to six trucks drove into the alley, each with one American and his guard. Yamada seemed to be in charge, and the other Japs were glad enough to get in on the good food. After a few weeks had passed, I was able to send good clothes to almost all the men at Fort McKinley. When my luncheon guests had finished eating, they would fill their empty mess kits with more food to take back to the men who could not come out. Before long they were bringing me notes from buddies in their camp. One such note, Yamada, himself gave me. It was signed "Bruce."

"Dear Madame: I have heard from the other men how kind you are. I don't mean to beg, but I have been hurt and need your help. While repairing a tire, the rim flew off and cut my face bad. Also my arm is broken, and the Nips will do not a thing for me. Yamada tried to get a doctor, but they won't allow it. Please help me in any way you can. Yours in Need."

I raided my medicine chest for gauze, cotton and adhesive tape, found two bamboo splints, and showed Yamada how to set Bruce's arm and dress his cut face. The kindly Nip not only took these things, but a note and money for Bruce in addition. He even hid some specially prepared food in his own mess kit.

About a month later, Yamada walked up the back stairs of my club with a strange American, very thin and pale, whom he introduced as Bruce.

"I'm still kind of weak," my visitor offered, as I made him sit down, "but I asked Yamada to bring me, so that I could thank you for all you've done for me and the others."

"Yamada has been very good to you," I commented.

"He is a white man... the best Japanese I ever met. Without his help and yours, I know I wouldn't have pulled through. Days went by and I was still bleeding."

Yamada, understanding the gist of Bruce's remarks, stood near us, all smiles. The scar on Bruce's face had healed well, and he reported his arm was almost as good as ever. We chatted about home in slang and pig-latin, and my visitor said he had guessed from the beginning what my true identity must be.

"Why is Yamada so good to all you men?" I queried curiously.

"I really don't know. Why don't you ask him?"

I turned to the Jap, and by dint of some effort, made him understand my question. He, in turn, got his point of view across to me. "Berieve it not hurting poor men. Roosevert bad. American bad, but dese boys my friends," and he grinned happily.

"But if you are caught," I tried to convey to him, "you may be shot."

His sole response was a shrug, another grin, and a pat on Bruce's shoulder.

We had a bad scare the following week. As I brought the food out to Yamada and the men in the alley, his captain walked past. I disappeared rapidly into the club. I was badly worried for more than a week, not only for myself, but the reprisals which may have been visited on the humane Jap and his prisoners. There were no more noon time visitors. Ten days after that unnerving incident, the telephone rang in the late morning.

"Prease to speak to Madame Tsubaki," came a Japanese voice.

"I am Madame Tsubaki."

I heard a loud laugh, then "This Yamada. Prease to bring food to park... radies toiret. Sugu! Hurry! Me and boys taihen himogii desu... very hungry."

I went to find Fely to see if she could figure it out..."Park... ladies toilet... food," she repeated "Sure, I know. There's a ladies rest room near the sea wall at the end of Luneta Park. Yamada must be waiting with his American prisoners behind that clump of trees over there."

We got together all the food we could find and packed it into a basket. Hailing a native rickshaw tricycle, equipped with a side car, I left for the spot. Spying two familiar trucks, I paid off the rickshaw boy, and started for the ladies toilet.

A cheerful whistle came from behind a high hedge. I turned and saw the beaming faces of Yamada and four Americans, Cimini, Bruce, O'Brien and my old friend Rizzo. They ate, and we chatted for about an hour. I learned that they all expected to be transferred soon to the Port Area Camp. I did not have a contact there at that time, but asked them to try to persuade a Filipino worker to bring me a note. In the meantime we agreed to meet on this spot every day as long as we were able to do so.

I asked Yamada how he had fared with his captain. He let me know that it had taken all the money he and the boys had to bribe the captain not to report him. The men added, that both he and they had been slapped by the said captain until he tired of the sport.

"Tomorrow when you come, I will bring all the money you think it safe to take, so that you will have it when you get to Port Area," I told them, as I left.

"Not over three hundred pesos," Rizzo cautioned, "It will be too hard to hide."

After two weeks, the word was "tomorrow is our last day."

"I wish we could have a big farewell party," I remarked gloomily.

"Me bring boys crub tomorrow," Yamada suggested. "Same time."

I realized that I was taking a big chance, but then it would be something these unfortunates could remember for a long time. One look at their eager faces was sufficient to let me know how eager they were for some honest-to-God food in decent surroundings.

When my visitors arrived on schedule, via the back door, we had placed all the small tables together. We served them fried chicken, baked beans, hot biscuits, fried capotes, vegetable salad, chocolate cake, coffee, beer and soft drinks. A present of cigarettes and money was handed to each prisoner. It was a thrill for me to entertain, just once, the right people in my club.

We had just finished eating and impromptu speech making, when Yamada's captain walked in through the back door! He walked up to Yamada and gave him a resounding slap in the face. "Baka!" the angry officer spat at his trembling subordinate. That means "fool," the supreme insult in Japanese. When you call a Jap that, he ordinarily froths at the mouth, for in his mind he considers it represents everything despicable that you think he is. Yamada took it with a fixed grin, while the big room emptied in a split second. The prisoners did not neglect to take along the uneaten food for some of their absent buddies, despite their undue haste in leaving.

I stood by, trembling, while the captain and Yamada engaged in a long conversation. After a while the officer's temper seemed to cool, and Yamada suggested "Madam, prease giving captain bottre good whiskey and hundred pesos. He be good captain then."

By means of comprehensive gestures, I urged the captain to take anything he wanted from the bar and handed him a hundred pesos with a straight face. He bowed politely and left. That was the last I saw of those prisoners, as they were transferred, as scheduled. Yamada still came to visit me on his days off duty. He never failed to let me know how hungry he was, and how his stomach hurt.

I could sympathize with him because I was in a similar predicament.

Decent food was gradually becoming more difficult to obtain. The Japs had long since taken over the only dairy, and even carabao milk which the doctor had ordered me to drink when I had first returned from the hills, was almost impossible to purchase. Canned milk, butter, lard, sugar and good meat were only memories. Eggs, if one could find them, sold for ten pesos each. Thus our diet was restricted to a little carabao meat or pork, a tasteless little vegetable known as "Chinese Greens," native potatoes, rice and mango beans, and rarely, bananas or papayas.

I had long since learned to get along with five or six hours sleep every night. As time went on, the knowledge that the Jap period for making arrests was between two and five a. m., seemed to keep me from falling into a deep sleep until almost dawn. Many a night the sound of marching feet and the subdued sound of sharp commands, brought me out of bed. My rest was also disturbed by urgent telephone calls from some of the underground group, early in the morning.

A "nervous stomach" caused by the sketchy diet, subdued excitement, growing fatigue, and the aura of fear which enveloped me, was aggravated by the occasional real drink I had to take at the insistence of some of the club's customers. The cocktails that the hostesses and I usually drank were harmless concoctions of calamanci juice with a dash of creme de menthe added for realism. I could not refuse a strong drink when a visitor ordered it and had it set in front of me, for even to Madame Tsubaki, a Jap wish was a command. More than once I reluctantly swallowed the fiery liquor under the duress of an unfriendly yellow hand clutching my throat.

A gnawing pain, not unlike that I had experienced in the hills, gradually increased in intensity. On the afternoon of September 30th, 1943, during a meeting of the underground group at my place, the pain became very severe, so I went into my bedroom and lay down. After a few moments when I started to arise, the misery was so intense that I screamed. People rushed in and somebody called my maid. She ran to summon my physician, Dr. Louis Guerrero, who only lived two blocks away, and he came immediately.

I learned later that my temperature was 106 degrees and my pulse weak when he arrived. I was rushed to the Doctor's Hospital. Dr. Guerrero called in one of the best local surgeons, who operated without delay, removing a perforated ulcer and about six inches of intestines. I dimly remember when I came back to this world Dr. Guerrero joked, "Too bad, you haven't got the guts you used to have." I faintly hoped that the residue was sufficient to carry me through whatever ordeal lay ahead of me.

I lay in a semi-stupor for ten days, being fed intravenously. On the eleventh day, I was given a piece of rice bread and an eggnog, but something of far greater importance makes it linger in my memory. Aunty, one of our workers, was standing by my bed, watching me eat, and joking about the difficulty I was having in masticating my food. She had met Sassy with the mail, and brought mine to me.

My nurse had gone into the hall at my request, so that my visitor and I could talk privately. We were about half-way through our correspondence when the nurse came hurrying in.

"There are four Japanese soldiers in the hall asking for you," she reported, pointing a finger at Aunty.

Military police! That thought flashed through both our minds.

"For God's sake! What shall I do?" wailed Aunty, panic-stricken.

"Give me those letters! Give me anything else that you have which may incriminate you! Hurry!" I told her.

She handed me her letters and several other papers, and these, with my own letters, I hastily stuffed under my bandage.

I had barely finished when four kenpei... military police... burst into the room and searched it thoroughly. I lay quivering, and they failed to touch my bandage, although they did look under my pillow and mattress. Aunty, like the brave soul that she was, marched mutely out of the door with the grim-looking quartette who took her to Fort Santiago.

Sick as I was, I worried, not only for the welfare of the poor woman, but over her ability to undergo the "examination" certain to be given her, without talking. The shock made me relapse into a state of semi-coma, and it was not until two days later that I awakened with a feeling that something was amiss. As my nurse entered and bade me "Good Morning!" I tried to reply, but the sound issuing from my lips was "Ood oring!" She laughed, but then with a puzzled look, inquired if I was joking. I shook my head negatively.

I was finally able to make her understand that I wanted to see Ramon Amusatague urgently, and he came within the hour. I told him in my semi-intelligible way about Aunty, and he promised to notify the others in our group. Then I handed him the notes from under my bandage and asked him to keep them intact for me. Alarmed at my condition, he called in my doctor and his father-in-law who was one of Manila's leading physicians.

The medicos examined my incision, called in and questioned the nurses who had helped with the operation, and there was a big hubbub. I could not understand most of the conversation which was conducted in staccato Spanish, but did catch the words "tetanus" and "sterilization." My pain was increasing, and before noon I was moved to the isolation wing of the hospital with a "No Visitors" sign on the door.

Food was denied me again, and intravenous injections were given me every hour. Two days later, I developed bronchial pneumonia. When I started to cough, I almost strangled, and the doctors administered oxygen. The "No Visitors" rule was disregarded to let a few close friends come to see me on the promise that they would not talk to me, or permit me to have speech with them.

By the fourth day, I was suffering convulsions, and only semi-conscious. In one lucid moment I remembered someone crying softly at my bedside, and I was able to turn my head enough to see Claring. I learned afterwards that she never left my side, day or night, although the doctors and nurses tried to make her go.

Much of what followed is hearsay. After five days of consultation between five of Manila's leading physicians, they walked out stating that they had tried every treatment they knew and all had failed. No anti-tetanus, serum was available, but one determined medico went to the Bureau of

Animal Husbandry and had some made. The next day, Dr. Guerrero administered 40,000 units in one injection to the dismay of my nurse who claimed
that it was ten times greater than the maximum dose she had ever given. I
had been abandoned as hopeless, and the courageous doctor thought the
shock might bring me out of the valley of the shadow, as all other measures
had failed.

He was right. On the following day, after I had received the third shot,
my jaws started to unlock and my temperature dropped to 103 degrees. My
good friend, Ramon, managed to find some sulpha tablets which were pul-
verized and given to me in powdered form.

My first impression on emerging from that long coma was the sight of
Claring and Father Lolar, regarding me intently, with tears in their eyes. The
kindly priest ordered me not to talk, but listen.

"God has sent you back to us because He still has work for you to do. Put
your trust in Him. He knows best."

The good father began to pray, and as I heard those beautiful lines of
hope in the Twenty Third Psalm, "Yea, though I walk through the valley of
the shadow of death, I will fear no evil; for Thou art with me..." I smiled faintly
to reassure him, and fell asleep.

From then on my improvement was rapid, and I was soon back in my
own room.

The first afternoon that I was allowed to sit up, I had an unexpected visitor. A worried little man in a shabby uniform, stood hesitantly in the doorway,
a big basket of flowers in his hand, and a broad smile on his face.

"Pass, friend!" I called weakly... and with a quaint little bow... in walked
Yamada.

Yes, Yamada, was a white man, despite the color of his skin.

CHAPTER XV

My Apologies to Sally

DURING MY ILLNESS, FELY HAD MANAGED THE CLUB very capably, and kept up the work of sending supplies to Boone.

I had dropped from one hundred and forty five to one hundred and fifteen pounds, and during a period of convalescence which lasted over a month, had to learn to walk all over again. I was able to go home in time for Thanksgiving, and I was thankful for my miraculous recovery, despite the fact that it cost me around ten thousand pesos and caused me to suspend my activities.

I celebrated my birthday, December second, by writing to Boone, and some of my "boys" in Cabanatuan and "Park Avenue" to let them know I was back on the job. A note came back from Port Area, signed "Scarface"... obviously Bruce.

"Dear High-Pockets: This is another SOS. Please send money with this Filipino boy. He can be trusted. He is a worker here with us. Enclosed is a complete list of all the men here. I knew you would want it, so I've been working on it for the past two months. We are loading ships for the Japs and whenever anything looks fishy I will tell you. One thing right now is that these Red (double) Cross ships of theirs are bringing in troops, not wounded soldiers. We are now loading one of these ships and I would swear the cargo is guns and ammo. Send this info on if you can."

Within a half hour the "info" was on its way to Boone.

Bruce's messenger came to me once a week thereafter, and I sent money, medicine and small packages of food. The day before Christmas a small cake went to me with a word of cheer about seeing him on the Glorious Fourth. That's the manner in which we prodded ourselves in the hope that the American forces would return, always setting some specific dates by which we hoped to be free of the hated Nip yoke.

Ichikawa, noted conductor and composer, who was a frequent visitor at our club, called to let us know that he was giving a party in the ballroom of the Bay View Hotel. He insisted that Fely sing for it. She begged me to come along, pointing out that many Nip big-wigs would be present and we might pick up some important news. I thought the idea was a good one, and accompanied her. We met colonels and majors galore, and finally a captain who seemed to be a contact worthy of exploitation.

"Dis be Captain Kobioshi san, and he has charge investigations at Fort Santiago," remarked Ichikawa, as he introduced us.

"You are Itarian?" Kobioshi queried, as we walked off together.

"Yes, of Italian parentage, but I was born here. I have never seen 'Bella Italia' unfortunately."

"It nice but I rike America more better. Maybe you rike visit that country when Nippon takes it?"

"Yes, I would. I have seen many movies of the United States. It strikes me as an interesting place to visit, but too crude to live in. Don't you think so, captain?"

"Decidedry! After we conquer America, I am to be head of government in northwest. You pick city you rike best in province, and I make you present of it. Would dat prease you?"

This sally was accompanied by a winning smile, and a display of my escort's buck teeth.

"That would be most generous of you captain," I quipped. "I think I have one in mind. I have seen pictures of Portland, in Oregon. I hear it is called a city of roses, and they are my favorite flower."

"Portorando wirr be yours, Madame Tsubaki," he assured, patting my arm.

This banter continued intermittently throughout the evening. The next time I wrote Boone, I told him just for a laugh, how Japan was planning on dividing up America, but I had some real data to send him at the same time.

One evening the commander of a Japanese submarine flotilla came into the club. When Fely found out who he was, she came to me and suggested, "Wouldn't he be a good one to work on? He admires you and wants you to come to our table."

Unfortunately the commander was an individual who drank sparingly, and talked less. I brought up a number of subjects, but they met with no response. When I had about given up all hope, the unexpected break came as we were about to close for the night.

"So sorry we not staying in Manila rong," he volunteered.

"I tink I rike know you more better. Your singing very nice. Can you dance as nice you sing?"

"You would have to be the judge of that, commander. I am so disappointed you must leave. Not immediately, I hope." "Tomorrow afternoon, if finish repairs on our submarines." I assumed a sorrowful expression. My companion noted the rueful grimace, and with a twinkle in his eyes added:

"Dere one ting make me stay here a day ronger." Then he told me how when visiting San Francisco, he had seen Sally Rand do her fan dance. "If you do the same dance for me and my staff, I bring dem here tomorrow night."

"Oh, can you really arrange it?"

"Hai, I can say repairs not finished my satisfaction and I need anoder day."

"It's a deal, commander. How many will be in your party? I must know so that I can reserve places."

"Prepare for forty. I naturarry bring onry officers."

I thought "Forty officers means a nice mess of subs. Wait until Boone gets this." Before I slept that night, the information was on its way by carrier to my Babes in the Woods.

The next morning, I went into a huddle with Fely and Memerto. I told them of my problem, which was further complicated by the fact that I had never seen Sally Rand do her famous dance. Fely, the tireless costume designer, started looking through my wardrobe.

"This old pink slip," she reported, displaying the garment, "will make a pair of scanties and bra to start with."

Memerto offered to split some bamboo to make frames, and suggested that if we covered them with tissue paper they should make flimsy but passable fans. I had been saving a roll of American toilet paper for some sort of a nebulous emergency. "This is it!" I thought, and brought it out of my trunk. Cut into strips, it served its purpose. I hurried to the Escolta for other trimmings, and we worked most of the day to turn out what we hoped was a creditable copy of Miss Rand's costume ... or lack of it. David covered the baby spotlight with rose-colored paper. When the pianist arrived, and with Fely coaching, we rehearsed an improvised dance.

That night, the commander and his forty guests almost lost their eyesight, according to Fely's report, straining their orbs to determine whether I was really nude behind the fans... as they hoped, or wearing tights... as they feared. As I danced, I used a Japanese phrase, now and then, purposely mispronouncing it. This was a standard way of amusing our guests who always failed to grasp that any foreigner could really understand any of their language.

Fely ran in while I was changing to my evening gown.

"One of the men told the commander they would leave right after your dance," she reported, "to make the ships ready for an early start."

"Heavens! Then they must be sailing early in the morning. Go back to their tables and hold them until I get there."

As I passed Memerto, I gave him the signal to spike the drinks. I glanced hastily into the kitchen and saw Pacio waiting to take off. I knew that he had arranged that day for a banca to take him across the Bay, and thus shorten his trip into the hills.

"Tell me, did you like my dance?" I inquired.

"Hai! Hai!" chorused my guests enthusiastically.

"I'm going to miss you very much," I lamented, as I sat beside the commander, "Perhaps you, too, will be lonely. Would you like me to write you? I might send you my picture with the fans."

He smiled at the suggestion.

"Wait while I get into my costume again and get my fans ... and my camera," I cajoled.

Fely and Memerto "took" many pictures. Film had been unobtainable for some time and was therefore awol from the camera. When the "photography" was finished, I casually asked where I should send the pictures.

"So sorry you can not write to prace I going," the commander deplored, "for big war raging in Soromons now. I come back maybe two months. My ships onry patched up. Much work yet to do on them."

Leaving Fely to keep our guests amused, I excused myself, stating that I had another specialty prepared for them. In my room, I speedily reduced to writing all that we had learned, gave the note to Pacio and started him on his way.

"Tell that radio man I will stall these Japs as long as I can to give you more time to reach him before they shove off. Hurry as you never have before, Pacio."

Taking my remarks literally, he started down the back steps, three at a bound.

I quickly made another change to the beaded Parisian creation; so heavy that I wore it only for singing. Telling the orchestra to play softly, I warbled "Some of These Days." My rendition did not equal that of the inimitable Sophie Tucker, but it served its purpose. Memerto's drinks, plus more rapid-fire entertainment had the desired effect and there was no more talk about leaving. I wanted to hold them until Pacio could reach Boone... and that radio set... which if nothing unforeseen prevented, should be eight in the morning at the latest.

The Nipponese steadily became noisier and more intoxicated. Then the commander decided that he must dance again and again always with me. This was in violation of the orders posted on our wall by the military police, for the Japanese high command had long since forbidden such frivolity to officers in uniform. That did not worry the commander, but despite his high spirits, I noticed that he glanced occasionally at his wrist watch. As we executed an elaborate dip, I managed to strike the piano hard with our clasped hands, successfully smashing his time-piece. He was very angry for a few moments, while I apologized profusely for my apparent clumsiness. I told him not to worry as I would keep track of the time for him. He smiled again, and as we resumed dancing, cautioned me to be sure and tell him when it was two o'clock as he had to prepare to sail by four.

"Don't worry," I counseled, patting his shoulder, "We must close at midnight because of the curfew. You still have plenty of time."

All of our other patrons had left by the witching hour, so I instructed Memerto to lock the doors and extinguish the outside lights. We closed the windows to deaden the noise outside and prevented our lights from being observed. Then we performed our entire repertoire of floor shows, meanwhile pouring drinks into the revelers so fast that they forgot all about the time. Once started, the going was easy, for Japs do not have a white man's capacity to hold his liquor. At six a. m. although many of his staff had passed out happily, the commander was still on his feet. I then suggested that they should leave, but another thirty minutes ticked off before they were all out and on their much-delayed way. After repeated fond farewells, I dropped into bed exhausted, praying that we had seen the last of them.

We had, save only one. A month later a sub commander came in and related gloomily that theirs had been an ill-fated voyage. Every sub in the flotilla had been lost along with their crews. He had been picked up by a Japanese fishing craft, and transferred to a Red Cross ship en route to Manila. Insofar as he knew he was the sole survivor. After he had finished his lament, he insisted that I join him in endless toast to the departed spirits of his comrades, and soon became very drunk.

His moods varied, and when I sensed that he was getting a mean streak I would pour a drink and say "Here is to the best navy in the world, the Japanese Navy... Bottoms up." This delighted our patrons, who laughed and joined the toast. These deluded persons thought that I meant the bottom of the glass, but my employees smiled, knowing that I was referring to the Nip naval vessels. So both were happy.

I learned that Aunty had been released from Fort Santiago about two weeks after her arrest. She was tortured a bit, but her captors had no real evidence and as she did not talk, they released her. It seemed that a vindictive neighbor had reported her to the military police, due to the fact that she had many visitors both day and night. Our group avoided her after that, arranging to meet her only when essential, through Father Lolar at his church or hospital. She resented our aversion, but we had no means of knowing if she was being shadowed, and could not afford to take any chances.

Runners from the guerrillas continued to bring me new assignments, sometimes arriving at very inconvenient moments. If they came during business hours, a waiter would make some comment indicating that something was amiss in the kitchen. I was asked to locate and describe various Jap ammunition factories and storehouses. It was up to me to note every new Nip face, ascertain the mission that had brought its owner to Manila, the length of his stay, his date of departure and destination. Much of the information that I forwarded to the guerrillas was proverbial Greek to me. They evidently liked it for the inevitable reply was, "Beans very good. Send more."

One evening as I was trying desperately to entertain a new arrival, he suddenly leaned toward me and ordered, "I hear you are Itarian. You must sing for me your rovery native song 'O Sore Mio!' I have been Itary. I understand."

"O Sole Mio!"... that was a poser. I knew the air, but not the Italian words, and very few of the English ones. I tried to beg off ... said I had a cold... the pianist did not know the number. I could not admit my inability to sing what was probably the most well-known folk song of my "native land." I delayed action until I was able to get a few more drinks into my insistent guest, hoping that the liquor would deaden his sense of perception.

Finally, I went to my long suffering orchestra and instructed them to play the accompaniment very, very loud... and corny. I made it plain that they must drown out my voice. Then with a killing glance at the Italy-smitten Nip, I broke into song. No one could have understood a word save for my shouted "O Sole Mio!" but when I finished my friend pounded on the table, stamped on the floor and bellowed "Viva! Viva!" It dawned on me that it might be advisable to lose no time learning the Italian words of this song... I did not want to be in that spot again. It might not work.

One night we were favored with very few customers. Fely seemed to know the reason, as one of our early patrons had told her.

"The Japanese are making a movie called Dawn of Freedom, and shooting some of the scenes tonight on the Jones Bridge. It's about their occupation of Manila, and they are using American prisoners for extras."

We were sitting with a rather mild little Jap, Mr. Azioka, and I suggested, "Let's go down and see what it is all about." Azioka chimed in, "It's a good idea. I take you."

As Fely and I changed to street clothes, I asked her, "Do you think we should go with Azioka? I had the idea of trying to get some money to the prisoners."

"Azioka will be okay. He might get us in where we could not go alone," she commented. "With him, it's anything for a laugh."

The three of us started off in a carromata. Large crowds jammed the street near the bridge, so we had to get out and walk. Japanese cameramen were grinding away, and guards kept spectators off the bridge. Azioka talked our way past them, and we followed him to a good advantage point. We stood next to several truck-loads of Americans, and it was a simple matter to toss them cigarettes and matchboxes containing the usual peso notes. Azioka thought this was very funny and tossed cigarettes along with us.

Our chaperon knew one of the cameramen, and after getting the story behind the picture, explained it to us. It was to be a propaganda film showing the kind, brave Japanese in Manila, and the cowardly American fleeing in panic, running their cars and trucks over women and children.

I watched my chance and asked one of the prisoners "Where did you get the new uniform?"

"The Nips gave us all new ones for this picture," he informed, "They will take 'em right back after it's over, but we do get extra chow for this work."

Learning that he and the others were from Fort McKinley and Bilibid, I said cautiously, "I'm High-Pockets" and told him where to send a message, if he could get it out to me.

We remained until nearly curfew time. As we left Fely and I held up two fingers in a "V" sign and shouted "Keep 'em flying!" With roars of laughter, our Japanese friend mimicked us. The boys, headed back for their hell-holes, grinned and waved back.

I slept well that night, satisfied with my work in handing about a thousand pesos to the men in those matchboxes. If that picture is ever shown in the United States, some of those unfortunate men may be criticized for making their appearance before Jap cameras. It would be unjust and unfair to judge those pathetic creatures who sought "extra chow" and a little break in the bitter monotony of their imprisonment. I learned later that no American could be persuaded to play speaking, or bit parts, in that ludicrous and foul-smelling Japanese version of the "Dawn of Freedom."

If the Nips had only known the truth, they would have been aware that by the grace of God, the sun was about to rise on a real dawn of freedom for the oppressed people around me.

Chapter XVI

The Kenpei Take Me in Tow

ONE MORNING I WAS AWAKENED AT EIGHT BY THE persistent ringing of the telephone.

I heard Lerry say in her gentle voice; "The cookies are about ready."

"That's fine. I'll be out and bring the new recipes, I promised you," came my code reply.

At that moment I heard the unmistakeable sound of a throat being cleared.

"Do you still have that bad cold, dear?" I queried.

"No," she told me, "I'm feeling fine again."

After another minute or two of impersonal chatter, we hung up, both knowing that my telephone had been tapped. I had long since been warned to be wary of this Jap surveillance.

I knew that my good luck had been stretched like a rubber band, and did not know at what moment it would snap. Lerry's call had meant that Sassy was ready to leave with the Cabanatuan mail, and it must be prepared.

I took time out for breakfast with my baby. She was still lonely for Ah Ho, the amah whom I had dismissed. She had babied the child too much, and long hours of listening to the woman's pidgin English had seriously handicapped Dian's ability to speak English properly. Even now as I admonished "Eat plenty of rice and get fat," she echoed cheerfully "Etom plenty lice and gettem flat."

The child was very shy and reserved with her new nurse... Pressa, my former house cook. I had to see to it that the child ate her meal of rice bread, carabao milk and papaya. Presently Dian observed "Bitola cookie velly nice," which made me take time out to do some teaching. "Yes, Victoria cooks very nicely. Now, say it that way, dear." The meal over, Pressa took Dian's hand, and off they went on their way to impressive, shady Dewey Boulevard.

I sat down at my desk and began the task of reading and censoring the Cabanatuan mail. In their eagerness to cheer the prisoners, people would frequently mention names or express sentiments which, falling into the wrong hands, could be highly incriminating and dangerous. We also made duplicate lists of all letters and amounts of money enclosed. One I kept, and the other Looter smuggled in to the senior American officer.

He checked the incoming mail against his list, so, if anything failed to arrive, we could put a tracer on it.

The telephone clamored again. This time, it was Mr. Makino of the Shinbun... a newspaper big-wig.

"Madame Tsubaki? Prease to prepare the best froor show for tonight... and prease you must give most pretty hostess for my tabre. I bring most honorabre guest, the General Sato."

"How wonderful! How kind of you, Makino san," I cooed to the journalist in my most saccharine tones. "Leave it all to me."

Back in my room, I asked myself a woman's eternal question "what to wear?" I had quite a collection of evening gowns of varying vintages. Boots had brought several of them out of Santo Tomas, sent by internees in exchange for food.

"Fely!" I called to her, "how about scaring me up a new frock out of a couple of old ones?"

In happier times, that girl might have been a fabulous dress designer. I left her busily slashing into a coral silk jersey with a high neck and long sleeves, and tossing about assorted trimmings, rhinestones, artificial flowers and bits of tulle. That evening several Nip patrons audibly praised the new creation, which was form-fitting, clinging, cut with a very low back and a halter neck.

About six-thirty when the staff had all reported, I called them into my office.

"Listen carefully," I ordered, "Tonight is a very important one for our work. General Sato is coming and we must treat him royally. I'm not sure, but I have the feeling we may get some vital information. I don't have to tell you what that may mean to us all and the ones who depend on us. Fely, see that the general and his whole party drink plenty. Listen when they talk to each other and remember every word that you can!" Memerto cut in, "I will help them to talk. I will spike their drinks little by little."

"Yes, Memerto," I approved, "do just that. Now, Fely, and all you girls, leave the questioning of the general to me. I'll watch for the right moment to pry something out of him."

"I'll do the hottest hula that he ever saw," Fahny volunteered. "It should make his liquor work faster."

"That's fine," I concluded. "Now remember, tonight's floor show must top everything we've put on so far. Give, all of you!"

I met the journalist who ushered in the general and his staff, at the door, bowing low and murmuring "Kom ba wa" which means, "Good evening."

When they were seated and their refreshments had arrived, I started the party by taking the conventional first sip from the general's glass. Then tiny Fely, radiant in the beautiful pale, yellow kimono Ichikawa had given her, and a coronet of flowers binding his wealth of long, dark hair, went through her repertoire of Japanese songs. The charm of this act was the finished artistry with which this girl put the sentimental ballads over, making her auditors feel that she was using the words without grasping their meaning.

As the entertainment progressed, I noticed a Nip named Kamuri, sitting alone, very quietly, in a corner of the room. This slant-eyed wolf from Manchukuo had been dubbed "Tarzan" by the girls because of his constant boasts of his physical prowess. When he thought that I was not looking his way, his burning eyes followed my every movement.

General Sato seemed to enjoy every minute of the show. After my final song, he requested "Old Black Joe" saying that was his favorite tune. Remarking that I wanted to take a brief breathing spell, I sat at his table and drank a cocktail in his honor.

"Taisho Sato san," I cast my bait, "I hope that I will have the honor of singing for you again before you leave Manila."

"Ah, Madame Tsubaki, so sorry. I reave in two days on Red Cross ship," he replied, taking the hook.

"How can you travel on a Red Cross ship when you are, fortunately, in such wonderful health?"

"Easy to do. Stupid Americans not rook dere for me. Have to reprace General Tanaka at Singapore."

That admission was sufficient for me. I rendered "Old Black Joe" with gestures and my guest of honor was highly pleased. As the party left, and we made our farewell bows, I was thinking happily of all the food and supplies I could scrounge for the guerrillas with the evening's unusually large take.

After the door had closed on my departing guests "august" backs, I signaled to Pacio to follow me to the kitchen. There I hurriedly scribbled everything of importance Sato had told me, and dispatched the boy to the hills.

When I returned to the main room, my elation vanished abruptly when my eyes met the burning orbs of Kamuri, still sitting in his corner, and obviously sulking from neglect. This would never do. The well-dressed Nip civilian had been a faithful customer for at least a year. About five feet eight inches, minus the traditional spectacles, well-educated; a muscular man, he was not unattractive for a Jap. One soon tired of his unceasing boasts about his athletic achievements, his family in Manchukuo, his ancestors, his business acumen and his executive ability. In short, Kamuri liked Kamuri.

A guerrilla messenger had passed the word to me several days before, that this egotist was someone worth watching in the hope that information could be procured about his "battery-factory." This establishment was thought to be a blind for some other activity. I was glad that I had paid a bit of special attention. I seated myself at his table, and smiled brightly.

"My duty is done now toward the honorable general," I murmured. "Now I can enjoy myself a little, perhaps."

"How about making me enjoyment?" suggested "Tarzan."

"Would it please you if I sang something just for you?"

He nodded. I gave him "I Cried For You" with all the schmaltz at my command, and when I had finished he seemed to be his usual jolly self once more. As I returned to his table, he asked "Obe san, will you honor me with dancing?"

"Hai, arigato gozai masu," I answered demurely, a Japanese woman's obsequious way of saying "Yes, thank you very much."

My companion fancied himself a waltzer. As the orchestra softly and dreamily played the "Blue Danube," I began to talk about his factory. No dice. I returned to the subject a second, and then a third time,

"Why you so persistent," my partner demanded testily. "If I did not know you so intimatery, could think you maybe a spy."

My heart was pounding under Fely's creation, but I parried, "Kamuri san, you just say that because you don't want the men in your factory to see me. You're jealous. Well, I promise not to flirt with any of them if you will let me come. I only want to see if you are really the big businessman you always tell me you are."

At this point my wolf began to show his fangs.

"If you rove me," he propositioned blandly, "you be my sweetheart. You come have supper tonight my hotaru." After a cautious look around the room, he planted a hasty peck on my bare shoulder.

"Not tonight," I countered. "Ask me again after I've seen your factory."

It seemed to me that the orchestra was playing endlessly. As we whirled around in dizzy swirls, Kamuri kept insisting, "Hotaru first... factory after," while I ogled him and urged that it must be just the opposite procedure. The floor show put an end to our argument.

Fely and Fahny did their Moro dance. Fahny, taking the man's part, sat on the floor playing the native drums, while Fely circled around her, the bells on her graceful ankles tinkling, while her silver-banded scarf floated alluringly about her.

I wound up the large evening by singing "My Man" in what I hoped was a creditable imitation of Fanny Brice's unique performance, not forgetting a few provocative glances in Tarzan's direction. Kamuri left with considerable reluctance, after pressing a special gift of fifty pesos into my hand, and whispering amorously, "I see you tomorrow."

Tomorrow, I thought, the factory... and then. What after that?

I had temporarily dismissed all thoughts of my ardent suitor, when early the next morning I received the first and only personal request John Boone ever made of me. Would I arrange for his baby's christening in Manila? His wife was now on the way he wrote. To John and Mellie, both good Catholics, it was tremendously important to have their little son duly registered... war or no war... Japs or no Japs...and they wanted to name him after my husband.

I went at once to Father Lolar in his Malate church.

"Now, that's wonderful news altogether," he beamed. "And it will be you holding the blessed child as godmother."

"Father, would it be okay, when I'm not a Catholic?"

"My child, in war time there's no need to be quibbling over a good woman to stand sponsor for a brave man's son."

So it was settled, and I dashed over to the Amusatague home to ask Lerry for the loan of her boys' christening robe. Her sons had both been christened in her husband's robe, now thirty five years old. She took it from its box... two yards of luxurious cream silk and real Spanish lace... complete with attractive bonnet with long fading blue streamers.

"It will be pleasant to have it used again," Lerry said quietly. "I think we may never have any more children. Our work grows more dangerous every day, and anyone who turned in Ramon to the Japs would be..."

"Don't worry, honey," I interrupted. "Your husband is a brave man but he has excellent judgment. He will not take needless risks."

The dauntless Mellie arrived on schedule, her chubby baby in her arms. She had made the trip from the hills as I had done fifteen months before, over the mountain trails by night and then by banca across the bay.

"John wanted so much to come," she said wistfully.

"Of course, his son's christening..

"Oh, no. I think it was more to see your night club."

Standing in the ornate baptistry, I was thrilled to hold this tiny morsel of humanity in my arms, beautifully clothed in the borrowed finery, and to hear him given the old American name of Phillip John Boone. A brave man's son... and if Phil had lived... I thought that maybe by now, we too, would have been proud parents. It was difficult to hold back the tears.

When I returned to the club I found a note, to telephone Mr. Kamuri.

As he answered the telephone, he was apparently perturbed, "Madame Tsubaki, where were you? Come my office, at fourteen o'crock. It is forbidden thing I doing, just for you."

The Nip was awaiting me in the doorway of his plant. He took me through the front showroom and his private office, trying to persuade me that this was all it was essential for me to see. I was in no mood for lengthy explanations about trivia. Pretending to be in a high dudgeon, I fairly screamed at him, "So! You were only fooling me. Never mind! We'll call it all off. You agreed to show me the whole place," and started to walk out.

Kamuri called me back.

"Okay, okay. You win, but you must never say what you see, or it be," and he drew a stubby finger across his throat, "death for me... your friend. Remember, rittre fox, if Kamuri find you speak, I hate you then rike I rove you now. When Kamuri hates, it's bad."

He gave me a pair of dark glasses to wear, then led me into the factory where a number of Japs were hard at work. One glance told me the story... intricate machinery, turning out bullets of varying calibers.

As I thanked him he said, "You much satisfied now? Tonight I win. I see you rater at crub."

At home, I hastened to code a report on my visit, and sent it to Boone for relaying to Darwin. The carrier also carried the wanted items listed in a message that Mellie had brought down.

That evening at the club I endured a waking nightmare. I avoided Kamuri and kept thinking of what to say to him at closing time. Finally the boys began turning off the lights. There was no useful purpose to be served by delaying the crisis any longer. I went over and told him as pleasantly as possible that he must excuse me. Dian was not well. I would be compelled to visit him some other night. He sat sullenly, without replying. Then I rambled on stupidly, saying something about a headache. That did it! His yellow face flushed, and he jumped up, grabbed me by the wrist and pulled me through the door toward the stairs. I cried out. He slapped my face and kept on pulling me along. Memerto hurried into the hall and called:

"Senora, what will I tell your husband when he gets here and does not find you?"

The faithful boy had remembered my reiterated tale of a mysterious husband on another island.

"Call the military police," I screamed. "And as soon as my husband gets here, tell him where I am."

Memerto understood my bluff and started toward the telephone.

"Baka yo noi!" exploded Kamuri, releasing his grip. A second later he kicked me, and walked out raging. I bolted the door, raced upstairs to my room, and once in that haven, promptly fainted.

The next day, with my mission completed, I ruefully inspected my black and blue bruises. I would have settled for a very quiet evening on the following night. But alas, soon after opening time, Kamuri dashed in like a raging lion, and proceeded systematically to break all our mirrors, electric lights, about fifty glasses, plus several chairs and bar stools. The other Nip patrons watched impassively while the reverberating sounds of shattering glass and splintered wood filled the room. Not satisfied with his devastation, the maddened Nip tore down most of the drapes.

The military police finally arrived and took Kamuri away.

I don't know who called them. There was no desire on my part to become involved with the kenpei, although technically under their protection. Even when the going was extremely rough, I always felt that the less they knew about me, the better off I would be.

It was about this time that I overplayed my hand in the planting of food and money for the "Park Avenue" prisoners. I arranged with a sympathetic

Chinese confectioner to have a thousand peanut candy bars made up, and placed the whole lot of them along the road before daylight.

Someone probably informed the guards for that very morning the line of march to Nichol Field was rerouted, and our friends never again passed Claring's little house on the corner. I felt depressed about this, and earnestly hoped that the men did not think we had become tired or afraid, and so let them down.

Then the Nips picked up Claring and took her to Fort Santiago. She had some Japanese friends, spoke the language slightly, and was ready with a glib story that she would counter-spy on the local underground for the Nips. This earned her a "temporary release," and she slipped off at once to the hills.

A friend dropped by the club, and whispered that he had succeeded in "unreconditioning" his radio set by means of a clever little gadget invented by another group member. I hurried to his house. Finally we heard a commentator from San Francisco, speaking slowly and clearly; "General MacArthur's troops make new landing in Dutch New Guinea... Liberators bomb Guam by daylight... MacArthur and Nimitz batter Truk ... Army and Marine planes rain two hundred and forty tons of bombs on Japs in the Marshalls..."

Our men were really on their way! The Yanks were coming, and "The Time" would come! We took down the wonderful news, and the next day it was in circulation by means of a flood of typed "underground" sheets.

May eighteenth... and Pedro, one of our runners dashed, panting, up the back stairs. He had helped himself to a truck and rammed it along the eighty mile long road from Cabanatuan, to arrive in Manila before the jerk-water train.

"Senora High-Pockets," he gasped, "Sassy on train with mail basket... all the prisoners' letter! She doesn't know Japs found out about Looter!"

"How did that happen?"

"Americano prisoner out with carabao cart on wood detail fumbled. Dropped package. Guard shot him."

"What happened to Looter?"

"Oh, senora, she ran and ran, and got to the hills. Don't worry. Mutt too... he is gone."

"I'm glad of that," I told Pedro absent-mindedly while I was thinking, "Well, at least we were careful in seeing to it that there were no real names and addresses."

Then it flashed into my mind that Sassy's safety was in jeopardy. What if she was suspected and followed? Something had to be done, and that without delay. Then I suddenly conceived a bright idea.

"Get two or three boys and meet Sassy's train," I ordered. "Spot her and close in right behind her. Two of you start a fight. Tell the third man to grab her bag, make sure that he is not followed, and bring it here."

The plan worked successfully. In the interim I called every member of our group that I could reach and alerted them for possible trouble. We did not have long to wait.

Two days later Helen Petroff, a Russian, married to an American sailor, was arrested and taken to Fort Santiago. A letter to her from her husband was among those seized from Looter. This was the second missive we had carried for Helen. The first time I instructed her to sign her proper name and address it to her husband, but to select a code name and ask him to do the same for future communications. The possibility existed that she may not have heeded my warning, and, that in my last hasty censorship I had overlooked her dereliction. I tried hard to recall what my oversight, if any, had been, but that was now water over the dam. Helen was a nice girl, but not the caliber of such thoroughbreds as Boots or Screwball.

"The Nips will make her talk," I opined despairingly. They did.

Another day, another arrest. This time it was German. As our best typist, Fancy-Pants had turned out the last news sheets about the American advances.

A muddled train of defiant and apprehensive thoughts raced through my mind in rapid succession. Sleep was almost out of the question, and food was a tasteless something that I forced into my gullet to sustain life. My reaction was akin to that of a person sitting helplessly on a powder keg with a slow fuse burning its way to the touch-hole. I wondered repeatedly where and when the next blow would fall.

The next day... May twenty-second... I knew. Ramon Amusatague was arrested. I was confident that Ramon would not talk, and would face any ordeal that confronted him in the best tradition of his proud Iberian race. I wondered how Lerry and the children would fare, for I knew that the Amusatagues had been consistently giving away more money than they could ordinarily afford. I had been so closely associated with this couple that I was certain the net would soon envelope me.

I called a brief, secret meeting of our group. Each and every one of them was coached on what to say, and what not to say, if, as, and when... While I was talking, the hum of voices in a corner of the room became audible.

"What's going on here?" I demanded, "Let us in on it." The knot broke up and came over to me.

"Listen, High-Pockets," Dr. Atienza advised, acting as spokesman. "You're sure to be arrested next, and we don't want that to happen. We say you must go the hills with Dian, and let the guerrillas hide you."

The temptation was great, and I had recently given much thought to it. I had but to pack a few belongings, take Demyon or Pacio as a guide, then a trip by banca across the Bay, and over the hills to Boone's outposts. Somehow or other, I could not bring myself to do it. I felt that I owed it to the memory of my departed to remain and help his former comrades, regardless of any serious consequences to myself.

"The Japs have nothing on me," I bluffed. "If they take me in, it will only be for some stupid questioning. I'll be out in a couple of weeks. Why, Boone says that the invasion may take place in six months, and when it comes we will be needed here more than in the hills."

The die was cast!

One by one, all present told me in substance, "If you are determined to stay and take it, we will follow your example."

"That's settled, then," I told them. "Now go home, clean house, and wait for further orders."

At home, I plunged into house-cleaning zealously. Memerto and I worked feverishly, removing all papers and evidence pertaining to our activities, from their hiding places in the loft and behind loose boards. My most precious documents, my American passport, Phil's army papers, valued souvenirs such as the "receipts" from prisoners we had helped, and the "bullet with my number on it" were entrusted to Fely. Her sister, Flora, carried them off at once, and buried them, packed in bottles and tin cans, in her father's backyard in Quezon City.

That night, I did not close my eyes until sheer exhaustion made me sleep near dawn. Every sound seemed like Jap footsteps; every silence was unbearable.

May 23, 1944. At nine, Dian and I were having breakfast. I had sent Pressa for more rice bread and was coaxing the child to eat. I had just sweetened my coffee with the pinocha we used for sugar, when the rapid thudding of boots on the stairs let me know that I must expect unwelcome visitors!

Four stocky kenpei... military police... with drawn revolvers ran into the hall. Two remained on guard at the threshold. The other two advanced and poked their weapons into my ribs.

"Jitto shita cri!" one of them barked. That's the Nip way of saying "Don't move!" which translated into good American-ese means "Hands up!"

They ran their paws over my body to see if I was carrying any concealed weapons.

"You are Madame Tsubaki?"

"Yes."

"Take us to your office, High-Pockets!"

"May I get a girl to look after my baby?"

"Hai! But no try get away. I no mind shooting woman."

I looked for Fely, but she was out. I went on to Flora's room, my two guards trailing me closely. Flora was sleeping soundly. I shook her awake and whispered to her to take care of Dian, because I was being arrested.

"No whisper!" commanded one of the M. P.'s, grabbing my arm.

As I turned to leave, my lips formed the word "Boone," and Flora, pale and wide-eyed, nodded her head slightly.

My captors took me into my office-bedroom, and ordered me to open my desk and trunks. They had a suitcase with them, and tumbled my club accounts, treasured makeup and canned goods into it. The Nips explained that they were only taking evidence and all would be restored as soon as I was cleared; I was only to go to their office "for questioning."

The impatient kenpei wanted me to come with them as I was, clad only in my house-coat, but I persuaded them to let me change. Partially screened by the closed door, I donned a slack suit and socks. I kept thinking that it would be best for Dian and myself if I did not kiss her goodbye.

As I was led away, I turned to look back. Flora was there, and Dian was still sitting at the table. The child looked at me, and then at my uneaten food, her dark little head cocked to one side.

I managed to smile at her and said, "Be a good girl and Mummy will be home soon." The pressure on my arms told me that the police were about to drag me away, so I straightened up and walked out.

During the many bitter months that followed, the sweet little puzzled face of my baby lingered in my memory... not to mention the thought of the uneaten breakfast which built itself into a sumptuous feast as time passed.

CHAPTER XVII

An Unwilling Guest at Fort Santiago

My CAPTORS PUSHED ME RUDELY INTO A CAR and we drove away. I thought that we were going to the dreaded confines of Fort Santiago, as other seized members of our local underground had been taken there. To my great surprise we turned into the grounds of the Japanese Administration Building on San Luis Boulevard, only two blocks from the Club Tsubaki.

I had visited this structure before, first to help Louise procure her release from Santo Tomas, and then when I renounced my "Italian" citizenship. I had passed it many times and noticed the small guardhouse at the gate. Now I was hustled into this little lock-up, and shoved unceremoniously into one of the four empty cells it boasted... ducking my head as I passed through the Japanese-sized door. It slammed shut and I was left alone.

A quick survey of my cell showed that it was devoid of any creature comforts. It had a large barred window, covered with heavy screening, high above my head. By dint of jumping I could get a brief glimpse of the sky. The benjo... that's what the Nips call it... was strictly their style... a hole in the floor. It could not be flushed and a small, continuous trickle of water flowed through it as the sole concession to sanitation.

When I became weary of pacing and jumping, I sat down on the floor, my back against the wall. Several hours dragged by, as I marked the flight of time by surreptitious glances at my small diamond wrist watch which I had managed to tuck into my bra. When I was being hustled out of the club, I had managed to get it off my wrist without being detected. I wanted to slip it to one of my employees, but could not get close enough to them, so into the "high-pockets" it went.

I suddenly realized that I was very thirsty, and was about to pound on the door and ask for water, when I heard the sound of an automobile stopping. "Bampei! Bampei!" someone shouted for the guard. Within a short space of time, this wizened individual unlocked the cell door, entered and tied a blindfold over my eyes, then stood me against the wall at the far side of the cell. The sound of many footsteps followed, and the clank of metallic objects being brought into the coop.

Instruments of torture? My dry lips moved as I prayed for strength and courage.

A voice came from my right: "Sit down, there's a chair behind you."

In front of me, another voice: "High-Pockets, we are in a small room as you know, so there's no need to talk loud. Answer our questions truthfully, and you may soon be out."

"Yes, sir," I answered. "I will do my best."

Both invisible inquisitors spoke excellent English and their voices sounded vaguely familiar. I wondered if they had been patrons of the club. One of them sounded like George Takara, the journalist that spoke such perfect English and had attended college in the States. For reasons of their own, they did not want me to know their identity, hence the blindfold.

First Voice: "We know that you are not Italian. We have called the Italian Consulate and they will not vouch for you. We also know that you are not using your right name. So let's start with that. What is your right name?"

"It is true that I am not an Italian. I am an American by birth. If you look in the files of the Bureau of Vital Statistics, you will discover that about a year ago I renounced all former loyalties and embraced Philippine citizenship. My status is that of a Philippine national. I am using my right name ... Dorothy Fuentes."

First Voice: "Then why are you sometimes called Claire?"

"That is my middle name. I am Dorothy Claire Fuentes." I frankly wondered how they found out my real first name, as I had not used it since my return to Manila. Only a few old friends of pre-war vintage knew me by that name, and I had even educated them to call me "Dorothy."

The second voice cut in: "Do you deny that you have written and received letters from prisoners in Cabanatuan?"

I hesitated for a few moments while this raced through my mind "They know the name High-Pockets, so they must have one or more of my letters, either from Cabanatuan or Boone. I must not involve Boone." Then I replied, "Yes, I did write a few letters to Cabanatuan and received some answers."

Second Voice: "Now we are getting somewhere. I shall read your last letter, and then you can explain." A pause, then, "Dear Everlasting... Now who is Everlasting?"

"I don't know."

The words were barely out of my mouth, when I was struck in the temple with a doubled-up fist.

Second Voice, raging: "Uso wo itte kudasai, masu ne!"

First, ditto: "Calm yourself, she does not understand much of our language. My colleague just said 'Don't lie to me!' I echo his sentiments. You don't expect us to believe that statement, do you?"

I felt dizzy, but managed to retort firmly: "I have spoken the truth so far. Why can't you believe me now?"

Second Voice: "Then tell us how these letters got back and forth from Cabanatuan to you."

"There's a Filipino boy who came to my house every few months. I don't know his name."

Bang! Another blow on the side of my head that made me see stars, followed by a shower of kicks on my shins from heavy boots. Tears came to my eyes and I pressed my hand against the blindfold to blot them out.

Second Nip: "We can hand you something worse than kicks and slaps. We can do some stamping in places that will really hurt. Tears will not help you. You have taken on the job of a man, so you must face the same punishment. This is no fight between man and woman... it is Nippon and America. We represent one, and you, it seems, the other. Now are you going to talk or shall we really go to town?"

I realized that Mutt had made his getaway to the hills, and that it could do no harm to give his name.

"All I know about the boy is that he is called Mutt."

I gathered from the silence that this item satisfied them. First Voice, shouting close to my ear: "Who is Papaya?"

"Never heard of him."

Another brief spell of quiet, punctuated by the rustle of papers, then Second Voice returned to my letter: "Dear Everlasting: I was glad to hear that you received call and feel so much better. Will you please send out demijohn..."

First Voice, interrupting: "Who is Cal?"

"Cal is the abbreviation for calamanci, the lemons that..."

"Now you can't think we are that dumb! Cal is an American name and so is John. We believe that John Demi and Cal Demi are two men you've been trying to sneak out of the camp." Then I was slapped on both cheeks... hard. This kept on until I fell from the chair. Someone yanked me back into it.

I did not want to sob, but it was hard to control my voice. "You both appear to speak English well. Look in a Webster's Dictionary, if you have one. You will find the word 'demijohn' there. Ask any native if they do not call their lemons calamanci. That should prove that I was telling the truth." A brief respite, some Nip jabber, the sound of a door opening and closing, more Jap palaver, the door opening and closing again, the faint sound of pages being turned, then "So desu!" the Jap verbiage for "That's so!"

Second Nip again: "You did tell the truth there, now keep right on telling it and you won't get hurt. Now let's get on. What is the real name of Chap Bob?"

I tried again, to tell them that I did not know the real names of any of the men in Cabanatuan.

Number Two: "Don't try to make me believe you are sending in money to men you don't even know. In America, they would call such men 'pimps' and they would have an equally contemptuous name for you. You don't want to he called that, do you?"

"I can't help what I am called. I only sent money and medicine to sick men. I did not send a letter to Chap Bob."

First inquisitor: "The note is addressed in ink, so we shall soon see. Here, take this pencil! There is a paper here! Now write, 'Chap Bob'."

A pencil was slipped into my hand, which was guided to a sheet of paper. I had not typed the name on his note, but used pen and ink. I tried to disguise my writing, but being a natural scribbler, at times barely able to read my own scrawl, the task was a difficult one. When I had finished, my interrogators both laughed.

Commented Number One: "It is a hard job to fool anyone when a person writes as badly as you do. It's yours all right. Take that... and that... and that... for your lying!"

The triple "thats" and a few more of their close relatives were a rain of blows on my head that once more sent me to the floor for the count. When I had recovered and was again in my chair, a cigarette was poked into my mouth and lighted, while the "cooing" dulcet tones of Number Two coaxed: "Maybe you are just nervous. Just smoke and think for a while." As I puffed, they talked to each other in Japanese.

Beware of the Nips, when they try kindness, I thought. By this time I was so fighting mad that none of their tactics... friendly or ruthless... were going to make me change my story.

Then they started in again. "You do know Sparkplug and Fancy-Pants, don't you?"

"Yes, I know them. I met them when I was a volunteer nurse at the Remedios Hospital."

I knew that Ramon and German had been apprehended and a denial was useless.

"It would do no good to say that you did not know them. We have them both and before we get through we will have the rest of your ring. They have told us all about you, so you might as well tell us what you know about them."

That was an obvious lie. I knew Ramon and German too well. They would die before they would talk.

"I don't know what they could say about me," I told them, "except to say that I have sent money, letters and medicine into Cabanatuan."

"They say you are also doing guerrilla work. What do you say to that?"

"It's not true, so I am sure that they would not say that."

"We know you were doing guerrilla work and so were they. Speak now and we will let you off easy. If you persist in being stubborn, I will see that you get the limit. We can bring your child here and make her suffer too. Maybe that would make you talk!"

As I mentally voiced a prayer that Fely or someone else had spirited Dian away to safety, I persisted "Even if you bring my baby here I would still have to tell you the same thing, because it is all true."

Second Voice (wearily): "So you still stick to your story. We will leave you here, and I hope you rot in your lies. There will be plenty of time to think over what is good for you. When you decide to tell the truth, call a guard, and he will send for us."

This "sweetheart" gave me a few parting kicks. There was a sound of steps and the cell door closing. A guard came in and removed the blindfold. He carried out three chairs and a table that had been brought in for the investigation, locked the door and left the swirling world to darkness and to me.

My thirst increased, but no food or water appeared. About nine o'clock, I lay down on the filthy floor, pulled the housecoat I had brought with me over my head to ward off the mosquitoes, and tried to sleep. Soon after daybreak I heard the guards talking outside.

"Mizu, kudasai!" I called, using some of the very few Japanese words that I knew, which meant "Water, Please!"

The conversation ceased. One of the guards came to my cell door.

"Baka!" he spat at me, and walked away.

At noon, a ragged little Filipino boy, about nine years old, was brought in and placed in the cell across from me.

"Why are you here?" I whispered, when the guard left.

"I stole some food and clothes from a Jap house," he said quietly. Then raising his voice he sobbed, "Oh, my mother will be worried about me when I don't come home tonight!"

"Don't cry, son," I comforted, "They won't keep a little boy like you here long."

The guard obviously heard our conversation, for he returned, barking "Domare!" (Nip for "Shut up!"). Bellowing "Spy!" at me and "Thief!" at the youngster, he launched into a lengthy tirade in Japanese. After that my fellow prisoner and I exercised more caution when we talked.

No food or water that day, until a new guard came on duty at six p. m. After much pleading and cajoling on my part, he reluctantly gave us each one small cup of water. At noon on the third day, we received a gob of rice about the size of a tennis ball, and one cup of weak tea... but no water. By midnight I was so crazed by thirst that I cupped my hands, plunged them into the toilet trickle, and drank greedily.

A sudden harsh laugh shattered the quiet of the cell. I turned and looked into the taunting slant-eyes of a Nip guard, enjoying my desperate plight. He hastily summoned a few of his fellows. They took turns peering in my cell door, and the small building resounded with their shouts of unrestrained mirth. I was so mad that I cried myself to sleep.

The next day new guards came on duty. They walked in to look over their prisoners, shout "Spy!" and "Thief!" then left us alone. I forced myself to walk around the cell for exercise. While doing this, I noticed something shiny in a crack above the door and pried it out with a bobby pin. It was half a safety razor blade. With this treasure safely hidden in the cuff of my slacks, I spent the rest of the day figuring out how to make use of it.

Late that night, when all was quiet, I started cutting into a board at the back of the cell. The rainy season was just beginning and frequent thunder storms deadened the sound of my frenzied labor. It was almost dawn when I finally stopped and went to sleep.

The daily "meal" still consisted of one rice ball. If we were lucky now and then, my small neighbor and I could get as many as three cups of water during the day, but no more. No soap or wash water. I pestered the guards about this every day until one of them, mopping the hall, threw his whole bucket of dirty water over me.

Two more nights passed and I had the board almost cut through. Then I started on the one above it, trying to make an aperture large enough for my body. We had complete blackouts from dusk on. My thought was, once through the hole, I could easily crawl through the barbed wire fence, and there were no tell-tale street lights on Taft Avenue to disclose me to the guards.

On my fourteenth night of confinement, during a lively thunder-storm, I pushed with my feet and my two boards gave way. I found to my great disappointment that the wall was a double one. That night, I started to work on the two opposite boards of the outside wall. They were thick and it was a slow job. After a while I was obliged to quit, as my fingers were too sore to continue. The skin of my knuckles was raw... almost bleeding. I took the precaution to set the cut boards carefully back in their proper place.

The next day I managed to whisper to my little friend, "If you get out, go to the Club Tsubaki just up the street and tell them Madame Dorothy is here. Ask for Fely and tell her to get my baby to Boone." I told him that he would be rewarded with money, and could faintly hear him repeating the message over and over.

Alas, for my premature plans for escape. An hour after I talked to the boy, two military police entered my cell, half-dragged and half-carried me to a car, and drove me to the dreaded confines of Fort Santiago.

I was taken into the office; duly mugged and fingerprinted by Captain Kobioshi who once promised me the city of Portland. Routine questions were asked regarding my name, age, nationality, my parents' names and address, even their telephone number. After a perfunctory search, during which my precious watch was not discovered, I was thrust in a cell with six other women.

Our coop was about seven by twelve feet. The benjo was a hole in the floor, with a pan underneath, obviously removable from the outside. I was relieved to see a water faucet. At least I could drink all the water I wanted, and even wash... without soap.

My cell-mates consisted of two American nuns, their coifs and light tropical habits sadly bedraggled; a young Chinese girl named Carmen; and three German Jewesses... one elderly, one talkative, and one who had been, ironically, a delegate to the League of Nations Conference at Geneva.

Our food consisted of a level saucer of fishy-smelling rice gruel, thrice daily. It usually contained a few worms and plenty of grit. Sometimes, for a change, we discovered a few potato peelings boiled in it.

I found that my cell was one of sixteen, facing an open court. The side and back walls were solid, but the front was made up of parallel bars and a small door. A guard paced constantly from one end of the courtyard to the other, stopping at each cell to peer in. The guards were changed every hour, and a new shift took over every four days.

A strong light glared in the cells day and night. For twelve hours a day, from seven to seven, we were compelled to remain sitting on our heels in the traditional Japanese fashion. Then came relief for during the other hours we were permitted to lie on the floor.

The prison regulations called for complete silence at all times. Men have not been able to prevent women from talking since the inception of mankind, and now a few Japs did not stop us. We became adept at conversing in rapid whispers during the few moments after the guards had passed. Thus, by snatches of whispered conversation, I learned my jail-mates' stories.

Carmen's husband had been picked up on an unfounded charge of spreading propaganda. When she arrived with a parcel of food and clothing for him, a Japanese officer propositioned her. When she rejected the Nip's advances, they arrested her, also.

The Jewesses were there chiefly because of the Nazi-inspired hatred of their race, and strange to relate, the two nuns were also innocent victims of their persecution. The former League Delegate, a cultured and travelled lady, had been convalescing from an illness in the convent at Baguio. She brought a note of greeting from one of the resident nuns, to Sister Trinita, a teacher at the Assumption College. Sister Brigida was casually mentioned in the missive. En route to deliver the message, after her return to Manila, the lady met two Jewesses whom she happened to knew, and stopped to chat. A pair of unduly suspicious Jap M. P.'s, noting her sociability, came up and examined her handbag. They found the note which read in part "Butch has presented us with more dependents." When Sister Trinita was harshly ordered to decode the message, she could only blushingly tell the truth... Butch, a pet cat at the Baguio convent, had given birth to kittens. Naturally, no Jap would believe that story! So the addressee of that innocent message, a nun whose name was casually noted in it, its carrier and two acquaintances whom she chanced to meet on the street, were booked and held on suspicion of subversive activities.

All of this information came to me a bit at a time, as the frequent changes of our guards kept them observant and alert. They were always ready to punish any prisoner they caught talking, or not in the prescribed kneeling position without good reason. We were allowed to rise only to get a drink or use the benjo. This was very embarrassing as the guard frequently stood and watched us. The only protection that we had was a small screen about two feet high, and our heads towered above it. It was sufficiently disconcerting to have the guards stare at us during such moments, and they added to our discomfiture by laughing and making uncomplimentary remarks. If we offended, a guard usually contented himself with one blow on our head with his short club. If however, the culprit was hesitant about coming forward to receive her punishment, she was soundly trounced in the same manner as the male prisoners.

Ours was the only cell containing women. When I arrived there were probably two hundred men in the fifteen other cells, and the moans of those poor devils came constantly to our ears, as they were beaten every day without cause.

My cell mates had been incarcerated from two to four months. They looked thin, weak, and were afflicted with lice and fleas. It was not long before these pests moved in to taste the fresh meat of my hide. Sister Brigida had been suffering from anemia when jailed. Despite her misery, the nun's fortitude was admirable, as she fingered a rosary improvised from a knotted rag, and never complained.

As an almost daily routine, the women, and then the men were allowed out of their cells for a shower, with about two minutes allotted for this pseudo-ablution. This procedure consisted of running through a little stream of cold water from a hose attached to the roof of a three-wall cubicle. We threw our clothes across the top of the partition, dashed through the trickle, shook ourselves, and dressed. We did not feel any cleaner after this performance, but looked forward to it because of the chance for exercise, fresh air, and relief from the tiresome kneeling position for a few minutes. The guards climbed on boxes or anything else they could find to play the role of Peeping Toms when the women showered. Their giggles and pointed remarks about our figures did not make a hit with us, and we pretended to ignore them.

There was a small shed for the guards' use when off duty, in the court in front of our cells. It was equipped with a radio which they frequently tuned in to broadcasts from the States, and it was thrilling to hear snatches of American news and music. Our whole day was brightened when we heard that Tojo's entire cabinet had resigned. We even managed a forbidden laugh upon hearing the fashion note that "If the women's skirts keep getting shorter, they will be blouses." Some of the guards knew a little English, and virtually all of them could speak Tagalog. Luckily, I had slight knowledge of this dialect, and with the few Japanese words at my command, could make myself understood. One of the guards was obviously a ladies' man, and he won our hearts one night when he slipped us a teaspoonful of sugar rolled in a piece of newspaper. We divided it seven ways so that each could have one delicious taste. On another memorable night, he presented us with twenty one shelled peanuts. It required strenuous self-control to make three peanuts last one hour, but most of us exercised it.

After some time had passed, a new sergeant, whom I recognized as an old acquaintance, was placed in charge of the guards. This non-com had visited my club several times. I greeted him by his name... Yamashita... and he answered civilly, "Hai, Madame Tsubaki, I remember you. You arways good to me. Is dere something I can do for you?"

"Yes," I replied hopefully, "Could you go to my club and ask Fely for soap? That is what I need most."

Although my statement was true, my principal thought was to get word of my whereabouts to her.

"I see what I can do," Yamashita promised.

Two nights after, very late, the sergeant came quietly to my cell, called my name, and handed me a small package.

"Hide it," he cautioned, "Don't ret guards see, or dey ask how you get. That make big trouble for me."

"Arigato, gozai masu," I gave thanks, making a deep bow, and for once, in my heart, I meant it.

While one of the women kept watch, I opened the package and found to my joy, a bar of laundry soap, a small bath towel, a tooth brush, and a small tube of tooth-paste. I felt like a millionaire, and Carmen cried from sheer joy. When we showered the next day, we all had a good soapy bath, a shampoo, and brushed our teeth. Yes, we shared the toothbrush! After that splurge we introduced rationing. We allowed ourselves the use of the soap to wash our hands and face every day, but reserved it for general bodily use on a weekly basis. The tooth paste was strictly on a weekly rite.

Late in June I was sorry to see my good friend Ramon brought in. I waited for a chance to speak to him at the time when all prisoners were lined up in front of their cells and counted after the daily shower. When an opportune moment arrived I spoke quickly, asking him about the others who had been arrested. What about German? Where had they been all this time? Why had he just been brought to Fort Santiago?

"German became sick... very sick... and they sent him out to a hospital," he whispered rapidly. "I guess they didn't want him to die before they were through questioning him. We have both been kept in separate cells in a place near the old brewery. His cell was across a narrow hall from me, and we could talk at times. I took all the blame at our investigations so he could get out. There was no need for both of us to stay in, and he was too ill. Mutt got away, I am sure, so use his name if necessary."

"What happened to Papaya?"

"They know she is Marie, and have her old address, but she has moved. We think she is safe some place. Use her name if you must."

I felt a trifle better after those few hurried words with Ramon. Our stories would tally at least, in the event of future investigations. My friend was in the cell next to mine, and his proximity was comforting. I managed to slip him a piece of soap wrapped in half my towel. It was easily accomplished. When one of the Filipino boys came that night to clean out the benjo, I passed the small parcel through the hole to him, and asked him to slip it through the benjo hole into Ramon's cell.

One Filipino chow boy, who brought our food from the kitchen in another building, was not a prisoner, but a paid employee who returned home each night. One day for my benefit, he made a motion with his hand, as though writing. I understood the gesture and whispered, "Will you take a note out for me?" He nodded.

I wrangled a pencil from a benjo boy, and while Carmen kept watch, wrote a note to Fely on a scrap of old newspaper. I asked if Dian was safe with Boone, and begged her to try to smuggle in some food to us as we were slowly starving to death. I told her to let Ramon's wife know that he was here, and also to make use of any of my things in any way she fancied. After awaiting an opportunity for several days I managed to slip the missive to the chow boy, letting him know that Fely would pay him well if he brought me a reply.

The next week dragged past, without results. Finally the boy pressed a scrap of paper in my hand as he was bringing in the noon chow, and I was being taken out for a shower. Fely wrote that she had heard of me through the little boy who had been my companion in the guard house. I learned with joy that Dian was well, happy, and safe with Boone. Also that Boone had asked the local underground to do what they could for me, and keep him posted. The Japs had returned after my arrest and located the club. They had even found and taken a bottle of champagne hidden for a celebration when "The Time" arrived. Then, wonderful news; Boone had written that the Americans were decimating the Japs on nearby islands, and the American return was scheduled to take place soon. "Hold on and pray," Fely concluded.

Our cell was so overjoyed by the news that we managed to remain quiet with difficulty. I still had the pencil stub and a scrap of paper. I copied the war news and passed it through the hole to the benjo boy when he arrived for his nightly chores. It spread rapidly through the gloomy fortress and morale soared.

I feel certain that many a despairing soul, chin up-tilted, prayed that night as never before.

CHAPTER XVIII

The Sons of Heaven Torture and Try Me

THE TOOTHPASTE LASTED TWO WEEKS, and the soap one week after that. Our pests continued to multiply... flies, mosquitoes, bed-bugs, lice and fleas. The nights were a nightmare as big rats came through the benjo hole, and large flying cockroaches over-ran the cell. The guards would not give us any repellent to get rid of these nuisances. Our main occupation was to find and exterminate these creatures, but it was a losing battle.

Seven more women were crammed into our little coop before the end of June. It was not possible for all of us to lie down at once, and we had to take turns. Half of us would rest until midnight while the others stood against the back wall; then we changed positions. None of us were therefore able to get a full quota of sleep, and the nights became as endless as the days. The stifling atmosphere made us perspire constantly and the dust clung to our bodies. Our principal pastime was a contest to see who could roll the largest ball of dried skin and dirt from her arms and legs.

One night, while I was awaiting my turn to lie down, a guard stopped and asked me if I would like a cigarette. I said that I would, and he gave me one. However, when I asked for a light, he laughed and walked away. I kept that cigarette for three days, trying vainly to get a light. Finally, exasperated beyond endurance I threw it away. Occasionally we could snatch a fleeting puff from a lighted butt dropped by a guard near the shower. If they caught us in the act, they would knock it out of our hands. We wanted to smoke badly, for it helped deaden the ever-present pangs of hunger.

At the end of July, the female prisoners numbered twenty-two and we were moved to a larger cell... about fifteen by twelve feet. There was room here for all of us to sleep at night, lying spoon-fashion. When one turned, the rest of us had to follow suit. The number of prisoners in the fortress had doubled, and this served as an excuse for our jailers to cut our rice-slop down to two cups per day. We became constantly thinner and weaker, and heard that the deaths among the men averaged one to two each day.

The elderly Jewess was certain that she would be the first woman to die, but seemed to hold up better than some of the others. She could be quite humorous at times. One day a guard stopped to chat with us, and she asked him to take a message to her son who was an inmate of Cell Four. The Jap could not understand English very well, and kept saying "Nani, Nani," the Nip word for "What?" She brought the back of her hand to her mouth as though kissing it, cradled her arms as though holding a baby, raised four fingers and told him "A kiss for my baby in Cell Four."

The guard thought that she was saying that she wanted to kiss him. Infuriated, he reached his arm through the bars and struck her on the head with the butt of his gun. Carmen pulled her away from the gate, and told the Jap what the woman really meant. He came from Formosa, hence was able to understand Carmen's explanation made in Chinese. When it dawned on him what was wanted, he laughed heartily, then went to Cell Four and threw a kiss to the woman's son. He was very friendly after that. If he happened to be on duty when it was our shower time, he would let us take an hour, and give cigarettes to those who wanted them.

We were told about the middle of August to expect an officer who would visit us for a special inspection. When he arrived, it was none other than Captain Kobioshi with whom I had joked about a post-war trip to America. I told Sister Trinita and Carmen that I knew the officer and intended to ask him to start my investigation. Both were much alarmed and begged me not to act rashly, telling me that investigation was only a Nip synonym for torture. I made up my mind quickly that I must take that chance or else become slowly demented, sitting and rotting in that hell-hole.

"Captain Kobioshi," I called without any preliminaries, as he neared our cell, "You know me... Madame Tsubaki. Please will you find out why my investigation has not been finished? I want to have it over with and get out, so that I can be with my child."

"Hai!" he retorted brusquely, "If you ready, I have it continued. It so happens, Madame, your baby not home." He walked close to the bars and snapped, "Where is she?"

"I don't know," I asserted. "She was there when I was arrested."

"Baka!" he spat, and walked away. I felt so relieved at the thought of some action that I almost cried.

Kobioshi had me brought to his office the next day. He let it be known that if I would tell the truth and answer all questions, I had nothing to worry about and would be released.

"I will do anything you say," I told him meekly. "If I can only get out of here. I've been here for three months and I can't stand any more."

I wanted to convey the impression that I had reached the breaking point (as they hoped) and would tell all.

The captain called in another officer who resembled a chimpanzee, and retired to an inner office. I knew that he would listen, as the partitions were only half-walls, and wondered what strange quirk in his oriental mind made him evade the task of questioning me. My new inquisitor produced about fifteen of my letters to Cabanatuan. Also he showed me a chart of names.

"Now, Miss High-Pockets," the ape-man began, and he spoke flawless English, "we know that you head this group. We also know that Spark Plug is

Amusatague and Fancy Pants is a man called German. We don't know who Papaya is? Who is he?"

"Papaya is not a man, but a woman. Her name is Marie."

"I'm glad that you decided to speak the truth," commented the ape-man, and exhibited a paper with Marie's correct name and old address on it. "Now," he continued, "tell me about Mutt."

"I met Ramon first at the Remedios Hospital," I narrated, giving the answer Sparkplug had told me to use, "and he is the one who sent Mutt to me. Ramon said that I was to trust Mutt with notes and money, but not ask him any questions."

"Okay, who is the woman, Looter?"

"I don't know much about her. I only saw her once and that is the only name I knew her by."

"Well, what does she look like, and where can we find her?"

"She's a tall, thin, very light Filipino girl who lives near Cabanatuan."

Looter was short, plump and very dark, but my answer seemed to satisfy the Jap, for he continued:

"Now, Miss High-Pockets, you will decode all these letters which bear your signature. The first one is to Everlasting. Who is he?"

"I don't know him by any other name."

We were now right back where we left off three months... or was it years... before. The Nip glared at me in disgust, then shouted to the guard outside the door. They exchanged a few words in their native lingo. Then the guard walked in, picked up a thick bamboo rod, and began beating me on the head, shoulders and back. I finally fell to the floor, and he stopped. I slowly pulled myself back to a sitting position on the chair, rubbing my bruises.

"That is only a sample of what you will get if you keep on lying to me," the chimpanzee warned. Then followed the same monotonously reiterated queries and the same replies that I knew nothing more about Everlasting. That was my story and I stuck to it through the three severe drubbings that followed.

At last the simian-like official said wearily, "Okay, we will come back to that later."

"Now who are Cal and John Demi?" he shouted suddenly, kicking me in the shins with his heavy army boots, "We know these are two of the men you were trying to sneak out of Cabanatuan. You can't deny it!"

"My God," I thought despairingly, "Do I have to go through all that again?"

Speaking slowly and keeping my voice level, I explained as convincingly as I could that Cal was the abbreviation of calamanci and that demijohn is a large bottle. "I was sending sweetened calamanci juice in to the camp in demijohns," I concluded.

"That same crazy story," the official screamed, "You lie! You lie!"

He slapped me in the face repeatedly with his open hand. The blows stung me into a quiet fury, and although tears came to my eyes, they did not fall. The noise brought several more Nips into the room. The inquisitor barked something at them in Japanese. Two of them went out, and came back with rope and a piece of hose. It looked like the dreaded water-cure was coming next.

"No! Not that!" I protested, "I'm telling you the truth. Look it up in your dictionary! Please, not that!"

My tormentors paid no attention to my plea, and lashed me tightly to a long bench in a prone position. The hose, connected with a water tap in the hall, was rammed into my mouth. Guards held my head so that I could not move it when the gush of water came. I held my breath. A Nip noticed this and hit me in the abdomen. I gulped the water down... drowning on dry land. My head began to spin... the room went round and round... then oblivion.

I returned to consciousness aware of a burning sensation in my legs. I opened my eyes slowly and gazed dully at the leering slant-eyes who were untying me. Then I noticed that they had removed all of my clothes except my panties and bra. My wet slacks were draped over a chair in front of an electric fan. I wondered if they had found my watch, which I had wadded in a remnant of my old house coat and carried in my bra, but a quick touch of my hand showed me that it was still safe.

The monkey-man noticed my glance at my badly burned thighs and then at my slacks.

"They will be dry when you go back to your cell, so no one will know what happened. You are not to tell anyone, or make any mention of the fact that we had to burn you with our cigars to bring you around."

They let me rest for a few moments, then the inquisitor suggested sneeringly, "Perhaps you feel like telling us the truth now about the two men, Cal and John Demi. Or would you prefer more water?"

"Bring on the water," I sobbed, "I have told the truth."

I was tied to the bench once more, and the water forced down my throat. I passed out more rapidly this time. I came to, lying on the floor, with one of the guards whipping me with a split bamboo rod. The investigator was turning the pages of a little book. He looked up, and spoke almost politely: "High-Pockets, I see here in the dictionary that you were right. Demijohn is a large bottle with a small neck. So sorry. You will be taken back to your cell when your clothing is dry." Then, glancing at his wrist watch, he commented, "It's six o'clock. I'm tired. I've had enough for one day."

"Brother," I thought dully, "That makes us even."

I had been taken from my cell at nine that morning and "dinner was served" at four p. m. My thought was of food, not my current misery. When I returned to my cell, thoughtful Sister Trinita had kept my food safe, and but for her kindness I would have gone without food until the following morning.

Frequently when prisoners were out of their cells for investigations at meal time, their cell-mates would eat the absentee's portion. They could scarcely be blamed for this apparent greed, for we were all starving, and the absent prisoner's return was quite uncertain. When we only numbered seven, we played fair. Now with twenty two women in one cell, the only rule was the survival of the fittest. I was therefore grateful for the nun's kindness, and after wolfing my food, I tried to smile at the others when they evinced curiosity as to the things that occurred during my "examination." I did not talk, and they soon gave up the attempt to quiz me.

After a week's respite, another investigator who resembled a bull-dog took me on. He was a Nipponese "Mr. Five by Five" with blood-shot eyes, an underslung jaw, and large, protruding buck teeth. This canine-faced individual apparently spoke no English and his alleged interpreter was not very helpful. As I sat and waited for the inquisitor to finish perusal of some papers, the interpreter busied himself with a pornographic Nip magazine, and insisted on showing me the pictures in it. When I tried to ignore him, he laughed, and attempted to force me to look by pinching my arm or leg.

Dog-face suddenly jabbered, and the interpreter began "Give me right name... River... Chap Bobu... Reft Fierd... Wopu... Ditto..."

"These men are American prisoners of war in Cabanatuan. I don't know their right names."

The inquisitor kicked me before I finished talking. I turned to the interpreter and asked why the man took this punitive action if he could not understand what I was saying. This was duly translated, and the answer came back, "He tink you rying anyway. He insist on men's right names."

I repeated that I did not know them. The interpreter seized one of my arms and tied it behind me to a chair. Then he produced several .25 caliber Jap rifle cartridges from his pocket, inserted them between my fingers, and asked the question again. As he talked, he squeezed my hand, and the agony was excruciating. I screamed again and again "I don't know! I'm telling you the truth!" The pressure and my wails increased in intensity, as the sharp points of the bullets bit into my flesh.

I finally fainted, and came to on the dirty floor. The two men picked me up and shoved me back into the chair. My hand had commenced to swell, so now they used the other dig it, replacing the cartridges with large pencils. The resulting agony was not quite so bad, and I remained conscious while this session went on for two hours. Then while the interpreter went out to lunch and bull-dog napped in his chair, I remained tied to mine.

When the interpreter came back, he disdainfully tossed me a native orange. I remained in my uncomfortable position for another hour while the inquisitor left for his noon-day refreshment; then returned and talked with the interpreter for several minutes. That so-and-so then explained that I could have many advantages if I would cooperate. The investigator would stretch the questioning over a long period during which time I could enjoy a nice, clean bed in his office, plus the same food Japanese officers received and as much as I wanted.

"I am cooperating all that I can," I replied, disdaining these privileges given to squealers. "I don't want a long drawn-out investigation for food or anything else. I just want to get out and be with my baby."

Both men thought this statement was very funny and laughed heartily.

"I see by this record from your first investigation," commented the bull-dog, speaking good English, "that your baby is missing. Now if we can't find her, how can you?"

I still fail to grasp the reason why he went through the farce of employing an interpreter. At the time I was both surprised and angered by all this unnecessary knavery, so I remained silent.

"Take this fool away," he ordered. "I'll send for her later when she decides to cooperate."

I attempted to conceal my swollen digits from my companions in misery, as we had a mutual understanding not to add to each other's woes. My hands pained me so much that I could not sleep, and tried to find relief by soaking them in the water from our tap. A guard noticed my nocturnal activities, and demanded to know why I was not sleeping. I showed him my hands, and he exclaimed "Taihen warui desu!" (Very bad!). He went away and returned shortly with salt and hot water in which I soaked my hands, getting some relief. This humane guard was only on duty for one hour, so I had to resort to the tap again before the pain finally diminished. In the morning my hands were discolored and too stiff to use; one of the women was obliged to hold my saucer of food up to my mouth.

The next day I heard some new prison gossip via the grape vine, to the effect that General Lim, a Filipino officer was being tortured daily. Another guerrilla leader, Colonel Baha, was spread-eagle and flogged unmercifully with a thick rubber hose wrapped with barbed wire, while his wife and four children were forced to watch his punishment. I witnessed this inhuman brutality twice and was happy when death came to the Colonel's rescue, thus baffling the Japs who had been unable to wring any information from him.

When my hands were almost normal again in size, although a weird yellowish-green in appearance, I was called for another examination. This time I had the entire menagerie... Chimpanzee, Bull-Dog, and two new burly guards.

As I entered the office, it came as somewhat of a shock to see Ramon seated at one end of the table. I was ordered to sit at the opposite end. The guards stood at the door, and the inquisitors sat at one side of the long table with stacks of books and papers between them.

"We have brought you two together so we can get your stories straight," the Bull-Dog began. "High-Pockets you say that you gave your first letter to

Mutt in July of 1943. Sparkplug says that he did not meet Mutt until August, 1943. Now which one of you is lying?"

"I could be wrong," I admitted. "I did not make any note of the exact date."

That seemed to satisfy them. They talked back and forth in Japanese for about half an hour, rustling through a number of papers.

"Ramon says here you also gave him money for Cabanatuan. Why didn't you mention this?" demanded Chimpanzee suddenly.

"It was so long ago, I had forgotten. Besides you didn't ask me."

That flippancy earned me a cuff alongside the head.

"I'll read one of your letters to you. Then you explain it to us," Bull-Dog stated.

As he read the missive, I felt like kicking my bruised and battered carcass, for it was an excellent example of how a person continually exposed to the bright face of danger, becomes careless.

"Dear Ditto: Thanks for telling me about yourself. You asked about me, so here goes, I'm an American gal, running a Jap night club, and all the money I send you comes from the Nips..."

The Chimpanzee suddenly exploded in action. Face contorted, and eyes blazing, as though he were a maniac, he kicked and beat me until Bull-Dog stopped him. Through it all he screamed, "You stole money out of good Japanese pockets and gave it to illiterate American barbarians. I should kill you! KILL YOU!" By now I was cut and bleeding in so many places that my sole wish was to die and get it over with.

When the Chimpanzee had stopped gibbering, Bull-Dog continued, "The Babes in the Woods say that things will start popping right after the rainy season. Now decode that!"

"I have relatives in the country. They will shoot fire-crackers on the Fourth of July."

This was a silly answer; the first thing that popped into my head. They accepted replies like this, but the truth, never! It really meant that the guerrillas had stated the American invasion would begin in September when the rain stopped.

Bull-Dog: "Well, who is your relation in the country? If you are an American, so is he. Who is he?"

I knew that a beating, or worse was in store for me if I did not give a satisfactory answer. I wracked my numbed brain to think of someone who was dead... or safe. Nothing came to me. While I hesitated, Bull-Dog ordered that Ramon be taken back to his dungeon.

"Who is he?" It was now a shout, repeated again and again.

I could not trust myself to speak for fear that I might say the wrong thing. A guard tied one of my hands behind me, and Chimpanzee seized the other. I suddenly jumped from the agonizing pain of something sharp being driven under a fingernail. I saw the guard swing a hammer, and then knew that each time Bull-Dog reiterated his query, a nail was being driven farther into my finger.

I had a sudden inspiration. Eddie Hart! In Boone's last letter he had told me of an American so named, who had fled from Cavite to hide in the hills, only to be unmercifully tortured and killed by the Japs.

"Stop!" I shrieked, "I'll tell you! It's Eddie Hart!"

"That's better. Now tell us all about him," this, from Bull-Dog.

"He has been here on the Islands for many years. He ran the Dreamland Cabaret at Cavite. He has been living in the hills of Bataan since Manila was evacuated. Now and then a Filipino friend of his brought me a note from him, and I sent him things from town."

"I give up, High-Pockets," Bull-Dog announced disgustingly. "You tell the truth for a little while and then you lie like all Americans."

"Yes, we might as well stop," Chimpanzee agreed.

During the next three days, I languished in my cell, hoping to see Ramon again. The old dungeons, black, damp and foul, dated back to the old Spanish days, and it was horrible to think of him down there. Every night, I vainly asked the benjo boys for news of my comrade, and on the fourth evening learned that he was back in his cell. Next morning. I watched to see him taken out for a shower, but he did not appear. The benjo boy told me that night, "Ramon tortured very bad in dungeon. He paralyzed in one leg. No can walk."

I shared this news with the other women and they all offered to pray for Ramon. Under Sister Trinita's guidance, we took turns, day and night, keeping a continuous prayer going.

When September arrived, the food became scantier and filthier; and the death roll was increasing. No women had succumbed as yet, but in the night we frequently called to each other to make sure that all were alive. We set hourly watches, day and night, to pray and bolster up our weakest sisters.

We were plagued by diarrhea, and my condition became so bad that I begged the guards to let me see a doctor. Finally the prison doctor did examine me and said that he would send medicine the next day. His "prescription" came in the form of a notice tacked by a guard on the cell door. When I asked the Nip for an explanation, he informed me, "Doctor say no chow go in, no — come out. So no eat untir stop!"

My hunger became so unendurable that I begged the other women to give me some of their food. Most of them were afraid to let me even have a swallow, for fear that they too, would be deprived. The two nuns and Carmen gave me little tastes from their saucers. On the fourth day of this "cure" I could no longer keep the kneeling position and asked the guard's permission to lie down. The women would not stand for that surrender.

"Do you want to die?" Sister Trinita whispered harshly, as she slapped me, "Every time a man lies down in the day time, that's his finish. You know that. Now sit up and take your turn at prayer." I sat up.

At two in the morning, I was awakened by a guard kicking me in the ribs none too gently. He grabbed my hair, jerked me to my unsteady feet, and took me to the office where my last quartette of torturers awaited me.

"Are you still going to continue telling us lies?" the Bull-Dog bellowed.

"I tell you the truth, but you won't believe me."

"Well, sometimes when a person is awakened from a sound sleep, we hear the truth," the Chimpanzee offered, "So we will try you again, and this is your last chance."

There was substance to his statement about clarity of thought when awakened from a sound sleep in that inferno. Between the time that the "tenko" bell rang at night, and its companion ring in the morning, I was usually so exhausted from the cramped position of the day, that I slept as though under the influence of a drug. I knew that I must think straight and kept repeating this caution to myself.

The Japs let me remain standing. I was so weak that I kept shifting from one foot to another, and finally one of the inquisitors motioned for me to sit on the filthy floor. I was grateful for this opportunity to lean against the wall and rest my aching back. The Nips sorted over many papers, and talked between themselves for a long time before they deigned to take further notice of me.

"We have proof and your word that you were sending things to the American prisoners," Bull-Dog stated quickly, "and we also know that you had contacts with the guerrillas in the hills. That is what we want cleared up now."

"I have been approached for money to help the guerrillas, it is true, but I did not help them," I informed, thinking that they may have been referring to the time when the Nips sent a Filipino boy to my club with a spurious note from "Captain Bagley."

These words had been barely uttered when one of the investigators picked up a piece of board and rained blows on my back, arms, and the side of my head. They stunned me, but did not completely knock me out. He was screaming words that seemed meaningless while this was taking place, and my dulled consciousness finally grasped their import "... so you see the men at Cabanatuan told me that you had been getting information from the guerrillas and passing it on to them. What do you say to that?"

I assumed that the Nips had intercepted some of our news sheets prepared by German for distribution to the prisoners of war. I felt certain that none of the grateful men in Cabanatuan would betray us. With this comforting thought in mind, I vehemently denied that I had sent the news sheets or knew anything about them.

My nose was bleeding freely and blood was oozing from a cut on my head. As I contradicted this last charge, Chimpanzee slapped me in the face and blood covered his hand. He wiped his digit on the wall, picked up some old paper to remove the rest of the gore, and then tossed me some dirty old paper to remove the blood from my face.

"Why do you persist in denying contacts with the guerrillas when several officers in Cabanatuan signed a paper stating: that you had sent them all the guerrilla news?" Bull-Dog persevered.

I was almost certain that no officer of the United States Army would sink so low, and that this was a palpable lie. I clung to my story that I knew nothing about guerrilla activities or news, despite further beatings.

"High-Pockets, you are impossible. How can you deny this charge when we have the proof?" Chimpanzee finally snorted, "Well, there is nothing else left to do but go ahead with your execution."

He looked at his colleague, who nodded his agreement. A guard was called in from outside, and a few sharp orders given. The man left the room, returning with what looked like a soiled tea towel, with which he blindfolded me. Then someone took me by the arm and led me as I stumbled out of the room, along what seemed like a long corridor, and then down many uneven stone steps.

A musty, damp smell assailed my nostrils, and I could feel a cool breeze blowing in from the Pasig River. I guessed that I was being taken into the dungeons, and many tales of nameless horrors perpetrated in this terrestrial sub-section of hades passed through my mind in rapid succession. I knew of the unspeakably mutilated bodies found floating in the river, which were said to have been cast out from these ancient dungeons.

I stopped listening to the Nips who kept telling me of this last chance to save myself and began talking to God. "Yea, though I walk through the valley of the shadow of death, I will fear no evil for Thou art with me..." I told Him that He knew best. I was finally roughly pushed to my knees, and heard some vague comment about dying for my country.

"Bow your head," and I recognized the Bull-Dog's growl.

"We don't like to do this, but you must die unless you speak the truth. You have two minutes to decide."

"Two minutes to pray," I thought, and asked Our Lord to give me courage, watch over my loved ones, and grant success to the arms of the United States. I felt the cold, sharp steel of a beheading sword laid tentatively against my neck and then lifted.

"This is it," I thought... and then mercifully blacked out.

When I regained my senses, I was painfully aware that I was still on this earth, for I was being dragged by the heels over a rough portion of it. I struggled to regain my footing; the guard released his hold, and permitted me to do so. I realized that it was dawn and we seemed to be near my cell. Once there, I slumped to the floor and wanted nothing better than to sleep, as I was exhausted. A young Filipino girl next to me was moaning and rolling from side to side, and I smelled the nauseating odor of burned flesh. Sleep was out of the question, so I arose, took a wet rag and bathed her head. She was doubled up in agony, and I could not get her body straightened out. The other women petulantly told me to leave the girl alone and let them sleep, but I ignored their protests as she was in great misery. I persisted in finding out the cause of it, and she finally told me.

She had been one of General Lim's carriers, and had been caught while attempting to smuggle money and letters to him in his covert in the hills. This heroine, would not betray the general, even though he, too, was a victim in this hell-hole.

This slim, seventeen year old girl had been taken out for investigation a few minutes after I had been summoned. When she told her examiners that she was unaware of the contents of the letters found on her person, and refused to make any statements incriminating the general, the Nips tortured her in a ghastly manner which shamed the contemporaries in the Gestapo.

Several wet sacks were laid on the floor, after which the Japs removed most of the girl's clothing, and compelled her to lie on them. Then a long rod with an electric cord attached, was rammed into her vitals and the current turned on. When she screamed in agony, the juice was switched off, while her tormentors asked questions about General Lim. When she did not respond to their satisfaction, the ordeal continued.

The spirits of the old Dons said to haunt those dungeons must have wrung their ghostly hands in glee that night, for that brave girl suffered the tortures of the damned and did not squeal. I was glad to miss my much-needed sleep to help such a deserving patriot.

The next morning my cell-mates wanted to know what had happened, but I would not talk. I was still unable to determine whether I had called the Nip's bluff, or whether they had relented at the last moment. I shuddered at the thought that I might face the same hideous torture as that meted out to the Filipino girl.

At noon on September twenty second, we were returning from our shower when an intensified humming came from overhead. American planes? The guards acted as though our hopes were well-fulfilled for they herded us back to our cells, and placed double locks on the doors. One of the women managed to lag behind to find out what was literally in the air.

"What did you see?" was our universal query.

"Planes! About five hundred or more, I guess," she reported. "They are so very high that they look like specks."

The humming became louder; then came the angry buzz of diving planes and the devastating detonations of bursting bombs. Excited guards ran through the corridors shouting for us to lie flat on our stomachs. I cautioned the other women to hold their mouths open and keep their fingers in their ears. The floor quivered incessantly and it seemed as if the walls would cave in at any moment. The bombardment lasted for an hour, and despite the potential danger to our persons, we were elated to know that the Japs were beginning to feel the effects of American retribution. Our exultation soon vanished for we were not given any food that night. The next day we were informed that as "punishment" for helping those bad Americans, we would be fed only once a day.

Captain Kobioshi came and told me that the Nips had captured Papaya. She would be with us at nightfall, but he warned me not to talk with her. He took me to his office where I was forced to repeat all that I had told the other investigators. Everything was duly written down; then I signed the document and placed my right thumb print on it, as instructed.

"The case is closed," Kobioshi stated as I left. "You will not be called again until your case comes up for court martial."

Marie was brought into our cell about seven that evening, and she told us plenty in hushed tones. "The Americans have landed in Leyte. A large American task force is headed for northern Luzon," and much more encouraging news. I enjoyed a good laugh at the stupidity of the military police. It seems that some of them had peremptorily ordered Marie to move out of her house by sundown, so she hastily gathered her belongings and moved next door. The kenpei failed to notify their associates, and Marie, unaware that she was the object of an intensive search, calmly lived in her new abode, until accidentally apprehended.

The next day American aircraft dropped more lethal eggs, and from then on bombings became a routine performance.

About a week after my last talk with Kobioshi, I was ordered to bring along my scanty belongings and follow the guard. I found Marie and Ramon in the office. Their money and jewelry was returned to them from the safe, and we exchanged glances, believing that this might indicate we were to be released. We were soon disillusioned for we were handcuffed and thrust into the back of an officer's car. Ramon could not walk and we virtually had to carry him between us. Due to his inability to shave, he had grown a crop of long red whiskers.

The Japs, evidently curious to see what damage had been wrought by the bombings, drove out of their way down Dewey Boulevard. All the beautiful trees which once lined that formerly magnificent driveway were now gone. I saw that the former American High Commissioner's residence had been hit; one wing was completely destroyed, and the rest of the structure badly damaged. I noted joyfully that most of the piers were smashed and the Bay was filled with the broken hulks of Jap vessels.

We entered the familiar gates of Fort McKinley and were driven to the old Post Exchange. There our shackles were removed and we were handcuffed separately. Without delay we were led into a large room dominated by a platform on which there stood a long table. A colored lithograph of Hirohito, draped with a Japanese flag, looked down on three grim-looking officers seated at the table. I assumed that they were our judges.

A captain designated to act as interpreter, took his place beside us. He called Ramon first, instructing him to bow low and approach the judges. Ramon did this with some difficulty, and then the charges against him were read in English. Ramon was shaking from weakness and pain, and toward the end I doubt if he knew what was being read. When asked if he was guilty, he replied "Yes" in a barely audible voice, then collapsed in a chair.

Marie came next. She bowed, and stood to hear her charges read. When asked to state whether or not she pleaded guilty, she hesitated. The interpreter shouted that she must show respect to the court. "Yes, guilty," she admitted reluctantly.

I, in turn, went through the same farce.

We were then taken out into the hall. I found a seat for Ramon, and covered his shaking knees with a towel I had brought along. The poor soul was burning up with fever, and his days were obviously numbered. I tried to bring back some of his old spirit.

"Don't let them get you down," I comforted. "The American invasion has started. We are going to win. All of this will soon be just a bad nightmare. Think of Lerry and the boys. You can't let them down."

"I'm trying, High-Pockets, but I get weaker every day. You're just a skeleton yourself," he answered feebly, then dozed off in the chair.

After about a two hour wait, a guard came from the court room and ordered us in a can I asked him about the verdict, and he drew his hand across his throat, saying curtly, "You patay!"

I knew the ominous meaning of that Tagalog word... die.

"Where are we going now?" I queried as we drove off.

"Biribid! You patay!"

Bilibid, despite its grim name, held no terrors for me, because I figured that death would bring a speedy end to my seemingly endless ordeal of starvation, torture and illness.

Marie began to sob, but Ramon, when I took his warm hand and pressed it reassuringly, did not respond. He, too, like me, felt that we were the living dead.

CHAPTER XIX

Number 920 Awaits Her Doom

WHEN WE ARRIVED AT THE MASSIVE, GRIM PILE that is called Bilibid, Ramon was unable to get out of the car. A trusty was called to assist him into the prison office. The Nip officials curtly informed us that we had lost our names, and henceforth would be known by number only. Ramon was assigned Number 919, I was given Number 920, and Marie, Number 921.

Our registration completed, a guard was summoned to take Marie and me to the women's cell. He carried two olive-drab bags about the size of a pillow slip, with draw-strings at the top. We walked from the office into a beautiful patio replete with flower beds and a fountain, before entering our cell block. Several Japs followed us out of the office, and we wondered why we had such an unusual escort.

We soon found out. We were taken into the shower room; ordered to strip, shower and don the uniforms that were in the o. d. bags. They were actually men's grey pajamas with "Medical Corps, U.S.A." stamped on the backs.

As we waited for the men to leave, one of them snapped, "Sugu!! Hurry!! We do not have arr day!"

Marie and I both hesitated, despite his remark.

"I give you one minute... then we tear your crothes off!" the head guard bellowed.

Then I grasped the reason why we had such an interested circle of spectators. It was clear that the head guard meant what he said, as his satellites closed in on us, gaping and leering. Marie burst into tears, but I was too angry to cry.

"Come on, make it snappy," I advised. "We may as well get it over with."

I still had my watch inside my bra and wondered how I could keep it hidden from our argus-eyed audience. I turned my back for a second, and this sufficed to get the watch out and rolled into a corner of the rag I used for a handkerchief.

Once stripped, we rushed into the shower, and emerging, scrambled into the over-sized pajamas. The sleeves of the coat were so long that they concealed my hands, one of which still clutched the watch in the rag. We were compelled to leave our shoes in the shower room, and were taken down the corridor bare-footed.

Marie and I were locked in a cell, next to one where I saw Ramon half lying, his red beard straggling across his chest.

Our cell was about five by eight feet square, with a benjo hole and water tap such as we had at Fort Santiago. An open barred wall in front and a large window at the rear covered with heavy screening, promised protection against the mosquitoes. We found no lice or bedbugs, and this was a relief.

The food ration arrived twice daily, at first in American army mess kits, and later in coconut shells. It consisted of either a rice ball garnished with a few pieces of seaweed, or a dried fish the size of my little finger. As time passed we realized that we should have appreciated the "minnow" for the fare soon dwindled to one rice ball a day, either with or without a cup of weak tea. We had been warned not to drink from the tap as the water was contaminated, but we ignored that caution on days when the Nips did not give us tea.

Morning and night we stood "tenko"... our numbers were called and we answered "Hai!" from our cells. I listened intently each time at roll call for Ramon's weak response. On the fourth day, Number 919 did not answer, and a few minutes later we were commanded to face the rear of our cells. This order indicated that a prisoner was either being brought in, or a corpse carried out. I bent down and peered under my arm. I managed to get a fleeting glimpse of a stretcher carried by two Filipino prisoners, and thought that I saw a patch of red beard.

The wall facing Ramon's cell had a crack in it. I had found a sliver of lead from a pencil in a crevice in the floor. I hastily scrawled a note on a piece of benjo paper "If Ramon A. Number 919 is gone, knock once," and pushed it through the crevice into the next cell. The answer came back promptly... one knock. When the mess boy came, I managed to make him understand my query "Is the Spaniard with the red beard dead?"

"Hai!" he retorted, indifferently.

My first thought was to send word out to Lerry, but as all the work at Bilibid was done by Japs, I knew that I did not have the faintest chance of communicating with the outside world.

Marie and I were alone for two dreary weeks. Then three Filipino women were brought in... two young sisters and a middle-aged woman. They had been caught carrying money and supplies from Manila to two guerrilla chiefs... General Lim and Colonel Straughn. They told me that General Lim had been sentenced to death, and was now also in Bilibid, awaiting execution.

The third week, Florence Smith, an attractive young American mestiza was placed in our cell. Florence and I became good friends immediately. While the others cried and complained, Florence and I exchanged recipes, and we let our imagination flow freely. One of our favorites was "Waffles a la Bilibid" which called for wheat flour, eggs, cream, cheese, butter and bacon. When our rice ball arrived we would pretend that it was one of our delicious concoctions.

The guards now subjected us to a new and exasperating annoyance. Our food arrived smoking hot, but our tormentors made us sit and look at it until it was cold. Then they would shout "Jaimaru!" a corruption of the Nip word "Hajimaru!" which means "Begin!" If a prisoner ventured to start before the signal, the food was snatched away. Now and then the tea was hot, and that helped, although it was little more than yellow water.

Florence and I often joked with the Jap mess boys (also prisoners) and now and then wrangled extra tea. If a prisoner died early in the day, his name was not scratched from the mess list, and his portion came to our cell block. We prevailed upon the mess boys to give it to us, and we divided it equally. I found myself wishing that if someone had to die, that they would conveniently select the morning hours.

After the first month about one to four deaths occurred daily among the approximately two hundred men in our cell block. The men were fed on the same basis as the women, but they were beaten more frequently. I received only one drubbing, and that was when I was caught talking to Florence. The same "No talking" rule effective at Fort Santiago, was also enforced here.

We dreaded the days when numbers were called out for transfers or executions. The guards shouted from the far end of the corridor, their English was poor, and we could not hear them plainly. There were times when I would catch "Nine two ..." and not be able to distinguish the last number. Again I would not hear the first number but a shouted "Twenty!" I had no recourse but to wait and find out, my heart beating in my throat.

Our kneeling time here was four hours longer than at Fort Santiago; from five in the morning until nine at night. We were so exhausted at the end of this daily ordeal, that once it was over, we fell back and were asleep almost instantly.

About one hundred Japanese prisoners, doing from one to five year stretches for violation of their army regulations, were treated as cruelly as we were, but their food was better. We envied their fare of steaming hot rice and vegetable soup, brought to them thrice daily. Now and then they received fruit or fish.

The bombings increased in violence and intensity, and I was buoyed up at the thought that the Nips were now on the receiving end. On days when there were no bombings, all prisoners were taken out daily for fifteen minutes of setting-up exercises. After lining up in front of our cells and being counted off, we were marched to the courtyard where a Jap sergeant put us through a strenuous drill, making us count aloud.

"Ichi... ni... san... shi... go... roku..." it became monotonous after a while. I was caught lagging in my exercises, and the sergeant let me know that they were intended for my bodily well-being. I rashly commented that if we were fed more, we would have the strength to perform the exercises properly. This unsolicited criticism earned me a hard slap and thirty minutes of extra exercise... solo.

While out in the courtyard we could hear the American prisoners on the other side of the wall as they counted off. Now and then I would catch a glimpse of some of them in the tower, and idly wondered if they could tell that I was one of their breed.

On November twenty second, after six weeks in Bilibid, I thought that I heard a guard call "9 2 0." He repeated the number distinctly, but even then I hesitated a second before I made the required response. Florence gripped my arm.

"It's your number, kid," she whispered, and helped me up.

"Hai!" I managed to answer as a guard came up, opened the cell and led me out of the cell block.

"You have court martiar in dat buirding," he remarked, as we approached one of the buildings. "When you go in, stand before honabre judges tabre and bow very row. Judges be five high men sent by Emperor review most important cases. They show you big honor."

"What happens then?" I inquired.

"I your interpreter," the Nip advised me. "I ret you know."

I pulled myself together and tried to walk steadily, although my weak legs almost refused to support me. We entered the room; I bowed as directed, and waited.

The five judges regarded me solemnly for what seemed a long time. Then one of the judges spoke up and the interpreter told me "They ask you have anything to say your defense. Dis your rast chance. Speak up."

I remained silent for a moment.

"Speak up!" the interpreter shouted, slapping my face. "Will you please tell the judges," I pleaded, "that I was only sending medicine and food to men who were less fortunate than I. I would have done this regardless of their nationality." One of the quintet commented on this, and I soon learned that he had inquired whether I would have done the same for Japanese prisoners.

"I have befriended many Japanese, and have made many Japanese friends during this war," was my answer.

When this was translated, one of the judges frowned and spoke sharply to the interpreter, who, suddenly struck me on the jaw with his doubled fist. I reeled against the table and spat out blood and half a tooth.

"Honorabre judge say," my erstwhile assailant elucidated, "you onry pretend be friends with Japanese so you carry on your cowardry work. Now answer 'guirty or not guirty'." Common sense dictated that any appeal to them would be useless, so I raised my voice and answered "Guilty."

En route to my cell, I asked "When will I know my sentence?" and was told that night or early the next morning.

Marie was taken out next and came back quickly. Then as though designed to give us courage, there came a terrific American bombing which lasted about three hours. We all lay on the floor as explosions rocked our cellblock like an earthquake. We could hear shrapnel from Jap anti-aircraft guns on the university buildings a block away, falling into the yard outside, and wondered when some of the pellets would come through the roof. There was no food that night.

The next morning a guard awakened Marie and me before daylight. He was carrying the two o. d. bags in which Marie and I had placed our clothes when we entered. He ordered us to change. Then we were led out of the cell, roped together, and thrust into the back of a car with the command "Keep your heads down." My interpreter-guard of the day before, rode beside us. I tried to look up to see where we were going and received a rap on the top of my head with a pistol butt.

When the smooth city streets changed to bumpy country roads, I thought that they were taking us to the old Chinese cemetery. I knew that most of the executions still took place there. I am not ashamed to state that I prayed hard, while my entire life seemed to pass through my mind in rapid review from childhood recollections to the present moment. I thought of past mistakes and how I would have rectified them if I were given another chance. My thoughts jumped to my family in the States. Then my beloved Phil... I would be with him soon ... I hoped, in a place where there was no more hunger, torture or disease. I idly wondered if some generous soul would provide for Dian's welfare. My bewildered mind searched for some comfort and once again the words were with me..."Yea, though I walk through the valley of the shadow of death, I will fear no evil for Thou art with me..." As I prayed, a profound feeling of peace and quiet descended upon me.

As the first tinges of a ruddy dawn gilded the horizon, the car slowed down and stopped. I heard the sound of heavy gates being opened. "You can rook up now," the guard barked.

As I did, a large sign over a gate met my eyes... WOMEN'S CORRECTIONAL INSTITUTION. I knew this to be an insular penitentiary, and it suddenly dawned on me that maybe we were not to be shot after all.

We drove through the portals and along a curving driveway to the entrance of a large, circular building. In response to the guard's imperative ring, a Filipino woman guard unlocked the gate and admitted us. The Nip ordered Marie and me to stand against the wall of the guards' alcove near the entrance. Then unrolling a long document, he read the court's finding:

"Because of the mercy of His Imperial Highness, the emperor of Japan, your sentence has been commuted to twelve years confinement at hard labor. If you try to escape, your time will be doubled and you will be taken to Japan to finish your sentence. If at any time you wish to retract your lies, send for a Japanese official. In such event, you may have a new trial, and if the court sees fit, you may be released or pardoned. You are to have no outside contacts. No mail. No visitors. No food sent in to you."

When he had finished reading this dictum, the guard-interpreter rolled up the scroll, and, with one last severe look at us, walked briskly across the hall and into an office marked "MRS. GARCIA, SUPERINTENDENT." After a few moments he reappeared, passed us without a glance, and left the building.

The Filipino guard locked and bolted the gate behind the Nip. As I heard the car drive off, I dropped to the floor and cried... my head on my knees... but my emotions were those of relief and gratitude.

While I sobbed quietly, I did not forget to thank Our Lord for His help and protection.

CHAPTER XX

"Yes, I'm Real, Sister!"

THE WOMAN GUARD TOLD US IN A NOT UNKINDLY MANNER, to step up to her desk and fill in three cards each, all of which read:

Name:
Age:
Father's full name:
Mother's full name:
Nationality:
Have you ever been in prison before?
Have you ever been arrested before?
Sign your full name:
Sign your full name:
Sign your full name:

I followed her instructions, and after writing "Dorothy Claire Fuentes" nine times, inquired as to the reason for the seemingly aimless repetition.

"So we will be sure that it's not a forgery," the woman informed.

A trusty was called. She took us into the next room, searched us, found the watch, and demanded that I turn it over to be placed in the safe. I had not kept this time-piece safe from the Japs all this time in order to consign it to the dubious safekeeping of a half-witted trusty. It was my sole link with my happy pre-war existence, and I did not intend to relinquish it without an argument. I insisted on seeing the superintendent.

Marie and I were conducted to Mrs. Garcia's office. That lady, a thin, neatly-dressed Filipino woman of about forty, was sitting very erect and dignified, behind her large desk as we entered. She did not raise her stern, pale face from some papers she was studying intently. Purposely so, I thought, to impress and belittle us. As we stood waiting patiently, Mrs. Garcia dipped her pen and began writing. I knew that all this assumed preoccupation was merely a pose, as I had trod the boards long enough to recognize a bit of ham acting. At last, our newest jailer, raised her head and imperiously dismissed the trusty.

"What are you charged with?" she demanded in a firm, low voice.

"Must you treat us like criminals, Mrs. Garcia!" I entreated, "We are here because we helped suffering fellow beings... American and Filipino prisoners."

Her impassive face did not change expression as she stated:

"Now get this, as I shall only say it once. I am sorry that you are here, but I'm compelled by the Japanese to treat you military prisoners exactly as they say. You will be treated the same as the rest of the other prisoners. You will receive no special privileges, so don't ask for any."

"Oh, senora, please! You don't seem to realize what we've been through," Marie pleaded. "We are almost starved. Can't you at least contact our friends for us and get us some decent food?"

"You heard what the Japanese official said," was the woman's cold reply, "No outside contacts. I must abide by that rule. Don't try to talk any of the insular prisoners into attempting to get you food. If I find out, both they and you will be punished."

The superintendent then took my watch, remarking that it would remain in her safe until I was released, and then terminated the interview. Our clothing... in my case, the tattered old slacks and shirt... was checked. I went bare-foot, and discarded my shoes, the soles of which had been tied on for many moons with strips torn from my old housecoat. We were issued uniforms; faded sacks of once-blue denim, with holes cut for the head and arms. The "uniforms" bore a big "M.P."

The trusty then took us to the "Military Brigade" as our dormitory was called, and introduced us as Dot and Marie to our eight other room-mates. We were allowed to talk freely and I soon learned their case histories:

Two French Canadian nuns, aged sixty and sixty-five years. Sentenced to fifteen years for spreading propaganda.

A pretty American girl named Margie. Two years for escaping from Santo Tomas, with only one more month to serve. Even after witnessing the execution of three men for this offense, this plucky girl had still gone over the wall.

American woman, about forty, doing six months for failure to report to Santo Tomas because of serious illness. Her time was up in another three weeks.

Three Filipino girls... propaganda... five to ten years.

French mestiza... propaganda... ten years. She had spent a year here and at the psychopathic hospital across the road, and was still slightly balmy.

I soon learned from my new companions in misery, that we had the run of the circular, one-story building, and its inner, open courtyard during the day.

There were three other brigades, similar to ours, for the insular prisoners... about one hundred and fifty women, ranging from fifteen to fifty, and serving time for offenses ranging from petty theft to murder. They were all walking skeletons, so thin that one could count all their bones.

I noticed that we had beds here... and what beds!... two wide planks nailed across the low saw-horses. I was issued a dingy, white spread, a grass-stuffed pillow, and a mosquito net which showed unmistakable evidence that it was inhabited by bed-bugs. My first act was to take all my alleged bedding into the sun, and scrub it with hot water wangled from a kitchen trusty. It was obvious that the insect pests from which I had been almost free at Bilibid due to the weekly cell disinfection there, were now back with me in full force.

We were each issued one eating utensil; a spoon, which we carried back and forth to the mess hall. To each two of us went a shovel, intended for use in the cultivation of a vegetable garden in the courtyard.

Florence Smith and one of the Filipino girls from Bilibid soon joined our brigade, each with a sentence of five years for propaganda. Here, comparatively safe from further "questioning" by the Japs, Florence confided to me that she, too, had loved and lost an American husband. He had been a flyer, shot down over Bataan, in the early part of 1942. This common bond of affliction welded us together into a close friendship. We worked as digging partners and, under Mrs. Garcia's watchful scrutiny, spent six hours a day battling with the stones and weeds in the courtyard. All of us labored thus, except Marie who had a system. Selecting the huskiest Filipino girl for her partner, she acted as supervisor while the girl dug.

At first we received three tablespoonfuls of boiled, dried corn for breakfast. Lunch consisted of thin, soupy rice and half a tin of boiled weeds, and then at five p. m. a cup of thin, boiled rice was doled out to us. This "luxurious" daily menu came to an end after the first three weeks. Then we were cut down to thin rice gruel for breakfast; a half portion of rice and dried, boiled cassava roots at noon; and boiled weeds with thin rice soup for dinner. As the institution's rice supply diminished, the cooks added more cassava roots, and then peelings which caused a skin rash.

When another month had passed, and the supper weeds became scarce, some of the trusties were allowed outside to chop down small banana trees. The heavy outer bark was discarded, but the inner trunk was grated, and boiled for us. It looked good ... like coleslaw... but did not taste like it, nor did it contain any nourishment. It was merely something to fill our stomachs and momentarily quiet that constant inner clamor for sustenance.

Mrs. Garcia continually insisted that we must make a showing with our "gardens" for the benefit of the Japanese officers who came each week for an inspection. Few of the moldy spinach seeds we were finally given to plant over sprouted, and these scrawny growths were invariably stolen and eaten raw by some hungry prisoner.

The mess hall where all of the prisoners were fed was about forty feet square, and furnished with three long tables and benches, with a serving table at one end. The military prisoners had a table to themselves. So we had plenty of elbow room, and that's all we did have plenty of in that room. The other prisoners were very crowded at their tables. A few of the more fortunate prisoners ate from tin plates, but Florence and I used coconut shells which we had hollowed out, and then given a high polish with wood ashes.

At the sound of a gong we all took our places, but remained standing with bowed heads. Then the oldest prisoner... doing life for the murder of her husband... asked the blessing. As the elderly murderess mumbled a prayer in a sing-song Tagalog dialect, the woman next to her... an incurable kleptomaniac ... would dart little glances around the table until she thought that she was unobserved. Then she would quickly grab for some food on another woman's plate. The grace-sayer, without missing a word, would reach over, slap the clutching hand away from its prize then take a deep breath and continue in a louder tone. Florence and I never tired of watching this little comedy, and placed many bets on whether the thief would ever get the grass ring. She never did.

I managed to weigh myself on the kitchen scales and found that I was down to an even hundred pounds; my normal weight being forty five pounds more. Marie and I frequently discussed ways and means of getting food, and she finally persuaded a guard to take a message to her mother and sister in Manila. They soon appeared, accompanied by a Nip guard from Fort Santiago, and my former apartment house manager, Senorita Del Rosario. Somehow... somewhere... along the line, someone had been bribed for they showered Marie with bags of food, soap and toilet articles.

"My dear Mrs. Phillips! What are you doing here?" Senorita Del Rosario gasped, when she recognized me.

"Please don't use that name," I whispered quickly, "I'm Dorothy Fuentes here. They arrested me for trying to help my husband before he died, as well as other prisoners in Cabanatuan."

"You poor child," gushed my former acquaintance. "I shall help you get out at once. I can do it. I will demand that they let you out. I'm assisting at Fort Santiago in an official capacity, and have a bit of influence. After all, I was presented to the Empress, you know, and my Japanese friends will do whatever I ask them within reason." Then lowering her voice she confided, "Is there anyone with money I can go to on your behalf. It will take plenty of money to influence some of the higher officers... but I can do it," and she favored me with a condescending smile.

"I'm sorry, but there is no money anywhere in my scheme of things, so just forget the idea."

"Well, think it over my dear, and now that I know you are here I will not forget you at Christmas time."

So that was her game... money. Marie told me that Del Rosario and another woman exercised considerable influence over Colonel Nagahama at Fort Santiago; the other woman allegedly being his mistress. Although I never saw or heard of Del Rosario again, I was not fearful that she would cause me further trouble as in the pre-war days Phil had been very kind to her. She had little money then, and he frequently bought food for her at lowered prices through the army commissary.

Marie's sudden affluence made her act very cool to me. She had convinced a number of the other prisoners that she was going to do great things for them in the future, and they fawned on her. She now grudgingly offered me a few spoonfuls of the food brought in to her. A few days later, when I asked her for a bit of the toothpaste which she had offered freely to all of us, she commented acidly, "Just this once. It must last me for a long time." I never asked her for anything again, although after that first visit of her family, food came regularly and she stored it under her bed.

Hunger does strange and horrible things to people, and one becomes obsessed by the very thought of food. One night when the strain had become almost unendurable, I called Marie outside.

"I don't want any of your food," I said bluntly, "but please tell me how you manage to have it smuggled in so that I can get some. If I can get a note to Fely or Pressa, I feel sure they will bring me some food."

"I can not tell you my contact, but I will send a note out if you write it," she promised.

This I did at once, telling Fely that I was starving.

I did not want to sink low enough to steal food, but some of the insular prisoners had no such qualms, and when caught in the act, they were placed in solitary confinement in a pigeon-coop screened in front and just high enough to stand erect, inside. One night a young Filipino girl, so punished, broke the screen and got out. She caught the assistant superintendent's cat, skinned it, and ate it raw. Next morning, she was caught trying to dispose of the feline's hide in the latrine.

There was another cat on the premises, and I began to look at it longingly. I did not drool, but did start to figure on ways and means of snaring and cooking a feline delicacy. After eating the meat of carabao, snakes and monkeys, plus the indescribable garbage ladled out to me by the Japs, I was ready to devour anything that would sustain life. Because my plight was as desperate as that of the Filipino girl, I went to see our grim superintendent to intercede for the culprit.

"Mrs. Garcia," I entreated, "Why do you punish a prisoner so severely for stealing food? Can't you see we are starving?"

"That's none of your business," the woman snapped, "I must keep discipline. There is not enough food, if you must know. We have barely enough in the store-room to last a month, even with the small rations you are getting. The Bureau of Prisons told me to expect no more from them. The Japanese admit that they have not even enough for their army, and from now on we must shift for ourselves."

"Then why won't you permit food to be sent to us? I can give you the names of many people who will be glad to help me, and whatever they send can be divided."

"The Japanese say no food for military prisoners without a permit. If your friends can not get a permit that is not my fault. As a matter of fact your friend Fely Corcuera has been here, but I had to turn her away because she had no permit. Incidentally, how did she know that you are here? Did you send a note out to her?"

"Did Fely have food for me?" I asked, ignoring her pointed questions momentarily.

"Yes, she did, but she had no permit."

"Permit! Permit! Permit!" I screamed, flying into a rage, "Is that all you can think of while we grow thinner and weaker every day? I will not tell you if I sent Fely a note. Find out for yourself!" and I ran back to my brigade.

That afternoon the assistant superintendent called me and asked, "Do you know a girl named Pressa?"

"Yes! Where is she?"

"She is at the gate, but I can not let her in as she does not have a pass. She says that she walked here all the way from Manila."

I imagine that the official noted the doleful look in my eyes for she added, "I took a message for you. The girl says your baby, Dian, is safe and well in the hills."

"Please, please, let me talk to Pressa," I begged.

My plea was not granted, but I was told that I might remain and catch a glimpse of my visitor across the courtyard. I saw Pressa crying, and pleading with the guard. I waved to her and she waved back; then motioned to my mouth and she nodded. I knew Pressa's capabilities, and was confident that she would not take that long, hot five mile walk from Manila, without smuggling something in to me if it was humanly possible.

That night as we were going to our brigade to be locked in, Pilar, Marie's pet trusty, motioned me away from the others. We walked into the shower room, and she told me "Stay here. I'll be back." Five minutes later she came into the dark room, pulled a small package from her uniform, and handed it to me. It contained a pop bottle of carabao milk and an egg sandwich.

"Eat it quick," she cautioned, "I'll have to take the bottle. Your friend Pressa gave it to one of the men guards on the outside gate. Here are a few cigarettes too, and she said that she will send you more. Remember! Don't ever breathe a word to anyone that I did this for you."

"Don't worry! I won't!" I assured, as I drank the milk and wolfed half the sandwich. I hid the rest in my uniform pocket and gave it to Florence who enjoyed the treat. It was the first bread and egg that we had tasted in months.

The next day I managed to talk with Pilar privately, and let her know that I would reward her handsomely if she would take a note to one of the guards on the outside gate and prevail upon him to deliver it. I told her that it was my intention to ask friends for money, that she and the guard would receive a fair share of it, when, as, and if they responded; and that I would remain silent. She agreed to try. I had optimistically anticipated her acquiescence, and handed her a note addressed to Judge Roxas, which I had in readiness.

During the following week I anxiously besought Pilar for news, with negative results, until one day she remarked, "The guard tells me that he delivered the note but the Roxas family are afraid to help you. Why don't you write to someone else? I'll get it out."

I could not believe that story about the Roxas family, as I knew them too well. I wrote a note to Father Lolar, asking for money and food, and gave it to the girl. After another week of suspense, Marie called me aside.

"I would not trust Pilar if I were you," she advised.

"What makes you say that?"

"Oh, I know what's been taking place. I just received a letter from my sister saying that she sent me a thousand pesos through Pilar and her guard friend, but I only received five hundred. My sister wrote that she saw Father Lolar a few days ago. Your note reached him, and he sent five hundred back. You didn't get it, did you?"

I started looking for Pilar, but she was evasive, and it took two days for me to corner her.

"What about my five hundred pesos from Father Lolar?" I demanded angrily, "You and the guard better get together. Either give me the money or some food."

The trusty looked guilty and frightened.

"I haven't seen the money," she denied, almost tearfully, "The guard must have kept it. If you give me another note to Judge Roxas, I will send it by a different guard... one that I know is honest."

I wrote Fely, and sent another note to Judge Roxas, stating that I had written to him previously, and needed money or food badly.

Fely sent me a thousand pesos and some cigarettes, with the explanation that there was no food to be bought. "We are subsisting on coconuts and boiled telenum leaves ourselves," she wrote, "I hope that this money may do you some good."

A few days later Pilar motioned for me to go to the shower room just before lock-up time, handed me a small package, and hurried away. Opening it I found a cup of red beans, a cup of mango beans, and six calamanci tied in a large handkerchief with the initial "M" in the corner. There was no note, but the "M" for "Mamerto" signified that the judge had not failed me.

Florence was overjoyed when I exhibited the proverbial manna. It was a Herculean task to get the beans cooked without detection, but we managed to accomplish it with the help of one of the nuns who had kitchen privileges.

By virtue of strict rationing the beans lasted four of us... Florence, a Filipino girl not in Marie's good graces, the nun and me... for four days. The lemon juice seasoned our boiled roots and weeds for six days.

The next week, Pressa smuggled in milk and four carabao meat sandwiches, through Pilar. Florence and I shared one sandwich each day, but this welcome nourishment only served to accentuate our gnawing hunger.

My physical condition had now become so desperate that I was ready for anything. I requested another interview with Mrs. Garcia and placed the issue squarely before her.

"You know very well that the Americans are going to return in the near future," I asserted boldly, "and when they do, you will be held responsible for the death of the military prisoners unless you relax the Jap restrictions and let us get food from outside. You are certainly fully aware of the fact that this is being done by some of the insular prisoners, and you have not interfered with their activities."

"How can this be done?" she queried, weakening.

"Let me send my watch out to be sold," I suggested, "I will use the money to buy food and share it with the military prisoners."

Mrs. Garcia finally agreed to my plan, stipulating that she would sell the watch. Shortly afterward, she reported its sale for fifteen thousand pesos, which due to the prevailing inflation, sufficed only to buy ten pounds of rice, three of sugar, one of beans, vinegar, coconuts and six eggs at one hundred pesos each. I learned later that the watch had actually brought thirty thousand pesos, and idly wondered why I had been compelled to high-pressure the woman to accept such a profitable deal.

One evening, Pilar came to my brigade at lock-up time, and whispered, "Look, I'm only pretending to lock you in. When you are sure everyone is asleep, sneak out, go to the bars at the end of the long hall, and whistle real low."

"The guard at the outside gate was contacted by a guerrilla officer. This man has a message for you. It's fixed so that you can speak to him about midnight."

It required all my self-restraint to avoid telling Florence about the exciting prospect in store for me, but I managed to keep quiet. I lay awake, listening as the big clock in the front office chimed out the slowly passing hours, and finally heard the long awaited twelve strokes. The heavy breathing of the other women indicated that they were sleeping soundly, so I crept out of bed and to the door. It opened easily, and I padded silently down the length of the darkened hall.

Standing before the bars there, I whistled softly and then tensely held my breath, but there was no response. I whistled again, a trifle louder. The dark bushes outside swayed slightly, a man stepped out, and came to the window. We conversed in whispers.

"High-Pockets?"

"Yes."

"Identify yourself. Who is Boone? What is his code name and position?"

"Captain John P. Boone... Code name, Compadre... Bataan hills near Dinalupihan."

"I guess that you're the real thing. Our group got the word about you from him, and we have a plan for your escape. The guard at the outside gate is one of our men. His name is Fred. I placed him here as soon as we heard where you were. Fred will get pencil and paper to you. Draw a diagram of the inside of your building, the walls, and the courtyard. Give it to him when you have finished, and he will fill in the rest of the compound. You can trust Fred and do whatever he says. He is getting impressions of the locks."

"Is my child really safe with Boone?"

"Yes, she is being well cared for. Don't worry. You will be with her soon."

With that assurance, the man faded into the night.

The next day Pilar handed me a sheet of paper and a pencil.

"Don't let anyone see," she cautioned, "When you're done, I will return the sheet to Fred."

I worked on the diagram every spare minute that I could, when unobserved. It was finished in two days. I met Pilar on her way out of the building with another girl to gather weeds, and arranged for her to meet me in the shower after lunch. At noon, there was a big commotion in the front office. Pilar and the other trusty had escaped! I was happy for their sake, but Pilar's defection made matters difficult. The men guards were not allowed to pass beyond the front office, and without her aid, I had no means of getting the diagram to Fred.

About a week later near midnight, I sat bolt upright on my saw-horses, thinking that I heard a soft whistle outside the high window. I slid out of bed, stood at the door, listened intently, and then suddenly became convinced that the sound was not a figment of my imagination. Using my spoon, I managed to pry the wire loose enough for me to reach and open the door from the outside; then hastened down the gloomy hall to the barred opening.

After my first soft shrill, the guerrilla came into the open, and stood silhouetted against the dark, blue sky. I had brought the chart and handed it through the bars.

"I want to tell you something," my unknown friend commenced, "and then see if you still want us to go through with your rescue."

"Nothing could make me change my mind, unless the Americans are near."

"That's just it. The Americans landed in Leyte some time ago, and today we had word of a second landing up north in Lingayen."

My impulse was to shout, but I whispered, "Are you sure? We have heard these rumors so often."

"I understand that, but this time it's true. The guerrillas up north have sent us messages signed by American officers. We are ready to help them when they strike here."

"Then I'll wait for them to liberate me. This plan may mean trouble... possibly shooting sympathetic people. Since I have waited this long, I can wait a little longer. Will you keep me posted?"

"Yes, I will try to come at least twice a week and tell you where the Americans are."

Back in the brigade Florence and I were whispering animatedly about the great news, when the sharp crack of a shot split the silence of the night. Then came the sound of men running and shouting. The lights were suddenly turned on.

"Someone get a fire started and boil some water," we heard Mrs. Garcia scream, followed by loud sobs, "Call the nurse! Call the priest! Hurry! Hurry!"

We soon found out the cause of her anguish. Her husband had heard someone prowling outside, and had sallied forth to investigate. His nocturnal curiosity had been his undoing; he did not regain consciousness and died within the hour. Rumor had it that the guerrillas sought his scalp because he refused to cooperate with them. Garcia's sudden demise did not cause us to shed any tears; it only confirmed our suspicions that he had been a collaborationist whose evil influence reflected itself in his wife's demeanor.

Events now began to happen in rapid succession. American planes came over every day, flying low, and it was a thrill to see the stars on their wings. The bombing was relentless. The Japanese anti-aircraft guns on the roofs of the orphanage and psychopathic hospital nearby were continuously in action.

On the first day of February, during a lull in the bombardment, the sound of orderly volley firing reached us. A Filipino guard from the psychopathic hospital let us know that Japanese soldiers had marched into the institution, ordered all the white patients outside, and mowed them down. He warned us that the same thing might happen to us.

Mrs. Garcia's attitude toward the military prisoners changed overnight. She even managed a wintry smile when I passed her in the hall. Our brigade doors were left unlocked now, and Mrs. Garcia posted an alert Filipino guard at the outside gate with instructions to press a buzzer whenever he spotted any Japanese approaching. This buzzer rang in the office, and at this signal the inside guard would shout "Soldiers!" so that the white prisoners could hide.

The difficulty with this plan was that there was a dearth of choice hiding places. My favorite one was under the small stage in the recreation hall. We had managed to loosen some boards there, and dived into our refuge whenever the warning came; at least once daily.

From February fourth on, we heard loud explosions which recurred at about one hour intervals, both day and night. The penitentiary stood on a hill, overlooking Manila, and from this vantage point we witnessed an eye-filling spectacle. The whole city seemed to be in flames. Vast columns of smoke and fire rose high in the air, and the never-ceasing sounds of battle came steadily closer. Bridges, schools, churches, factories, some of them not far off, were blasted in rapid succession.

At midnight on February sixth, my guerrilla friend came and reported that the Americans had liberated Santo Tomas.

The next day, Mrs. Garcia summoned the military prisoners and returned their clothes. My old slacks were unsightly, but I welcomed them as though they were a Parisian creation.

The scene of combat now moved too close for comfort and there was no surcease; day or night.

Early on the morning of February tenth, the prison priest came running into the courtyard, "I have seen the Americanos with my own eyes he shouted happily, "Deo gratias! It is true. They are here!"

We crowded around him; all asking questions at the same time. He related that while on his way to conduct an early mass in the hospital, he had passed airmail thicket and sighted the tanks and motors of an American unit. He urged Mrs. Garcia to let him guide the military prisoners to the troops.

"I can not hold you longer if you wish to go," that character announced in sugary tones. "But I think that you should wait until I can turn you over to an American officer."

A general clamor mingled with a few "Boos" silenced her for a moment, and then she added with one of her frigid smiles. "I, too, want a little glory. I want to be the one to tell the Americans how I have protected you all."

"Did you say protected?" one of the crowd quipped

Mrs. Garcia's reply was drowned in the raucous bitter burst of laughter which followed. We had a caucus on the spot and decided that it would be best to wait until our troops came for us.

I had been a prisoner for eight months and eighteen days, but the last few hours of tense waiting seemed to be the longest. About ten, the all-too-familiar shout rang out "Soldiers!" I was too far from the recreation hall to reach my good hideout without being intercepted. I dived under my bed, tearing the seat of my slacks as I did so. I snatched the spread from the saw-horses, covered myself with it and remained tense and motionless.

Shouts and laughter echoed from the courtyard.

"Americans! Viva los Americanos!"

Those magic words made me roll out so fast and incautiously that the same offending nail caught my slacks again and removed the entire seat. I snatched the spread, saronged it around me, and made a dash for the court-yard.

There stood ten of the tallest Yanks I had ever seen! I rushed up to the nearest soldier and timidly touched his arm. "Yes, I'm real, sister," he asserted with an assuring grin. Any doubts in my mind vanished when I saw that broad smile and heard that welcome Texas drawl.

"I just wanted to be sure... sure that I wasn't dreaming." My eyes were dimmed with happy tears.

"You're an American, aren't you?" the soldier inquired.

"You bet. Could I please kiss you?"

"Well, if you don't, I'm going to kiss you, sister. You're the first woman from God's country that I've seen in over two years."

The G. I. stooped over and planted a big kiss squarely on my lips. It almost took my breath away.

"How is it that you haven't seen an American woman for so long?" I managed to gasp.

"Because it's been that long since I left the States. We have been all that time getting here by way of Guadalcanal, Bougainville, New Guinea and a few other places. You better go in and talk to the colonel now, Miss."

"All right, what's his name?"

"Colonel Charles Young."

I walked into Mrs. Garcia's office. She was there, rigid and official as ever, sorting papers and handing our records over to the colonel. I started to explain who I was, and why I was in prison.

"Never mind, my dear," he interrupted. "That's all over. We will take you to Santo Tomas where you will be among friends again."

Before our little group left, the colonel asked us to sit down for a minute on the entrance steps, along with the prison official and guards, and let him take a picture.

I noticed that the fighting in our vicinity had subsided, and that the sounds of battle were now farther off. I recognized my guerrilla friend among the others waiting to guide us to the main road, and managed to shake hands with him! "Why do we need guides?" I asked the colonel.

"Because the Japs had this road mined to keep us out and you in. Luckily the guerrillas have been watching them for a long time and had the mines spotted."

We followed our guides in single file, treading gingerly around the dangerous spots. We reached the main highway without incident and found the colonel's jeep and a truck in readiness.

"Long live the guerillas!" I exulted happily, as I climbed aboard.

"You can say that again," the colonel responded, "It was due to their efforts that we reached you in time."

CHAPTER XXI

We Turn Our Faces East

WE DROVE ALONG THE SMOKE CLOUDED, traffic-infested highway, threading our way through a maze of tanks, trucks, and other military vehicles on their way to the rapidly changing front. It was not a tranquil ride for the ping of sniper's bullets, the staccato chatter of machine guns, and the burping of mortars came from all directions. We frequently saw G. I.'s tossing hand grenades into shallow, hastily-built air raid shelters where many Japs had sought refuge, and were fighting to the death rather than surrender. As we neared the Luneta, an overpowering stench from many decomposing corpses compelled us to hold our nostrils.

Upon arrival at Santo Tomas University, we found that everything was momentarily snafu. Internees released from other camps had been crowded in here, and many natives who had not been interned clamored at the gates for permission to enter. At the moment this ancient seat of learning was the only safe haven providing military protection, shelter, medical attention and American victuals. The sentry at the gate refused us admission, and Colonel Young was forced to convince the commanding officer that we were rescued military prisoners who must be given sanctuary.

We reported singly, to officers of the Military Intelligence Corps, engaged in counter-intelligence work, to be registered and billeted. After being directed to the administration office for meal tickets, we waited an hour in a chow line that was two blocks long.

As I sat down to devour the food placed in front of me, I could not help but think of a silly expression heard in my halcyon childhood days, to wit; "Just because you are getting it free, don't make a hog of yourself." Tinned meat, dehydrated potatoes, good Army bread, canned fruit and coffee... it was not easy to exercise self-restraint when I had starved for so long. I walked and walked afterwards to ease my amazed stomach, but it refused to be calmed. Eventually all that long-dreamed-of American food had to be charged off as a total loss. I ended up in a bed in a field hospital on a limited diet of soup and eggnogs.

Before night-fall my first visitor arrived... faithful little Pressa... and we had a joyous reunion.

As we talked a trim Red Cross worker inquired if I would like to write a letter home. I literally snatched the proffered pen and paper and started

"Dearest Mother and Dad..." Then I wrote a note to Phil's parents, and sank back exhausted.

Upon examination the Army doctors found me to be anemic, suffering from scurvy and several varieties of skin infections. My weight was down to ninety five pounds. When I washed my hair and gave it a long delayed brushing, it came out in handfuls. I had lost no teeth, other than the one knocked out during my last trial, but they were all loose. The dentist made me happy when he stated they would regain their former condition after I had eaten proper food.

The army authorities offered to send me home at once by plane, but I refused, telling them about Dian. I gave them Captain Boone's last known position, and they sent a radio message immediately. The answer came at once, from Major Boone, that Dian would be sent down without delay in the custody of two army officers.

When the child arrived three days later, she did not recognize me, and would have nothing to do with me. I was happy to note that she was sound and well, although considerably underweight. The next day when I took her with me to select dresses and shoes from the discarded clothing left with the Red Cross by departed internees, Dian thawed a little. "Are you my Mummy?" she asked dubiously, and when I replied affirmatively, she trustingly placed her thin little hand in mine.

While all of this was taking place, the battle for the Walled City continued. We heard the intermittent bellows of the mortars in position behind the University, firing into the holed-up Japs. After a while, the answering cru-u-ump of the enemy shells was less welcome.

The battle for the Manila Hotel raged for days. Our soldiers were obliged to mop up the Nips floor by floor, and room by room.

"We found the bastards hiding in closets, in bath tubs, behind closed doors, and even under rugs," a wounded soldier told me. "We would no sooner get one floor cleaned out and start for the one above, than the floor below us would fill up with skibbies again. There seemed to be no end of them," he finished, laughing.

"I'll bet that it wasn't so funny when it was going on."

"You said it, sister," the G. I. agreed. "One night after we had been fighting for four days and nights without any sleep and damn little chow, two of my buddies and I found ourselves on a floor that seemed to be entirely clear of Japs. It was kind of late and were dead tired, so we decided to go into a room and take a few minutes rest. We locked the door and flopped on the floor. We must have slept about an hour or more when a funny noise made me wake up. I called the others and we listened. It came from the next room and sounded exactly like snoring." The soldier paused to chuckle. "We crept as quietly as we could out of the room and to the next door," he continued. "My buddies had Tommy guns. They stood on each side while I gingerly opened the door."

"Well," I prompted, "what did you find?"

"Twenty Japs all asleep and snoring like hell. One of my buddies yelled 'Come on, you yellow bastards, we'll give you a break!' They came alive in a hurry and the lead started flying. After a while all of those monkeys were permanently asleep. That's how I got mine giving those lousy sons o' bitches a break."

As the days passed, the firing became spasmodic, and almost nil save in spots where a few Nip die-hards still held out. Manila was a shambles... wrecked and gutted buildings filled with decaying bodies. I wanted to see more of it, but my physical condition would not permit. I took short walks every day for the exercise. One day, while strolling with Dian near the main gate of Santo Tomas, I caught sight of a familiar face.

"Mona!" I called impulsively. "Where on earth did you come from?"

My former friend would no doubt have liked to pass me up, but there was no way out of her predicament. Her face lighted up with one of her well-known smiles as she came rushing up.

"Claire, you're alive! I'm so glad! I was certainly worried when I heard what happened to you last year."

"How have you been? You and George?"

"It's been terrible, but I managed to make out... Oh, George? He was taken into the Japanese army. I never saw him again."

"What a shame," I commented acidly. "What do you suppose happened to him?"

"How should I know? That's all in the past, and I don't care. When the Americans started bombing Manila I went out into the province and stayed until they took the city. Oh, those wonderful Yanks!"

"So, you've switched flags again."

"I don't know what you mean," Mena pouted, "had to lookout for myself during this horrible war, didn't I?"

"Yes," I returned. "We all did."

"I really must run along," she chattered, "came to have a shrapnel wound dressed. It's really nothing... but Pete... he's the cutest American lieutenant... made me promise to come in. Be seeing you," and she was on her way.

"Not if I see you first," I retorted sharply, and I meant just that.

I was really anxious about Louise. I learned at the administration office that the internees at Los Banos had just been liberated, under fire, and transferred to Montinglupe. I asked permission to go up there, and the army authorities gave me a pass which permitted me to hitch-hike on one of their trucks.

A nurse who had been looking after Dian while I was in the hospital, agreed to take care of her for another day or two. I made the trip to Mont-inglupe... a former men's penitentiary. It was a massive structure, and for a moment I thought my chances of finding Louise were slim. However her name was broadcasted over the loud-speaker, and I suddenly saw her running across the courtyard. We hugged, kissed, and cried a little. Bob Humphreys joined us, and when I noticed the love-light in their eyes, I was glad. Louise told me that they had heard about my arrest and never expected to see me again. They too had suffered, but that seemed forgotten in their current happiness.

Back at Santo Tomas, each day that we waited for repatriation brought its thrills and surprises. Claring Yuma appeared, safely back from the hills. She related that our "Park Avenue" boys had all been taken to Japan on prison ships.

Then came another thrill.

"Phillips... Claire..." came a voice paging me over the loud-speaker, "Come to the main gate. You have visitors."

I ran all the way, and found Sassy, Looter, German, Dr. and Mrs. Atienza, and Mr. Rigeness... Swiss. They were all smiling and waving, but looked much older and very emaciated. We sat inside a large army pyramidal tent, and talked for two hours... sometimes all at once.

I discovered that Father Lolar and the Mencarinis were dead. The good priest and his associates had been destroyed by the Japs during their final dynamiting and bombing. They died as they had lived... serving and consoling others. Then I learned that Boots and Rocky had been taken to Fort Santiago on Christmas Day. The survivors of our group had been able to keep tabs on them and knew that they were moved to Fort Santo Abod a few days before the Americans came in. The Yanks, searching the place discovered a pit with eighteen bodies in it. The only corpses that could be identified were those of Johnson of the Maritime Commission, and Dougelby and Larson, two businessmen. They were former American internees in Santo Tomas, who had been convicted of sending money to help the guerrillas. There was no trace of the beloved Mencarinis... Boots and Rocky.

My visitors let me know that The Doctor... Torres... had joined the guerrillas in the hills immediately after my arrest. Juan-Elizalde had died serving his country... after several months of torture in Fort Santiago and Bilibid prisons.

When my turn came to talk, I narrated how Ramon had died in Bilibid, and asked whether Lerry knew about it. German said she had been informed by a released prisoner, and was now in a private sanitarium suffering from a nervous breakdown. She was expected to recover eventually, and in the interim her sister was caring for her two sons.

I asked permission to go out to Quezon City, to recover my papers. Dian and I stood at the gates of Santo Tomas, and after stopping many jeeps, found one that was going our way. We received a very enthusiastic welcome at Fely's home, and we dug up my records. The papers were yellow and crumpled, but well preserved in the large demijohns which contained them. I wished that Chimpanzee and Bull-Dog could have been present so I could show them what a demijohn looked like... and then break one on their thick Nip skulls. All of my boys' notes were intact as well as the hard-won lists of men in the various prison camps. When I exhibited the latter to military intelligence officers, they made careful copies. I would not relinquish the originals... they meant so much to me.

The Great Day arrived when the loud-speaker announced the names of those who were to prepare and leave for the States in two days..."Phillips...Claire...Phillips... Dian..."

As the army transport sailed out of Manila Bay, and I saw the Stars and Stripes proudly waving over devastated Corregidor, my thoughts turned back to a happier moment four years before when I had voyaged into that same harbor, blissfully unaware of the cruel blows fate had in store for me.

I knew that it was only goodbye, not farewell. Phil was sleeping in a martyr's grave at Cabanatuan, and I thought of the well-known promise of General Douglas MacArthur:

"I shall return!"

THE END

Made in the USA
San Bernardino, CA
12 March 2020